# WOODSWOMAN

ANNE LABASTILLE majored in conservation at Cornell and holds a Ph.D. in wildlife ecology from that university. For the last five years she has worked independently as an ecological consultant, free-lance writer, lecturer, and photographer. She has made field studies of endangered wildlife and surveys of proposed national parks and wildlife reserves for private companies, the Smithsonian Institution, and several foreign governments. Anne LaBastille is the author of scientific and popular articles in *National Geographic, Audubon Magazine, Reader's Digest, Biological Conservation, International Wildlife,* and other publications. She serves as one of ten international jurors for the J. Paul Getty Wildlife Conservation Award.

Anne LaBastille was honored in 1974 with the Gold Medal of the World Wildlife Fund International as Conservationist of the Year.

# Anne LaBastille

# WOODSWOMAN

 *A Dutton* **dep** *Paperback*

E. P. DUTTON | NEW YORK

To Major

For information contact: E. P. Dutton, a division of Penguin Books USA Inc., 375 Hudson Street, New York, N.Y. 10014.

*Library of Congress Cataloging in Publication Data*
LaBastille, Anne.

Woodswoman.
1. LaBastille, Anne. 2. Natural History—New York (State)—Adirondack Mountains. I. Title.
QH31.L15A34 1976 500.9'747'53 75-34071

ISBN: 0-525-48565-1

Published simultaneously in Canada
by Fitzhenry and Whiteside, Ltd.,
Toronto

Photographs are by the author,
unless otherwise specified.

15  17  19  20  18  16

# Contents

# I

## No Home

The freeze-up on Black Bear Lake is a prelude to winter. The freeze-up is a prelude to hardship. The freeze-up is a prelude to loneliness. It begins on a November evening as a filigreed fingering of ice along the shoreline. It greets me in the morning as a rim of ice around the boat hull and a skim of ice atop the water buckets. Some nights the ice forms halfway across the lake; but, come morning, it shatters into a trillion thin shards beneath waves and wind. The freeze-up takes its time. The freeze-up is implacable. There is no stopping it. The freeze-up is an event as important in nature as the solstices, equinoxes, full moon and eclipses. It affects the living patterns of many fish and wildlife species. And it dramatically changes my life-style on this Adirondack lake where I live alone in the log cabin I built myself.

Motoring down the lake in my small aluminum outboard boat, I "feel" how heavy the water has become, how dark, how turgid. The propeller seems to be churning syrup and the boat handles sluggishly. At a few degrees above freezing, water is actually denser than at 32 degrees. God help me if I fall out of the boat. If the shock doesn't kill outright, the cold water will do so within three minutes.

One rainy, blustery night during my first winter at Black Bear Lake I jumped into my boat at the empty public landing, my poncho waving wildly in the wind. By mistake, I had left the gearshift in forward, something I almost never do. Fumbling with the flapping poncho, I forgot my usual routine to check if the engine was in neutral. I stood, straddling the seat, and pulled the starting rope. The engine roared into life, the boat lurched forward, then careened sideways. I fell heavily upon the gunwale, narrowly missed losing my balance and dumping over backward into the lake. Getting the boat under control once more, I started to tremble. Imagining a frantic lunge for shore, the entanglement with my poncho underwater, the circular chase by a runaway motorboat, I resolved to be more careful in boats during freeze-up.

On another November night I took two buckets and a flashlight down to the lake for water. Snow was whirling through the air and heavy waves pounded the dock. The unexpected sound of a boat came through the storm. Strange. I had seen no camps occupied over the weekend at my end of the lake. I shone the flashlight over the water, and minutes later, a dangerously overladen boat pulled alongside. Five frightened hunters squinted into the beam.

"We're lost!" shouted one.

"Can you help us out? Guide us down the lake?" yelled another. "We've been circling for half an hour and can't find the way."

I ran up to the cabin and grabbed gloves, parka, and poncho. Already I dreaded the trip. Starting up my motor, I asked two of the hunters to come into my boat and I placed the torch so the boat operator behind would not be blinded. When we got down to the public landing, they jumped out, stamped their feet, and wiped off their rifles. The hunters were relieved to be back to the safety of their cars and to have escaped from the storm. The oldest man pressed a five-dollar bill in my hand. I protested.

"Please, take it," he said fervently. "Take it for your gas."

I turned to go. By now, pitch darkness had descended and the snow had thickened. Alone in midlake I lost sight of land. My only sense of direction was the gale buffeting my back. Never had these 1½ miles seemed so long or perilous. I tried to estimate where the rock shoals, the island, and my point of rocks lay so as to avoid a sheared propeller or a smashup. I'd have hated changing a pin or rowing up the lake in this weather. After a fifteen-minute run, I turned right 90 degrees and trusted to luck I was about opposite my land. Not a light anywhere on Black Bear Lake. Even my own cabin was dark, for I always turn off my propane gas lamps whenever I go out.

Frigid waves lashed the side of the boat, drenching me with spray which quickly turned to ice. Inching toward shore by dead reckoning, I just missed smacking into the granite rocks off my point. I cut off the 10 horsepower engine and poled to deeper water and the dock. Back inside the toasty cabin, dripping dry in front of the Franklin stove, I removed the mushy five-dollar bill from my pocket and stared at it thoughtfully. Should I have accepted it? Should I have gone at all? I spread it out to dry near the stove and shrugged my shoulders. Such decisions are always made in favor of helping one's fellowman up here in the North Woods.

A few days later, I found myself helping out another person during freeze-up. An elderly couple were staying at their camp for the Thanksgiving holidays. The man had a heart attack. An emergency crew, boat, and ambulance were radioed in to evacuate him. His wife stayed on to close up and pack out their valuable belongings. She didn't know when, if ever, they'd be back. The night before Thanksgiving temperatures dropped to 10 degrees. The lake skimmed from shore to shore. This was probably the ultimate phase of the freeze-up. Ice was "making" quickly, relentlessly. Another night like this and the lake would be frozen solid until spring.

Breaking through half an inch of ice with my boat, I went to help this kind lady. Trunks, boxes, and suitcases were piled by the backdoor. They'd never fit in one boat on one trip down the lake. My neighbor was too anxious and too busy to leave her camp; yet hour by hour the lake was becoming more solid. I suggested that we load her boat full and tow it behind mine down to the landing. She worried over what might happen if the ice punctured my hull and the boat sank.

"I'll jump into yours," I reassured her, "and row back. Don't worry. We've got to move fast to get you out of here by dark."

I carved out a passageway to the landing by nosing the bow of my boat up on the ice, now almost an inch thick, revving the motor, and letting its weight break through. The noise was ear shattering and ominous as chunks crashed and grated against the thin aluminum hulls. Where the ice was too thick, I idled the engine and moved forward to pound through the ice with a metal oar. It took an hour to travel a mile and deposit the gear at the landing.

Returning for another load, I found my newly opened path already glazed shut with ice. We ate a quick turkey sandwich—our Thanksgiving dinner. Again I made a run with two boats, one laden with boxes and files. On the third trip, my neighbor was ready to close her camp and I took her in my boat to the landing, where her car was kept. It was almost twilight. We embraced sadly and I waited until I had seen her drive safely away.

A deathly hush lay over Black Bear Lake, save for an almost inaudible whisper. Ice making. I was completely alone. Stepping into my boat, I found that ice had surrounded it in that short period of time at the landing. I backed out into the passageway, sucking ice chunks under the propeller. The lake stretched ahead to the cabin a solid sheet of gray. My path was clogged and closed. A flicker of fear jabbed at my heart. The lake was making ice faster than I could break it!

The gravity of my situation suddenly struck. Could I make it back to my new home, or would I be frozen fast in the middle of Black Bear Lake? If the ice imprisoned me in the boat, there would be no way to reach shore. The ice would not be thick enough to walk upon, yet probably too thick to chop through with my oars. If only I had thought to bring an axe! It occurred to me that I could freeze to death overnight in my own boat within sight of the cabin.

Adrenaline pumped through me. I gunned the motor and rammed the boat up the narrow waterway faster than it should go. We had left my neighbor's boat at the landing, overturned for the winter. If mine sprung a leak or if the motor sheared a pin, I'd be in real trouble. My gamble was that the aluminum was strong enough to withstand the banging and crunching.

No trip has ever seemed so tortuous or long or lonely as my shattering, smashing, desperate sprint for home on that ice-making Thanksgiving night. When I finally reached the cove and shut off the engine, the silence soothed me like a benediction. Then I heard the faintest of whispers. Peering over the stern, I realized with a shudder that the ice had already sealed the path directly behind me. A cranberry-red sunset cast a forbidding

The cabin in early winter; open-air sun deck in foreground.

glimmer over the lake. I watched icy slivers and darts, fingers and bridges, projections and connections forming and joining and congealing on the water's surface. The ice was creating itself, spreading and hardening with incredible speed. I acknowledged for the first time the utter precision and cruelty of cold. I was witnessing the final freeze-up in all its awful, relentless, primal strength. I will never forget that phenomenon and how vulnerable a warm-blooded creature can be in its grip.

Through the gathering darkness I picked my way up the trail from the small dock to my cabin. As I opened the front door and stepped in, the familiar room with its cozy bark walls hung with furs and deer antlers, greeted me reassuringly. How quickly, I reflected, peril could be followed by beauty in the wilderness, each forming a part of the other. In this lonely cabin, my life-style had indeed been transformed from my earlier hectic, gregarious existence. How had it happened? How had I come here? I thought back over the series of events that had brought me to this log-walled home, this now ice-bound and winter-locked lake in the North Woods.

I had had no place to go. My own family were either dead or scattered, leaving me with no relatives to turn to. Even more critical, a divorce seemed imminent. For several summers I had worked side by side with my husband, Morgan, running a small resort lodge in the Adirondacks. Winters, we took a few select groups of nature lovers to Florida and points south on wildlife tours. We chopped wood, washed dishes, planned menus, taught riding, waterskiing, and skin diving; decorated hotel rooms; identified tropical birds and Indian ruins; and generally labored to keep our guests happy. It was a colorful life-style full of travel, people, and problems.

We had had very little privacy and a great deal of work in our married life. Perhaps this combination had gradually eroded our love. Meanwhile certain other changes had taken place and by early spring our marriage was coming to an end.

"You must leave before the Fourth of July," said Morgan tensely one evening. "I can't open and operate the hotel under this strain. You *have* to find some place to go!"

This ultimatum triggered a dramatic change in my life. Ever since a childhood spent near New York City, I had wanted to live in a Thoreau-style cabin in the woods. In high school, I had dreamed of camping and hiking amid forested mountains and clear lakes. In college, majoring in wildlife conservation, my professional goal had been to observe and study wild animals. And during my marriage to Morgan, I had craved a tranquil haven where I could write and relax.

Intuitively now, I made my decision. I would build a log cabin in the Adirondack wilderness. I hoped that a withdrawal to the peace of nature might remedy my despair. I reasoned that the companionship of wild animals and local outdoor people could cure my sorrow. Most of all I felt that the creation of a rustic cabin would be the solution to my homelessness.

Time was short. I had less than two months to find land, build a cabin, and move. I began looking at properties and "camps" (cottages) within a 25-mile radius of Lake Serene, as I shall call the village near Morgan's lodge. I checked over dozens of buildings, acres of land. I was offered elegant chalets; tiny hunting camps; a wooded island for $80,000; 100-foot lots in busy Lake Serene village; 400 acres of logged-over forest on a yearly lease basis. None of them were right for my pocketbook or my taste.

By chance, I heard about a large private estate on what I shall call Black Bear Lake. The owner had died and it was being broken into three parcels. Black Bear Lake was one of the most remote lakes to which one could still drive; yet it had no road around it. That should ensure privacy, I thought. In addition, there was no power line or telephone service there. This also appealed to my "back to nature" frame of mind. The price seemed very reasonable.

So on a sunny spring day in early May, I drove my pickup

truck and boat trailer to the foot of Black Bear Lake. Shoving a small aluminum boat into the water, I pulled and choked the stubborn 10-horse engine into life and cruised past forested shores, islands, bays, and points. No track or trail linked the dirt road and public landing to the property one mile and a half up the lake. Here and there a summer cottage or boathouse broke the sweep of woodland. I had learned that only one elderly couple resided year-round on the lake. The closest permanent settlement was 5 miles west over the mountain at the hamlet of Hawk Hill. Lake Serene lay more than 25 miles away.

Nosing the boat toward the wild eastern shoreline, I found a tiny cove with sand bottom. I tied up to a wythrod bush and started pushing through thick shrubbery and a tangle of young balsams, searching for the cement boundary markers. The real estate agent had said they were 400 feet apart somewhere between the patient granite rocks off the cove and the mouth of a small creek. In the other direction, there was almost a half-mile strip of primeval woods between Black Bear Lake and Beaver Pond, a small body of water which formed the back property line. Beyond it, thousands of acres of state Adirondack Forest Preserve stretched away. Surely I could find a site for my log cabin on this lovely piece of land.

Towering virgin white pines, red spruces, and balsam firs graced the property. Trees native to these mountains, they lent a tangy, pungent odor to the fresh air and sighed in the breeze. Back from the lake, this evergreen forest merged into hardwoods. Huge sugar maples, beeches, and yellow birches grew from the rich black Adirondack duff. Many of the trees stood 100 feet high with trunks 1 to 2 feet in diameter. Their ages ranged from 100 to 300 years old, maybe more. No axe had ever touched their trunks, no shovel had ever broken ground here. Clearly the land belonged to the trees far more than to any human being.

The sparkling lakes skirting this property were also native features of these ancient mountains. Cut and carved by thick ice sheets which sporadically covered the Adirondacks from 1 million to about 10 thousand years ago, Black Bear Lake and Beaver Pond are only two of some 2,300 lakes and ponds which adorn the area. Large granite rocks and shoals marked the shoreline. The rocky-sandy bottom, I knew, sloped to a depth of 40 feet. Brook trout, bullfrogs, beaver, and bullheads lived in the amber-colored water. It seemed as though no pollution had ever contaminated its quality, no erosion had ever corrupted its clarity. I had only to cup my hand in it to obtain pure drinking water.

I spent the entire afternoon exploring, checking exposures, imagining views through picture windows, estimating spaces between trees, gauging distances to the lake. By evening, I had a firm idea of where a cabin could be located and how it might be built. It must stand far enough from the lake to leave a fringe of firs for privacy and beauty. The balsams would make fragile black silhouettes against the stained-glass sunsets of Adirondack skies. Yet the cabin must be close enough to run down for a dip and see beaver swim by. Most important, the building would have to be put upon one special knoll where no large trees grew. Even though hundreds of board feet of lumber and dozens of stout logs lay locked in these behemoth trees, I vowed not to cut a single giant for my home or for firewood, unless it was absolutely necessary. The trees and I would be companions and coexist upon the land. At that moment, I also vowed never to commit an act which might pollute the lakes lapping on the tract. The cabin should face south and west in order to have the best exposure to sun (for warmth and brightness) and wind (for blowing away insects). My home would need a steep cathedral roof from which the heavy snows would slide easily. And, most critical, it had to be small enough to build by myself.

Tired of tugging my way through the underbrush, I sat down in the boat to rest and reconsider everything. A late afternoon west wind cooled me and cleared my mind. "West of the Wind" —already I had a name for the place. It was certain that I had the potential site and setting for a wilderness cabin. I really wanted this land. All I had to do now was buy it, find building materials, transport them here, and construct a cabin. A complicated task! Then through the whir of my preoccupied thoughts, the gentle trill of spring peepers slipped in to calm me. The setting sun was burnishing the spruces and throwing a path of liquid gold across the water. I started the outboard motor and backed slowly away from shore. An unexpected sense of relief and exhilaration grew as I chugged down the lake. I could feel that a part of me remained behind. Even without a house to live in, I had found a place to go.

Two days later I caught the midnight train near Lake Serene and went to New York City. Arriving at 8 A.M., I presented myself at an old, prestigious law firm where the arrangements would be made for the sale of property on Black Bear Lake. I was advised to come back after lunch as the attorney handling the estate was not yet in. I spent a nervous morning window-shopping, fingering my checkbook, and worrying what I'd do if the sale fell through.

At 2 P.M., I sat across an antique desk from a grayish-skinned man in a grayish-green suit. The stale office air smelled of old papers and too many luncheon martinis. In a hurry to culminate the deal, I signed my check, the deed, and covenant in a flourish without reading anything. I thanked the attorney and rushed out with my copy and a bill of sale to catch the 4 P.M. train back to fresh air and the mountains. I was the proud owner of 22 acres of Adirondack wilderness—the first land I had ever owned in my life.

Deciding not to cut any big trees on my land posed a major problem, both economically and logistically, in building a log cabin. I had to be extremely frugal until a settlement with Morgan was reached and my writing career launched. Without a road to my site, I had to find a way to get logs and lumber up

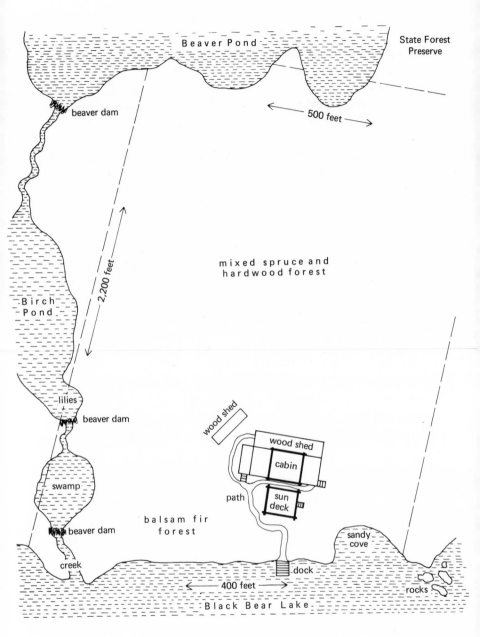

The Cabin and Its Land.

the lake. And lacking electrical power, all the work would have to be done by hand or using a portable generator.

Fortunately, the Adirondacks is a country of lumberjacks, both French Canadians and Americans. They have been cutting millions upon millions of hardwoods and softwoods off these mountains for years. In the old days, before New York State's Adirondack Forest Preserve existed, they cut the evergreens for spars, spiles, barrels, and boards. They peeled thousands of hemlocks for the tannic acid hidden in the bark. Today they are cutting both softwoods and hardwoods for pulp, paper, veneer, and furniture.

Fifteen miles from Black Bear Lake stood a large sawmill and logging company. I drove over to see Pierre, the young, square-shaped, iron-muscled boss. The French Canadian had the solution for my cabin. Pierre pointed to an enormous pile of spruce logs in his loading yard. They were 16 feet long, a foot or more in diameter, and had been cut in midwinter when the sap was down and the bark tight to the trunk. I was delighted. Their size seemed manageable—the weight would not be over 500 pounds per log. And I would not have to peel the logs. The image of soft, gray-barked walls was far more appealing than hard polished beams.

According to my rough calculations, the cabin walls would be 6 feet, 6 inches high, and the main indoor room 12 by 12 feet. This reduction in size from 16 feet was caused by leaving 1 foot of log beyond the walls at each end and by losing at least 12 inches in each notch where the log fit over its neighbor. The steep roof would extend 8 feet from both ends of the cabin itself so that small sheltered porches could be built beneath it. Figuring up the foundation posts, base logs, log walls, supports for doors, windows, porch beams, and roof, I estimated forty-five logs should do the job!

Shifting a toothpick aimlessly between tobacco-stained teeth, Pierre said, "Pick what you like. I'll truck dem to your lake." We did some bargaining. Finally, we settled on $600 for forty-five logs delivered to the water's edge. Pierre gave me a wink as he climbed into the cab of his enormous loader. "You good Frenchman!" he exclaimed. "You make good deal wit dem logs."

My dream cabin became a reality the day those forty-five logs tumbled off the logging truck and splashed resoundingly into the lake. My future home floated haphazardly, like so many of Pierre's toothpicks, a mile and a half from its destination.

Jockeying the motorboat around like a trained cow pony, I managed to round up the logs and half-hitch them together in two bunches. Slowly, ponderously, I towed them up the lake. It took two hours to pull each load. I had to be careful not to crash into the shore, run aground, or overheat my 10-horse engine. By midafternoon, all forty-five logs were bobbing gently within a log boom lashed to live trees along the shore just like a string of packhorses inside a corral fence.

At this time, it became obvious I'd need help manhandling the logs and erecting the cabin roof and floor. The local hardware store recommended two brothers who worked as a team. Bob and Dave were sturdy, taciturn carpenters, used to improvising and utilizing native woods and stones. They met me at Black Bear Lake landing with a portable generator, power saws, tools, plywood for flooring, 2-by-8s for rafters, and 2-by-10s for joists.

I groaned inwardly. I had read Calvin Rutstrum's fine book, *The Wilderness Cabin*, and had visions of hand-cut spruce rafters and ridgepole, rough-hewn pine floor planks, even cedar shakes on the roof. Bob and Dave had a hard time convincing me to use precut lumber on the cabin. Dave patiently explained that rustic construction, while esthetically pleasing, would take all summer and four times as much money to fashion properly. I needed a home as soon as possible.

"Come on, 'woodswoman,'" chided Bob. "Compromise!"

"Right," said Dave, sensibly. "*We'll* build the floor, roof, windows, and door frames from regular store-bought lumber. *You* can cut rustic log foundation posts and raise the log walls, all by hand."

Our first joint task, however, was to dig eight deep holes, mix cement, and fill the holes full of stones and concrete. The huge spruce posts would rest on these footings, thereby preventing rot. It was an odious job because Adirondack soil is full of rocks and underlaid with an indurate, obstinate, and impregnable substratum called "hardpan."

Soon we were ready to handle the heavy cabin logs. Dave rigged up a "king-pole" (a spruce pole attached at one end to the base of a huge tree with a pivoting pin and held up at an angle by a cable from the top of the king-pole to the upper trunk). A "come-along" (a small, hand-operated winch with cable and hook) was threaded through a pulley at the top of the pole. With this we could hook and haul logs out of the water, winch them up the steep bank, raise them in the air, and swing them over to the cabin site. It took a lot of muscle power to turn that winch handle. I thought my body was in good shape from doing countless chores at the hotel; yet I soon developed new and useful muscles.

Time slipped backward. I felt like a stubborn pioneer woman swinging her axe. I felt like a resourceful pioneer man guiding each log into place with a peavey (a wooden pole with metal tip and hinged hook for handling logs). I felt like a gleeful pioneer child hearing the thump as each new notched log slipped over the lower. I used only an axe for notching, an adze for dressing, and a chain saw to run between the logs. The latter buzzed off bumps and knots and snugged the beams into a tighter fit. Gradually the bunch floating in the lake diminished and four walls rose upon the knoll. Fragrant white spruce chips piled up on the ground. An enormous pride grew in me as I fashioned my own home on land never before occupied in the history of red or white men.

Then came the day when all forty-five logs had been snaked out from the water, and a small square structure stood under the spruces. It was time for a door and windows. I was getting tired of climbing over the stockadelike walls to get in and out. Rev-

I enjoy splitting logs for firewood.
(PHOTO: DAVID ALLEN HARVEY: CHIMERA)

ving up the chain saw, I cut out a doorway which led to the
back porch and two large openings for windows. One faced
south toward the lake, sun, granite rocks, and cove; the other
faced west into the sunset and fringe of firs along the shoreline.
The carpenters framed in these openings and gingerly installed
a half-glass door and two picture windows. They worked as if
handling priceless crystal.

"God help us," breathed Bob, "if we smash any panes after
bringing them 75 miles from the city by truck and then up this
lake by boat!"

While Dave and Bob did the more complicated carpentry required to erect the roof, I firmly nailed the thick plywood sheets
to the joists to make a floor. Then I began chinking the log walls
inside. Fluffy yellow fiberglass was pushed between the logs instead of the traditional oakum or sphagnum moss. I reasoned it
would insulate better than the old-fashioned types and not give
off any odor. Besides, I had no intention of gathering sphagnum
moss all summer with a basket on my head. The yellow fiberglass
contrasted beautifully with the gray logs.

Suddenly I had a home. I had a door to open or close to the
world. There were windows with peaceful views. I had four
thick, insulated walls and a sturdy, well-pitched roof. The floor
was flat and level. By using heavy lumber for joists and rafters,
the floor could hold a cast-iron stove and heavy bookcases, and
the roof could support tons of snow and ice. From the lake, one
could scarcely see the cabin, so perfectly did the gray bark walls
and green metal roof blend into the forest. Yet it lay only 38 feet
from shore. The only obvious sign of human activity was a small,
improvised dock for my boat and the rut grooved into the bank
where the logs had been winched. The original leafy denizens of
my land surely must have smiled down with a "well done" for
my rugged little bark-covered house.

A 12-by-12-foot cabin is hardly a mansion. I had hundreds of
books to move in and a desk to install. I needed a dresser for
clothes, cupboards for gear, and some furniture. Most important,

there must be a place to sleep. Even a single bed would have taken at least one-eighth of my precious floor space. I considered a hammock, a fold-down plank bed, a cot, a mattress atop the desk—none of these would do. I wanted a cozy, permanent resting place, preferably double, in case someday there would be someone to share the cabin with me.

Then I remembered the pioneers again. They had slept up in lofts warmed by heat rising from their fireplaces and safe from prowling wild animals. A sleeping loft was the answer. I suspended a ceiling across the open back porch and framed in one end with a wide window. Nailing a rustic log ladder on the inside wall, I had easy access (by possessing the agility of a red squirrel) to my bedroom. It was snug with a wide foam-rubber mattress, goose-down pillows, and heavy woolen Hudson Bay and Guatemalan blankets. At night I slept practically in the branches of balsam firs. Also, I cut a few boughs and laid them under the mattress so that their fragrance continually filled the air.

A kitchen was also imperative. All my appliances had to function on bottled propane gas. Fortunately, I found a gas refrigerator and a three-burner gas stove with tiny oven. These were set out on the open back porch under the sleeping loft. I soon realized that on windy or rainy days it would be unpleasant fixing meals here. The porch would have to be enclosed before winter arrived. For the immediate summer months, however, I could manage.

Even July and August in the Adirondacks have nights when temperatures dip near freezing and drizzly days are as dark as an eclipse. The cabin needed heat and light. The most efficient woodburning stove is a Franklin; so I purchased one in town. Then began a struggle to haul the cast-iron, cumbersome dinosaur home. The stove must have weighed 300 pounds and it took three men and me to get it in and out of the boat, up the hill, and into a corner of the cabin. How wonderful that first fire felt and sounded, snapping, crackling, throwing its warmth across the cabin walls. Aside from its life-supporting function, my Franklin stove was to become the main source of psychological comfort in fall and winter when days are short, bleak, and lonely.

Light was simple to arrange. Candles and kerosene lanterns sufficed at first, later augmented by gaslamps run off the propane system. They are far less glaring and noisy than Coleman lanterns, and make a mellow glow at night quite bright enough for reading, typing, or fine sewing.

The cabin had taken the month of May to build. Now, taking advantage of the long June nights, I began furnishing the inside. Again the chain saw proved indispensable for putting together rustic bookcases and little benches. A glossy black Boston rocker, authentic red, black, and white Navajo rugs, a gay red cupboard, two filing cabinets under a long smooth desk top, an antique cherry dresser—this comprised my cabin furniture. I took practically nothing from the dozens of rooms of furniture at Morgan's lodge.

It was July 1. My ultimatum was up. I resolved to be moved out of the hotel and into the cabin by July 4. In abandoning my life-style of the past several years, this American Independence Day would be as much a day of *personal* liberation as *national*.

I faced a flurry of finishing jobs. The newly hung door and window frames had to be painted dark green before hand-woven red and white Guatemalan Indian curtains could be hung. Cabin posts needed a good soaking in creosote to prevent rot or decay. The kitchen floor was stained dark brown so muddy boots would not discolor the plywood. Sheets of white cedar veneer were secured over the rafters, making a warm-toned, rustic ceiling. I nailed up deer antlers as gun, fishing rod, and clothing racks. A Mexican guitar and Colorado coyote pelt decorated one log wall. On the front porch, a couple of Adirondack-style rocking chairs and a Brazilian hammock swayed back and forth in the wind. A pot of red geraniums lent a cheerful touch. I set out fire extinguishers, a barometer, a maximum-minimum thermometer, and a battery-operated radio. Best of all, I arranged my library—

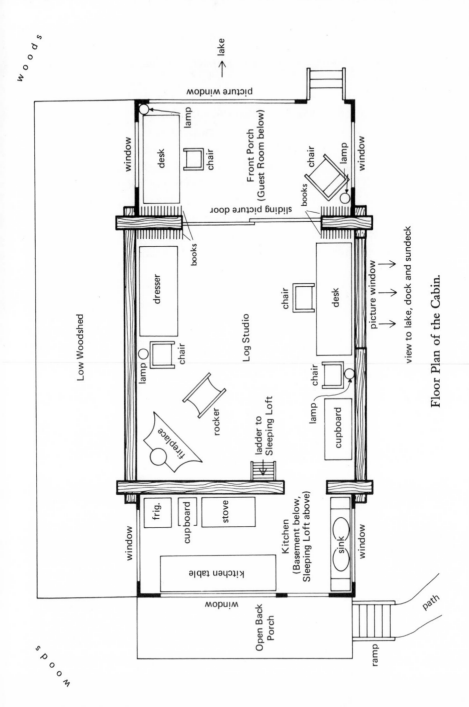

Floor Plan of the Cabin.

a complete set of *Encyclopaedia Britannica*, the *Journal of Wild-life Management*, the *Auk* (journal of the American Ornithologists' Union), the *New York State Conservationist*, *Webster's Dictionary* and *Roget's Thesaurus*, plus dozens of scientific references—in a multicolored array on rustic shelves.

My new home, the first *real* home of my adult life, was ready for occupancy. One of my first visitors, a single lady writer, left me with these memorable words: "Your log cabin is as softly outlined, as naturally brown, as proudly retiring, as completely indigenous in character as an Adirondack bear—a real, prepeople, independent bear."

Well, time would show just how independent I could be living in it.

# 2

## At Home

After spending several years married to an Adirondack inn-keeper, with the hustle, bustle, and strain of managing summer guests, staff, eight cottages, a dining room, fourteen fireplaces, a dozen hotel rooms, horses, boats, salesmen, chefs, and bakers, I viewed moving into my tiny cabin with mixed fear and antici-pation. It would be a tremendous change in life-style, albeit a therapeutic one. I would truly be alone in a cabin in the woods.

Just a step beyond my backdoor, stretched my "backyard"— 6 million acres. The Adirondack Park is larger than any other state or national park in the United States, and undoubtedly the biggest tract of wilderness left east of the Mississippi. The *state* part (almost half of the park) is legally designated as "forever wild." It has been this way since 1894. No building or road may be built, no trees can be cut, and hunting and fishing are care-fully managed by the State Department of Environmental Con-servation.

The *private* half is a patchwork quilt of landholdings owned by residents like myself, commercial enterprises, and big lumber companies. Yet essentially it is wild or rural in character. Many private lands are laced with public trails, canoe routes, beaches, boat-launching sites, hunting and fishing areas, plus the scattering of hamlets, villages, and a few towns. There are no cities in the Adirondacks. In fact, local people refer to that teeming, citified area *beyond* the mythical Blue Line surrounding the Adirondack Park as the "Outside." Those of us who live *inside* the park and love it call it the "North Woods." The Adirondack Park Agency seeks to protect the "forever wild" nature of the state-owned acreage and to regulate growth on private holdings through two farsighted regional land-use plans. These plans promise to conserve the quality of this exceptional mountain region for "natives" and "Outsiders" alike.

Nevertheless, silly spectral thoughts raced through my mind before moving into my cabin. My own side property lines meet two other private holdings, each comprising over 50 acres of woodland. My back property line touches directly on a 50,000-acre state wilderness area where no motorized vehicles, roads, or structures exist. And just across Black Bear Lake another such 60,000-acre tract lies. Would it be dangerous living under such remote conditions? Might an unwanted prowler break in at night? Although several private summer cottages dotted the lakeshore, no one could hear me if I screamed for help. The thick forest, wind, and water all contrived to insulate me from other inhabitants. What if a wild bear came into my outdoor kitchen, tearing open the refrigerator or ripping apart the gas lines? Black bears are common in the Adirondacks and have a notorious fondness for redolent kitchens and dumps. What if I slipped and broke a leg? Without a telephone, citizen's band radio, or car at hand, there was no way I could summon aid. The nearest doctor and clinic were over 25 miles away in the village of Lake Serene, at least a 45-minute drive in fair weather. Such were the silly spectral thoughts that raced through my mind before moving.

On the other hand, visions of uninterrupted mornings sitting at my desk, quiet evenings rocking by the stove, and living a simple and totally private life lured me unerringly to my new home.

The first evening I ate supper on the dock bathed by a golden sunset. A Rusty Blackbird creaked out his call from an alder bush and two Purple Finches warbled atop a tall spruce. Not a breath of wind ruffled the water. Barn Swallows were swooping down to the surface, plucking insects, and embroidering small circles upon the lake with each dip of their beaks. Brook trout were rising up to the surface, snatching bugs, and in contraposition, making the same lazy circles with their mouths. A doe and spotted fawn waded playfully through the shallows on the opposite shore a quarter of a mile away. Their ripples threw the geometrical patterns created by birds and fish into fragments. My wildlife neighbors seemed oblivious to my presence. It was comforting to see them all around. Sometime during that first night, I awoke with a start to the slap of a beaver's tail on water, and again at dawn to the drumming of a woodpecker on the front porch post. These "intruders" were welcome any time.

After that first week at the cabin, I began to relax. It was apparent that few, if any, people or bears were going to molest me. Nevertheless, I kept my .300 Savage rifle and 16-gauge shotgun loaded and a chain on the door at night. Every tempting scrap of garbage went out by boat to the local dump 3 miles outside of Hawk Hill hamlet. Most of my visitors were charming. Red- and White-breasted Nuthatches, chickadees, and juncoes began coming to the feeder, trilling and tooting their songs all day. A frisky raccoon scrambled nightly up a stump to tease suet from the wire-mesh holder. Soon the red squirrels were sitting boldly in the balsams scolding me. Was it *their* land, or *mine*, they seemed to say. How dare I erect this wooden square nest underneath their leafy round ones? As long as I kept the feeder supplied with sunflower seeds, they would permit me to stay.

One morning I surprised a snowshoe hare in its "form" or resting place only 50 feet from the cabin. It froze. I spent ten minutes noting every detail of its soft brown fur (due to turn white before winter) and its comically large paws (so superb at transporting this bunny on soft snow). No wonder it is called snowshoe.

Chipmunks dashed through the wood sorrel and bunchberries, over mossy logs, and under the witch hobble. They even ventured up my porch to the geranium pot but decided against eating the spicy leaves. One soon dug its burrow next to the back post. I estimated it took three weeks for the resident wildlife and me to become accustomed to each other and lose our timidity.

For all the water around my land, I couldn't figure out how to get it *inside* the cabin. Buckets of lake water sufficed for drinking, cooking, and washing dishes; but I wanted a steady source for laundry and fire fighting. First I tried driving a point into a low piece of ground near the cabin. I hoped to hit a spring or vein of clear cold water. After I rigged up a hand pump, all that came up was pail after pail of dirty "beaver" water, smelling of swamps and mud and rotting logs. So I threaded on another section of pipe and drove deeper. Giving a mighty swing of the maul, I broke off the pipe at the joint and lost the point. There seemed no way of retrieving it short of digging a 10-foot hole through duff, rocks, and that hateful hardpan. I abandoned the pump idea—and the point.

Next I searched through my woods for a spring, sump, seep, or creek. Nothing. There was no way to bring in a well digger and equipment, being so far from the road. Finally, I bought a gasoline pump, several yards of plastic pipeline, and a 50-gallon stock tank. By pumping water from the lake to the tank set high on a knoll, I had an efficient gravity feed system to the cabin. In addition, the pump and a long garden hose made an effective fire-fighting device.

My facilities that first summer were pleasantly primitive, refreshingly Spartan. I swam two or three times a day in the lake (starting with a dip at dawn in the nude) and washed my hair in that soft, pure water. I added a sink and cold-water tap for washing dishes in the open-air kitchen. There was a tiny outhouse with removable seat (which could be taken indoors to warm up) about 200 feet from the cabin. To my surprise, a well-meaning summer neighbor who lived half a mile up the lake delivered a huge, lion-pawed, enamel bathtub to my dock (I suspected he had been trying to get rid of it for years). It took four of us to heft the monster up the bank and under the cabin. Having no place to locate it discreetly and no hot-water system, I made the tub a receptacle for the chain saw, its tools, and gas can. Maybe some day I would install a hot-water heater and build a basement-bathroom.

On the first nippy August morning following a Canadian cold front, I could predict that my facilities would freeze solid come fall and winter. I'd soon have to figure out a whole new regime for getting water inside and protecting the cabin from fire.

One night, lying in the loft, I heard a tentative scratching and scrambling under the roof boards, but above the ceiling paneling. I listened intently. Suddenly a breath of air touched my face. The flutter of wings filled the loft. A bat! Aware that its superb sonar would keep it from actually touching me, I quietly opened the window screen. The bat flew frantically around for a moment, then zeroed into the opening and swished out. Half an hour later another bat went through the same performance. It looked as if they had taken up residence. I did not want the fetid odor of their feces in the cabin, nor these unsettling evening acrobatics. Next day I got a ladder and searched for holes around the eaves and ridgepole. In order not to imprison the bats under the roof and have them die there, I had to wait till their evening sortie before climbing a ladder in the dark to plug up the holes. It must have been successful, for bats never again flew through my loft. I often wondered where they *did* go to sleep after finding their free apartment sealed up.

Other wild neighbors which I tried to discourage were mice. Even the winsome eyes and immaculate underparts of the little deer mouse and the elegant, plush fur of the redbacked vole did not win my hospitality or affection. I found their droppings in the sugar bowl and rice box and their holes gnawed right through handknit sweaters and woolen jackets. Mice were definitely "personae non grata." Setting mousetraps with peanut butter became as familiar an evening routine as brushing my teeth. As soon as I had the outside logs chinked with cement, which sealed the cracks better, the cabin became less like a mouse condominium and more like a one-night mouse motel stop.

In the midst of getting acquainted with my wildlife neighbors, a number of human summer inhabitants dropped by to welcome me to the lake and share a cup of camp coffee. According to Adirondack tradition, most visiting is done in late afternoon. The visitors may arrive by guideboat, canoe, motorboat, seaplane, sailboat, or on water skiis, but etiquette demands that they wait at the dock (having made appropriately loud noises) until the visitee walks down and invites them into the camp. This is analogous to ringing a doorbell in the city and waiting for the front door to be opened.

One morning, to my surprise, a man arrived at the dock about 9 A.M. He tied up his boat and stalked straight for the cabin door. A series of obtrusive knocks told me trouble was at hand. Five minutes later, my dream cabin had collapsed. I was given notice of an impending suit by the attorney who'd arranged the sale of the property. I had broken a clause in the covenant which accompanied my deed to the land. It stated that no building could be erected within 50 feet of the lakeshore: my cabin stood at 38 feet. I was stunned! Foolishly, I had not even bothered to read the covenant (which was about 3 feet long and full of "legalese"). The land had been available, inexpensive, wild, and beautiful. I had bought and built quickly, desperate to have a home. And I had spared those tall trees by choosing a site where none grew.

The lawyer was adamant. He was determined that the law would *not* be flaunted at Black Bear Lake. The cabin *must* be torn down or moved; otherwise, I faced a court procedure. In my current state of sorrow and instability, I had not heart for battle or courage to face a court case.

A rapid calculation showed that the cabin weighed 14 tons—a tremendous weight to move. The logs were held together by massive iron spikes in every corner which would hinder dismantling or tearing them apart. Another quick survey showed that three or four huge spruces would have to be cut down in order to move the building away from the lake. My pact with the trees would then be violated. In addition, the land beyond the knoll dropped down. If moved sideways, horizontally, the cabin would be left sitting up in the air rather than nestling close to the ground as it did now. It seemed to me that it could be neither torn down nor moved save under exceptional conditions, and that either action would leave a grievous wound on the forest and land.

No amount of pleading—no arguments for the sake of preserving the trees—no conservation ethic could shake the attorney's preposterous demand. At that point, I acquired a deep contempt for the "letter of the law." Somehow, just somehow, the cabin would have to be shoved sideways *12 feet* to conform with the covenant!

One day, as if by a miracle, three friends came to call. Over coffee, I poured out my woes about the cabin. I had until November 1 to move it. Already August was old. My friends, a hotel-owning family, told me they were closing business right after Labor Day and would be glad to help. Ned, a jolly Scandinavian by birth, went into a huddle with his sons, Sven and Brian, on my breezy front porch. As canny as professional engineers, they plotted and calculated how to shift the 14-ton building. New foundation holes would have to be dug, fresh footings poured, and more spruce posts cut. Long, peeled logs, stretching from the old posts to the new, would provide the skidways. Brian quickly jotted down a list of tools we would need—hydraulic jacks, come-alongs, cables and chains, peaveys, spikes, mauls, and crowbars.

"Don't fret!" he assured me with a cheering smile. "We've got all this stuff at our hotel. If you have a shovel, you can dig holes. If you have a chain saw, you can cut those skid logs. And if you can find some old grease, you can lubricate those skidways for easy sliding! That's all."

Instructions given, they left me feeling more optimistic than I had felt for days. Three weeks remained for the preparatory work. First I felled those tall spruces which clustered about the cabin like friends. Indian-style, I sent a prayer winging upward to each before it crashed to the ground. Soon the forest floor was marred with stumps, roots, branches, and tops. I had no time to clean up. The eight new holes proved just as tough to excavate as the last eight. I shucked off my muddy clothes each night so weary that I could hardly climb the wall to my sleeping loft. Two gargantuan logs, each 40 feet long, were cut and peeled. My hands became callous, grimy, and sticky with sap.

Next, I went to a restaurant and a service station in Lake Serene. One place gave me a 25-pound tin full of old fat from their french fryer; the other, a big bucket of axle grease. I was ready for Ned, Sven, and Brian.

Labor Day arrived and the weather turned raw and rainy. Nevertheless, my friends showed up to move the cabin. They were not daunted in the least.

"We'll have this moved over in no time," said Ned, giving me a comforting pat on the shoulder.

"No time" took *one* day just to jack up the building and pry it loose from the foundation posts; *another* day to haul the skid logs to the cabin and lift them into place; *another* day to secure the skid logs to the old and new foundation posts, grease them, and set up the jacks, come-alongs, and winches; *another* day to nail cross-members to the cabin walls, windows, and roof edges so they would be less likely to shift; and a *fifth* day to move the cabin.

"Today's the day!" said Sven, grinning mischievously as he dabbed my nose with axle grease. "She'll slip across those logs

like a snake on a hot rock. You wait and see." With that he and
Brian each grabbed a come-along handle and started winching.

Ostrich-like, I sat inside during the entire transfer. I could
not bear to be outdoors with the men; straining with the steel
cables, listening to the creaks and groans, expecting to see the
posts topple over under the weight. Even indoors I waited for
windows to shatter or the roof to fall on my head.

The cabin inched across those huge skid logs, a distance of
12½ feet, in eight hours (that half foot was for good measure).
Nothing cracked, broke, or tilted. No one was hurt. So much for
the sturdiness of log cabins and good friends.

Now my home perched in the woods like a long-legged marsh
bird. It stood so high that there was space for a narrow guest
room, tiny basement, and a general catchall space beneath the
main log structure once the new floor was laid. My long mis-
used bathtub found a home and companion. It was squeezed into
one corner of the basement and connected to a gas hot-water
heater. My life-style was becoming less Spartan. But, I rational-
ized, how good those hot baths would feel on chilly nights after
working hard all day to clear up the mess. The cabin's original
posts, joists, and floor were still intact. I would convert them next
summer into a sun deck with rustic flower boxes around the
edges. All this extra space has proven invaluable, but at what
emotional cost!

I have a letter from that lawyer in my files. It states that my
dwelling conforms with the distance stated in that infamous and
neglected covenant—50 feet from the shoreline. He must have
sneaked over and measured. If I had caught him in the act, I
would have smeared that man with french-fry and axle grease
and tied him to one of those tree stumps for the bears or black
flies to devour. I couldn't have cared which!

Once again my cabin was ready for occupancy.

# 3

# Season of Splendors

Autumn in the Adirondacks is a season of splendors. By early September, all the cacophony and motion of summer—outboard motors, seaplanes, water-skiers, tourist traffic, canoers, backpackers, sunbathers, swimmers—abruptly cease since most of the annual 9 million transients through our mountains try to cram their visits in between July 4 and Labor Day. Now the mountains and lakes return to their normal tranquility and wildlife again appears.

On a misty morning in September I can step down to the lake and find damp paw prints and a sprig of pondweed on my dock. One hundred feet away a trio of otters may be fishing. First I see the hump of a sleek back, then a curved tail, then two rounded ears and bright eyes—no, four—no, six. It looks like an animal 20 feet long with two heads. Where does "it" begin and end? Could it be the Loch Ness Monster come to the Adirondacks? The mist swirls in the dawn breeze and obscures the otters for a moment. Then it separates and I see the three animals leap fluidly onto the rocks off my cove. Each holds a bullhead in its mouth. In the hush, I hear the crunch of bones. Breakfast over, the otters glide back into the lake to play more monster games.

In early evening the beaver sally forth, no longer skulking along shorelines to avoid motorboats. About 6 P.M. a big male swims nonchalantly past my dock. I try to be there, sitting quietly, to watch him. A smooth wake spreads out from his tail. This ripple moves across the lake, marbling the reflection of ebony hills, electric-blue sky, and rosy clouds. Moments later his mate follows, trailed by three kits. I sit bemused by the slow dissolving of colors back to mirrored perfection. Then a munching noise begins up the creek. I slip into my aluminum canoe (painted to look like birchbark) and paddle silently toward the sound. Five beavers are eating dinner, half-in, half-out of the water. They've gnawed down an 8-inch diameter yellow birch whose top branches are afloat. Each animal is chewing little paths around the trunk with its strong orange teeth.

The male sees me. He submerges instantly, comes up 15 feet away, and wallops the water with his tail. A few drops splash into my face. He begins a cautious circling of the canoe, hissing and snorting. The female joins the reconnaissance. The youngsters go into orbit farther out. For twenty minutes we are at a stalemate. I am a black and white planet and they are five suspicious satellites, circling, circling. At times I could touch one with my paddle. Finally, I break the suspense, back-water, and move away from their feed tree. The beavers relax and return to dinner. In a few days when they've devoured the bark and tender branches, I'll come back with my boat and tow the trunk home for firewood. After all, it *is* my tree.

Adirondack autumn days are usually mild enough at noon to enjoy some final sunbathing before winter. Sitting on the sun deck, I admire my flower boxes built of odd pieces of log slab siding. The hardy red and white petunias have not yet shriveled from frost. A sudden buzz and a Ruby-throated Hummingbird pokes his bill into a bloom. This may be his last day sipping nectar from my flowers in the Adirondacks. By September 20 he'll leave. Like a miniature jet he will fly south to his winter destination in Florida, Central America, or Panama. Then with a regularity as rigid as a Pan American trans-Atlantic flight, he'll be back by May 15. This tiny titan has an incredibly sensitive internal guidance mechanism which probably responds to the sun's changing light intensity, the earth's magnetic fields, and/or the stars' fixed positions. That, and a vitality so great that the bird can propel its 4-inch body across 1,000 to 2,000 miles of mountainous land and open ocean to a precise location by a certain date twice a year.

The only flying creatures that impress me more with their strength and mobility are the migrating Monarch butterflies. As I sprawl soaking up the weak sun, they waft past the somber spruces as gaily orange as any autumn leaf, yet infinitely more fragile. Updrafts toss them to the spruce tops; downdrafts plummet them toward the petunias. Still they push invincibly southward, some traveling 1,000 miles or more. For all their vast biological differences, their seeming vulnerability, I think these insects surely rival the hummingbirds in the power and persistence of their migratory urge.

On clear, frosty mornings, I'm awakened by the stentorian honking of Canada Geese flying low over my sleeping loft. They sound slightly hoarse, as if having just risen from their slumber on some cold and misty lake. All day, skein after skein wedge south, nudged by a north wind. As each chorusing group passes, I run down to the dock to count their numbers. By nighttime, still flying, the birds are unbelievably high. I listen from the dock again, bundled into a down jacket, gazing 5,000–8,000–10,000 feet up. Their honking has the haunting quality of distant French horns. My spirit soars up beside them. I imagine the mighty Adirondack Mountains dwindling into dark humps interlaced with quicksilvered streams and moon-spangled marshes.

How I wish to fly with the geese away from dreary November days, the "freeze-up," and cruel winter. Away from the loneliness, isolation, and anxiety bred by blizzards. Most every local person I've talked to grudgingly admits to an autumn apprehension. It is part and parcel of an Adirondacker's psychological makeup. The geese contaminate us with this strange depression on their southbound flight and cure us with their northbound. In between, we try to tolerate winter, each in his or her own way.

As soon as the sun loses its warmth each afternoon, I begin the business of laying up firewood for the winter. The Franklin stove will require 10 to 15 cords. Chain saw and ear mufflers in hand, I roam around the backwoods until I find a standing, dead hardwood tree. Yellow birch is best because it burns with the highest Btu's of any Adirondack tree and gives off a pungent woodsy aroma. Red and sugar maples or beech are second choices. Failing this, I cut spruce, but its resins tend to gum up the stovepipe. If there are no dead trees, I saw up live ones and wait a year for the wood to season before burning.

On a crispy autumn afternoon, there is no outdoor chore more pleasurable than cutting and splitting wood. The spunky roar of a chain saw—the growing pile of logs scattered among the ferns—the heft of my trusty axe—the bite of its blade into straight-grained wood—the special "thwang" when a section splits apart. That's woodcutting! In just a few minutes I work up a sweat and strip to a light shirt or bra. At the close of the day, I may even brave a plunge in the chilly lake to cool and clean off. That night my muscles will ache and fingers tingle, but I'll sleep deeply.

The hardest part of cutting wood is getting the logs to the woodshed. The forest is too dense and the ground too uneven to pull a cart, much less a horse and wagon. So, borrowing a custom from the Mayan Indians of Guatemala, I carry my wood with a tump line. I stack five to eight logs in a neat pile, lash them together, and swing them onto my back. The horsehide headband fits comfortably across my forehead. Using neck muscles eases the strain on my back and shoulders. I can carry almost twice as many logs with a tump as in my arms.

I feel a true pride at seeing my woodpile grow taller. Every fresh log means more hours of warmth. Woodcutting is homemade insurance against winter cold, costs nothing, and generates a flush of physical fitness. I often think of my girl friends who live in cities. They are slender and attractive, but they puff going up stairs and their upper arms and thighs look slack and unmuscled. That's another compensation for cutting wood. You sure don't need a girdle. Also, you can't stay terribly angry or worried over things for long when you split wood. Every blow of the axe can be sublimated into chopping off your enemy's head or punching the tax collector in the mouth.

With firewood so much on my mind, there's an opposite concern to consider—fire prevention. Living 1½ miles from the nearest road means no fire engine can ever come in an emergency. No fire boat exists on our sparsely populated, loosely organized lake. I check and refill all the extinguishers—foam, water, and chemical—and keep four buckets of water indoors at all times. Fireproof panels back the Franklin stove. Its pipe is well-insulated metal asbestos wrapped round with fiberglass and more asbestos paper. Winter, of course, is the most precarious season for fires since the stove burns constantly. The pump is drained and use-less. Two feet of ice cover the lake, and only one hole, chopped open daily by axe, gives access to precious fire-killing water. My fear of fire mounts almost to paranoia between November's freeze-up and April's breakup.

Fall brings the local inhabitants closer to one another. Cama-raderie increases as honking geese and keening winds remind us how sparsely settled our mountains are. "The Adirondacks are mostly populated with mountains," once wrote an astute ele-mentary schoolchild for a study unit. "People are only there second source of population." And only 125,000 permanent resi-dents *are* registered in the Adirondacks. Of the 107 towns and villages on private land entirely or partially within the "Blue Line" (or state park boundary), a mere 17 boast populations over 2,500. Contrast that to New York City only 250 to 300 miles away, with almost 8 million people within the city limits. In the city, I'm told, the average office worker sits within a ten-minute radius of 220,000 other human beings. Up in my cabin office, the nearest full-time residents are 5 miles away!

Early explorers, traders, and settlers went around this mass of mountains, taking the easy river routes which partially head up in, and embrace, the Adirondacks. The peaks were too tall and the swamps too wet, so they followed the St. Lawrence, Hudson, Mohawk, and Black Rivers. There grew the large upstate cities of Albany, Utica, Watertown, Massena, Plattsburg, and Amsterdam. Adirondack towns also developed on river banks and lake shores, but each one became a small satellite dependent on the lowland cities outside the mountains for major materials, food stuffs, medical services, and communications. Local residents make their living as lumberjacks, linemen, plumbers, carpenters, small shopkeepers, hotel staff, road crews, and mechanics. Theirs has always been a service-oriented society—service to the lumber companies, railroads, state land, and tourists. This has molded people who are staunchly independent, stubborn, reserved, suspicious of outsiders, but warmly supportive of local friends. "Locals," or "natives," they're called.

In fall, my shopping trips to Lake Serene triple in time. No one feels any pressure to attend to tourists.

"How've you been?" asks the urbane hardware store owner, as if we'd been on different continents all summer.

"Do you figure on a hard winter?" ponders the dour pharmacist, as I stop in for Band-Aids and Ben-Gay. (Both are necessary remedies for cutting wood.)

"Buying a new snowmobile this winter?" inquires the young, long-haired service attendant, when I drive in for gas.

These are the invariable topics of conversation. If I sit down in the diner for coffee, someone may start a bit of gossip by saying, "Say did you hear what happened to Bill last week?"

Thus, we catch up on the summer's happenings and reestablish our bonds of friendship or animosity. I find folks are relaxed and open at Lake Serene (a village of about 1,000 inhabitants) until hunting season approaches. Then, the tension of a new wave of tourists sets in again.

October 25 is the traditional opening day of big game season in the Adirondacks, or Northern Tier, of New York State. And it's big business up here! More than 150,000 hunters throng our mountains every year, spending an estimated $8 million for food, equipment, lodging, and services. This influx causes a new bustle of activity among the local shopkeepers and hotelmen. State Environmental Conservation officers prowl the roads and trails in search of preseason poachers or game violators. Residents either start oiling their rifles or begin securing their property.

It's time to post my 22 acres and protect them from trespass by eager sportsmen. I post my land because it is my private wildlife sanctuary, and no hunter or fisherman may disturb the animals here at any time. In a world where millions upon millions of people live in cities and suburbs, owning nothing, renting out a tiny space in which to live out their lives, I feel that having one's own land is a priceless gift. City folk have to define *their* territories through social behavior and the use of money. I can physically and visibly define *mine* by nailing NO TRESPASSING signs around my borders, much as a wolf marks his home range by urinating on special bushes and rocks. In a red and black lumberjack shirt, pockets bulging with flat-headed nails, hammer dangling from my belt, I walk the lines. Every hundred feet or so, a poster is placed on a prominent tree so that no one, however myopic, can cross these boundaries unknowingly.

Posting land is an ideal way to revisit cherished landmarks. I skirt past little Birch Pond to check on the yellow cow lilies and old beaver dam. No recent action there. Then I turn up a hill, following a well-worn deer run. Now the line ambles over hemlock-covered knolls and through sphagnum-carpeted swamps. Where it touches the shores of Beaver Pond, I always find the two corner posters torn to shreds by aggressive trespassers—red squirrels. Why, I'll never know. A lone Great Blue Heron stilts along the shoreline, and a family of Pied-billed Grebes dabbles in the shallows. I take a long draught from a tiny spring, then post the other half-mile line back toward camp.

Despite the signs, there are always arrogant hunters who flagrantly ignore them. On opening day during my first fall in the cabin, I heard a rifle shot right behind the water tank. Grabbing my .300 Savage off the wall, I then dashed through the woods in the direction of the shot. Three stocky Irishmen, clad entirely in red, faces flushed from exertion, stared at me.

"Gentlemen, this land is posted! You'll have to leave," I said sternly, cradling the rifle in my right arm.

"Aw, lady," replied one in a bantering tone, "we're just cutting across to state land behind here."

"Then why did you shoot?" I asked evenly.

"Couldn't have been *us!*" stated another, shifting the rifle in *his* arms.

A flutter of fear went through my stomach. Would they try to back me down and march right on through? Raising the rifle ever so slightly and easing off the safety, I said firmly, "This is a wildlife sanctuary. It's plainly posted. I don't care if you have to walk 5 miles to get around it, but you're not going across."

They hesitated a moment, then irritably turned and backtracked. "She might try a citizen's arrest," whispered one to the other. "Bitch!" muttered the third under his breath.

A far more frightening incident took place one foggy night in November. I was sitting at my desk writing, all the gas lamps glowing to dispel the spooky gloom. It was deathly still. Across the lake from my cabin was a brown and green camp seldom used except during hunting season. A gang of men had moved in on opening day and were still there. About 8 P.M. I heard a faint holler. "Annie, hello! Annie, are you there?"

I knew no one in that group. No other camps were occupied at my end of the lake. Could it be that someone was lost in the fog on the lake and calling for help? Yet only my closest friends call me "Annie." I extinguished all the lamps and stepped quietly onto the back porch. A low murmur of drunken voices carried over the still water. I crept down to the dock. Several grotesque shadowy forms, back-lit by a brilliant yard light, were weaving and jostling on their dock. It sounded ominously as if an aluminum boat was being launched.

Again, louder, "Annie, oh, Annie, are you there?"

This time I chose a shotgun loaded with buckshot from the cabin wall and sat down on the bank overlooking the lake. Perhaps seeing a darkened camp the men would figure I'd gone to bed and forget whatever plot or prank they had in mind. Certainly it would have been foolish to answer, and there was no one to call for help. The calling, clanking of oars in the boat, and jostling around the dock continued for half an hour. Then the men trooped into their camp and slammed the door. The woods dripped softly, the fog thickened, the lake steamed, the November night cooled. I held my vigil until almost midnight, considering that drunken hunters might be as unpredictable as rabid dogs.

Next morning I woke furious. Not only had my writing been disturbed, but I'd spent a sleepless night listening for trouble. It seemed wise to nip this incident in the bud and perhaps at the same time project an image which might prevent any future problems. I chose a beat-up stetson, strapped a .38-caliber revolver to my hip, and pulled on a pair of tall boots. Racing my boat full-speed across the lake, I jumped out and ran up to the door of their camp. "Bang-bang-bang." No answer. Finally, a puffy-faced man in quilted red underwear opened the door sleepily.

Before he had a chance to say anything, I burst out with, "What the devil were you and your friends up to last night? Yelling my name across the lake! I'm trying to write a book and did not appreciate the interruption. For your information, if anyone of you sets a foot on my land or even comes close to my dock without an invitation, I'll shoot first and ask his name after!"

I turned abruptly and strode away, hoping that my reputation as an ornery, pistol-packing woodswoman had begun. Evidently word spread, for no more hunters came close to the cabin for three or four years. Then, one late, windy afternoon, coming home from a long trip with a friend, we found a motorboat hidden up the creek. Tracks led across my land, right past the posted signs. Patsy and I pondered what to do.

"I'd like to catch those rascals," I told her. "Tying their boat right under a NO TRESPASSING sign is too much."

So we rowed their boat back to my dock, tied it fast, and carried their gas tank onto my porch. The hunters wouldn't be able to slip away without seeing us first. We sat down inside with tea and cookies. Patsy fidgeted. It was her first visit to the Adirondacks and she was nervous over the hordes of hunters, firearms, and vehicles. To a stranger from the city, it must look something like an armed invasion.

Just at dusk, two tall, muscular men stepped out of the balsams and yelled, "Anyone home?"

We both leaped out of our chairs. I opened the door while Patsy pressed close behind me, blue eyes round with apprehension.

"Are you looking for your boat?" I asked.

"Yes," replied the younger man politely Then he spotted the gas tank. "Did you take that?"

"I sure did. Can't you read? There was a posted sign not 20 feet from where you tied up. I see no excuse for your trespassing."

"We went into your creek because the lake was so rough," he explained calmly. "We didn't hunt on your land, Miss, but cut right over to unposted property."

Something in his manner disarmed me. I heard Patsy let out a breath of relief.

"Look," he said, "we're both state troopers and we wouldn't break the law. It's our first season hunting up here and we wanted to play it safe."

Patsy and I ended up inviting them in for coffee and spent a cheerful hour listening to tall tales. When they left, the older man asked, "Do you girls need help with anything?"

Next day, our two newfound friends and their two buddies,

four state policemen in all, brought my winter's supply of propane gas (eight cylinders weighing almost 200 pounds each) up
the lake and installed them at the cabin. I decided that not *all*
trespassers are bad guys.

Actually I have no quarrel with good hunters (provided they
keep off posted lands). Occasionally I hunt deer, and I enjoy a
venison roast as much as any sportsman or sportswoman. As a
trained wildlife ecologist, I recognize the important biological
role that hunters play in balancing wild game populations with
their existing food supplies and habitat conditions.

The whole topic of deer hunting, however, is a very touchy
subject in the Adirondacks. Many locals feel that our New York
State Department of Environmental Conservation is wiping out
the deer herd because they are far too lenient on the number of
licenses granted and too cocksure about their statistics and population dynamics. Conversely, the state game biologists maintain
that the lack of natural browse, deep snows, severe cold, and a
restricted winter range (only 20 percent of the total range) are
prime reasons for the low deer populations. The basic problem is
too many deer for the winter range to support, with resulting
malnutrition and starvation for the animals.

The Adirondack Mountains never were very good habitat for
white-tailed deer due to the dense and mature forests. After the
European settlers arrived, conditions changed somewhat. Clearings for small farms and cabins produced the grassland and brushland upon which deer thrive for food and cover. Wildfires
opened up more clearings. Gradually the large predators—wolves
and mountain lions—were exterminated. Later, rampant logging
operations and huge forest fires caused by careless loggers and
sparking trains destroyed still more forest canopy. All these fac-
tors changed the nature of the habitat and produced more and
better deer food.

Deer increased in the Adirondacks until about 1890 under
these unnatural conditions. Then the situation boomeranged.
The animals were prolifically fertile. They began to overbrowse
the winter range. Then they started dying of starvation. There

were massive die-offs. With the establishment of the Adirondack Forest Preserve in 1894, and its famous "forever wild" clause, state woodlands gradually began to recover from lumbering and burning. Gradually they returned to a more mature condition. Of course, less natural deer food was produced. Since the 1890s, our mountain deer herds, unlike those downstate in the Southern Tier, have followed a cyclic pattern. They build up for several years, suffer large losses from starvation in severe winters, then bounce back up again. The Department of Environmental Conservation attempts to regulate these cycles through human hunters (taking around 5,000 bucks annually in the twelve Adirondack counties). By harvesting more deer, including does, there is usually less winter starvation, hence a healthier herd in a more vigorous forest.

Every fall, there's one hunter—the mightiest of all—who pays no attention to posted signs, seasons, or game wardens Come

White-tailed deer in a forest clearing near Hawk Hill.

October, he starts stalking the skies, rising higher in the east each autumn night. His sword dangles brightly from his belt. His wide and imperious stance upon the horizon signals the end of our season of splendors. The sunny-yellow needles of tamaracks, last to turn, shiver to the ground. Now all the trees are bare. The hoots of Barred Owls echo through the frost-chilled forest. Along the mountain ridges, packs of coy dogs and coyotes howl under scudding clouds. Geese no longer honk overhead. One night the temperature drops to zero and the lakes glaze over with filigreed ice. Orion has leaped from the treetops to my cabin roof. Winter is here.

# 4

# Among My Closest Friends

During those first weeks and months at the cabin my close and constant companions were trees. I became intimately acquainted with every tree inside a 400-foot radius. What at first seemed like a dense stand of random temperate-zone vegetation—maples, spruces, hemlocks, beeches, birches, and pines—gradually introduced itself as an orderly congregation of unique individuals.

The "Four Sisters," a neatly spaced row of red spruces, stood practically within spitting distance of my sleeping loft. A trio of the same species clustered behind and above the dock, acting as friendly navigational aids against night skies. An enormous white pine leaned above the outhouse and another rose straight as a lighthouse on the point near the rocks. A forest of young firs graced the high shoreline from the side of the cabin almost down to the creek. Five more prodigious spruces loomed from a wet pocket of ground beyond the woodshed, while under them a few spindly youngsters stretched for the sun. I came to touch them all through trimming, pruning, clearing, cutting, admiring, and listening.

The first trees I got to know, and later draw strength from, were the mature, towering red spruces and white pines. These were highly skilled veterans, seasoned in survival techniques. They had started fortuitously as seedlings upon rich, sun-dappled patches of earth. They had escaped being nibbled by snowshoe hares, mice, grouse, or deer. They had shouldered past their siblings and finally pushed above the forest canopy into the free blue sky where swallows wheeled in summer and snowflakes whirled in winter. Here *all* the sunlight on any given day was theirs to activate the chlorophyll-laden needles, and *all* the rain of any given storm was theirs to wash the thick branches. These trees had survived attacks of smuts, aphids, mites, molds, beetles, galls, caterpillars, viruses, and the other miniature, life-robbing enemies of the plant world. They had also escaped being scratched by falling limbs, ripped by bears' claws, chafed by trunks, or rubbed by deer antlers. Likewise they had been unscathed by forest fires and bypassed by hurricanes. And so, in 1964, a goodly 300 years after their germination, they towered as invincible individuals of great character, lending dignity and beauty to my land.

I developed an amazing awareness of these trees. First, I noticed their noises. In wind, the spruces gave off a somber, deep, sad whoosh, while the pines made a higher, happier softer sough. After my initial surprise at the differences in sound between these two species, I began listening to other kinds of trees. Balsam firs made a short, precise, polite swishing; red and sugar maples gave an impatient rustling; yellow birches, a gentle, restful sighing.

Of course these strains of sound can be explained by the size, shape, flexibility, and thickness of leaf or needle. They can also be explained by the wind itself. I noticed distinct variations produced by the fresh westerly breezes, fierce north fronts, petulant south zephyrs, or stormy east winds. But the sound of the forest is more than this—just as a symphony is more than the sizes and shapes of the instruments, air pressure or touch which activate them to make music, and the players.

Next I discovered a whole assortment of tree scents. On hot, dry summer days, the balsams, spruces, and pines acted like giant sticks of incense, giving off a redolence which filled the air inside and outside the cabin. The carpet of dead needles, the dry duff, the trickles of pitch, the sun-warmed bark itself, all gave off subtle odors. The live needles tanged the air with what old-time doctors called "balsamifers."

The presence of this restorative odor is what made the Adirondacks a mecca for tubercular patients in the late 1800s and early 1900s. Whether the "balsamifers" did the curing, or the clean cold air, the long rests, the inspiring views, and the presence of such medical prophets as Dr. E. L. Trudeau, many mortally sick patients recovered in the Adirondacks. I know three men, all in their spry eighties, who came here to die in their thirties. They believe, as did Trudeau, pioneer tuberculosis researcher, that the resinous aromas produced by the evergreen forests helped cure them. Recent scientific studies have, in fact, revealed that the turpentine vapor exuded by conifers has a purifying effect on the local atmosphere and plays a part in keeping Adirondack air remarkably pure and healthy.

Another beautiful sensory experience happened to me in my forest of young balsam firs. On late summer afternoons, I saw the sun come slanting between the trunks. The light gave a glorious golden glow to the dense, dark copse. I began trimming off dead branches as high as I could reach with an axe. Whenever I nicked the bark of a trunk, I'd carefully daub moist earth on the wound to lessen sap flow and prevent the entry of disease organisms or insects. Off and on all summer I trimmed the balsam boles farther and farther away from the cabin until I achieved the desired effect. Then on a still September evening I perched on the porch railing, picking pitch from my palms, and watched the setting sun illuminate my fir forest. The sun shafts were straight diagonals of gold-washed air. As far as I could see, the balsam boles were straight black bars which threw black shadows onto the burnished-copper ground, golden-green moss, and bronzed fallen logs. My little forest had become a study in light and shadow, a stained glass window of gold and green panes with black bars, back-lit by the setting sun.

I experienced another quality of light on a dismal, dripping November day. It had rained for a week and the forest was totally drenched. My giant spruce trunks were soaked to charcoal-gray, their branches grizzly-green, the balsam boles inky-black, the ground tarry-brown, the pines pewter-gray. As Thomas Hardy wrote, "The whole world dripped in browns and duns." About eleven o'clock in the morning, the quality of light surrounding the cabin and trees was so watery that I might have been submerged somewhere in the North Atlantic. Each gust of rain felt like the surge of a swell, and the soggy forest looked like a stand of seaweed.

As I became more tuned into trees, I began to admire the enormous white pine near the path to the outhouse. I even oriented the entrance of the outhouse so that I could gaze at this tall, furrowed tree while sitting there. It was much better than reading *Time* magazine. In strong winds, the trunk would sway in a sinuous motion which combined the suppleness of a snake with the strength of an elephant. No rigidity to that pine. The thick bark, its multiple rings of wood, the very heart of the trunk all moved with a fluidity more animallike than plant. I drew closer to the tree and eventually came to stand against the trunk in order to watch those tons of wood bending lithely above my head. The grace and rhythm almost hypnotized me.

These friendly discoveries about my trees and the companionship which has been growing between us for years do not prevent me from using them at times for survival purposes. In a very practical way, trees have played an important role in my adult life, at times even a dangerous one.

Before I built my house from the bodies of trees, I used to help my husband, Morgan, cut wood for the hotel. We needed to put up at least 40 cords of firewood a year, besides bringing enough logs to the sawmill to provide lumber for the basic re-

Sun shafts filtering throug
my forest of balsam firs behind the cabi

pairs and additions of our buildings. With fourteen fireplaces to feed, eight cottages, a large main house, garages, stables, docks, and boardwalks to maintain, we had to cut a lot of timber each fall. And so I became a lumberjack, even being carried on the hotel payroll as such.

Coming from a populous suburb of New York City, I had never wielded an axe, revved up a chain saw, pulled a crosscut, or driven a wedge. After my first fall in the Adirondacks, however, I was able to cut and split 10 of those 40 cords, run a power saw, and operate the winch truck. I loved being a lumberjack, or "timberbeast." After a big breakfast, Morgan and I pulled on steel-shanked and -toed boots, grabbed heavy leather work gloves, and drove two trucks back into the woods over old logging roads. One truck had an iron A-frame which supported a pulley and winch cable for lifting logs; the other had a flatbed for transporting them. Locating an area of straight, tall hardwoods, we would pick a tree. Usually Morgan would start the chain saw and begin the cut while I stood back and watched the top. When the tree began to quiver, I would give hand signals which warned Morgan to stop the saw and dash away from the butt. He had to be careful that the severed trunk would not pinch down on the saw blade, kick back, or splinter as it fell. Then we both held our breaths and stood until the tree struck the earth with an awesome crash.

Once the tree was down, I usually darted up the trunk to the first limbs and began lopping them off with an axe. I worked upward until the trunk was too knotty or small to produce good firewood or lumber. Meanwhile, Morgan was busy sawing off the lower section into 8-foot, 12-foot, or 16-foot lengths which would be loaded onto the log truck. Later, at the hotel these would be blocked off into 18-inch sections for splitting, or taken directly to the sawmill for rough lumber, planking, and slab siding.

Switching off the ear-shattering saw and removing our ear-protector headsets, each of us started a truck. The winch truck was driven as close to the logs as possible and the flatbed backed up beside it. I would loosen the winch drum, drag the ⅜-inch steel cable out to the log, wrap and hook it around the butt end. Morgan would operate the controls from the cab of the winch truck. As soon as I made sure that the cable was running smoothly up to and through the pulley, I'd jerk my thumb upward in the signal, "All ready, lift up."

Morgan would start the cable winding on the drum and the log would be snaked through the woods. Once it was near the flatbed, Morgan slacked off the cable and I unhooked it from the log. Now a pair of heavy iron log tongs was hung on the cable hook, and I placed these at the center of the log.

Thumb up, I'd watch the 1,000-pound monster rise (hoping nothing would break just then) above my head. A shove this way or that aligned the log with the flatbed of the other truck. When it hung just right, I'd jerk my thumb down, "Let down." Morgan would lower the log by unwinding the cable. I hopped up on the flatbed and unhooked the tongs. A couple of chocks under the log assured me it wouldn't roll on my foot by mistake. Now we were ready to drag in another log, but before that, I had time to play a little game. In fact, it was the reason I preferred this half of the loading stint. Placing each boot inside the hooks of the tongs and grabbing the steel cable with my gloved hands, I would "ride" down from the truck bed to the ground, swinging like a monkey on a vine, as Morgan slowly let out the cable.

One morning, with six logs already on the flatbed, I was about to indulge in my usual pastime. As I grabbed the cable just below the pulley, my husband shifted the gears into "lift up" instead of "let down" by mistake. Before I realized what was happening, my glove and index finger were being ground up with the cable into the pulley. I let out a terrific scream. Morgan was so startled that he jammed in the brake, stalled the engine, and left me hanging. Continued screeching galvanized him into action. Seconds later the engine was running and I was descending to the ground. The shock of picturing myself being wound implacably through the winch like a mangled strip of hamburger almost made me pass out. I was afraid to pull off the glove. Morgan rushed me to a stream, dashed handfuls of icy water in my face, and plunged my right hand into the water. As it numbed from the cold, he gently eased off the glove. It was impossible to tell if bones were broken or tendons severed in the bloody wound.

The log truck was too heavily laden to make time, so Morgan carried me to the winch truck and drove flat out down the logging road. We had to cover about 35 miles of rough dirt and paved roads to the nearest clinic and X-ray machine. I was lucky. None of my fingers were broken or rendered useless. A couple of weeks later I was logging again, only this time *I* ran the winch truck and let *Morgan* hook and handle the logs.

Logging *can* be dangerous; however, this was the only accident either of us ever sustained during several fall seasons of logging. I gradually grew more adept with a chain saw. I could cut branches over my head, release trees tightly wedged against other trees, sever logs pinched together with an underhand cut, saw out planks, and even do some simple carpentry. This training, of course, made the construction of my log cabin possible and far easier than I ever suspected.

In those early days at the hotel, we employed Stan, an old-time lumberjack cook, as our off-season chef. He became my good friend. We whiled away many hours, he preparing roasts, me baking cakes, both singing lumberjack songs.

Stan taught me a tremendous respect for the early Adirondack timberbeasts. He told me of the prodigious appetites of these legendary men who wolfed down a dozen eggs and a stack of pancakes as tall as their boots for breakfast. He explained their incredible need for calories—over 6,000 a day—to pull crosscut saws for hours, ride slippery logs downriver, clear limbs, split wood, load logs, and drive horses in twelve-hour shifts. Stan would laugh when I came in ravenous from splitting firewood to devour slabs of roast beef and two pieces of pie.

"You eat like a cocker spaniel," he chuckled, "and your guests eat like toy poodles. You should have seen the meals I used to prepare for those lumberjacks!"

Stan also reminisced on logging-camp life. There was usually a shanty lined wtih narrow bunk beds, a cookhouse, and dining area. Silence was enforced at meals, except for requests for second, third, and fourth helpings, so as to lessen the chance for arguments and brawls. At night, the men would tumble into squalid straw-filled bunks. Often they would have to pluck lice from their hair by day. There were no washing machines in camp; but periodically, the cook, man or woman, would boil up the lumberjacks' clothes on a wood fire, thus removing some of the ingrained pitch, sweat, and soil. Timberbeasts worked all winter without a break (or a drink). They were without any transportation in or out except in emergencies. Then during a short spree in town, they might blow their entire earnings.

"God Almighty!" declared Stan. "What drinking sprees they used to go on. An 'Adirondack haircut'—that's what we called it. Some haircuts lasted three weeks!"

Logging hit the Adirondacks in the mid to late 1800's. Wave after wave of lumberjacks passèd through. Most came from outside the mountains, from the farming valleys and river bottoms. They were French Canadians, Swedes, Germans, Irish, and Welsh. Timberbeasts cut and snaked logs out of the woods with enormous, clever, patient horses. Winter was the best time for hauling logs via sled because the logging roads could be watered down and immediately turned to ice. This made it easier for the powerful teams to pull heavy loads. Logs were piled beside the closest lake, river, canal, or creek. Come spring, they were dumped into the water which was running abnormally high from the runoff. Then nimble loggers with caulked shoes, pegged trousers, and pike poles, "drove" the logs downstream to sawmills or railroads.

"Many a man lost his life on those river drives," mourned Stan, thumping a mound of sourdough for biscuits. "Once he fell in that icy river water, he either drowned, got knocked on the noggin' with a log, or was smashed up in a log jam. Jams were the most dangerous of all." Then he added cheerfully, "Say, did you hear about the lumberjack who turned up his heels at Tupper Lake last week? Clamps on his winch cable broke and a 1,200-pound log dropped on his head. Yes, indeedy, logging has always been dangerous work!"

Helping Stan stamp out biscuits with a cutter, I thought of all the logs that had lifted above *my* head back in the woods. A shudder ran through me. Then I considered that today's lumber-jacks really *do* have a safer, easier existence. They are protected by NIOSH (the National Institute of Occupational Safety and Health), they normally live at home, commute to work, eat better food, and use remarkable new power tools. On top of that, they can do their fighting and drinking on weekends. Adirondack haircuts have gone out of style. So have lice.

The other thing that is going out of style is the "rape attitude" of earlier days. In the 1800s, opportunists literally ravished the Adirondack forests. A lumberman's credo was, "If it grows, cut it." Clear-cutting and timber stealing were rampant. New York State led all states in 1850 in volume of timber cut. Due to this attitude, the Adirondack forest was swiftly devastated. Great tracts were cut—first the high pines and spruces to make spars and spiles (masts for sailing ships and spiles for docks), then the smaller softwoods for lumber, next the hemlocks for the tannic acid in their bark, and finally the hardwoods to provide furniture, veneer, tool handles, and other wooden merchandise.

Wildfires burned thousands of acres more. Sparks from logging camps and steam locomotives fell upon tinder-dry piles of branches, bark, and cull logs. The ensuing fires might smolder in the rich organic soil or leap into the crowns, burning for weeks without any control. People noticed that Adirondack streams and rivers were becoming "every year more slender and fitful."

The Adirondacks needed to be saved. Slowly public opinion turned toward conservation and legislators began to fight. In

1885, the state Adirondack Forest Preserve was created. Then in 1894, the famous "forever wild" amendment (Article 14) was added to the Constitution in order to protect the timber and watersheds of the Forest Preserve.

This legal gem reads: "The lands of the State, now owned or hereafter acquired, constituting the forest preserve as fixed by law shall be forever kept as wild forest lands. They shall not be leased, sold or exchanged, or be taken by any corporation, public or private, nor shall the timber thereupon be sold or removed or destroyed."

This far-sighted, totally unprecedented, wise conservation act is actually what made my dream of building a cabin in the wilderness—in the second-most-populated state of the Union—possible. Because of it, I have almost 3 million acres of untouched forest as my backyard. Without it, I shudder to think what scruffy piece of cutover land I might have purchased in my search for a home in the woods.

Today Adirondack trees still provide hundreds of thousands of board feet of lumber per year. Logging is our second most important industry up here, but it operates only on private holdings. Several large companies, such as International Paper, Litchfield Paper, and St. Regis Paper, employ lumberjacks. Timber is trucked to big mills outside the Adirondack Park. I often meet heavily loaded trucks bound for the Ticonderoga paper mill on the road to Hawk Hill. I always give them a wide berth, preferring to run off the shoulder and into a swamp than to match paints with a 20-ton truck whose stack of logs leans ominously over my small half-ton pickup.

Even though our Adirondack trees are protected from chain saws and axes on *state* land, they are still vulnerable everywhere to wind storms and lightning. In the great "blowdowns" of 1950 and 1954 trees toppled like pick-up sticks. Local events are still dated from these two most catastrophic hurricanes. On the eve of one less disastrous storm, I spent the entire night wandering through the woods. It was as warm as the tropics. That wild wind had blown up from Miami itself. High humidity soaked the air, swollen clouds gusted over the treetops, the air seemed spiced with scents from the Gulf of Mexico. I rolled up my shirt-sleeves and stopped by a stream to splash sweat off my face. The branches above me roared and thrashed. From time to time tall timber cracked and crashed to the ground. For one moment a three-quarter moon poured its wan light into the woods as monstrous blue-black clouds rent apart. I was too exhilarated to feel afraid, too thrilled to feel tired. The winds diminished around 5 A.M. Only then did I go to bed, still oblivious to the danger I had foolheartedly courted.

I awoke to devastation. Some sections of the Adirondack forest had been leveled as if by a scythe. Trunks lay crisscrossed in places up to 20 feet above the ground. Some of the finest mature timber in the Northeast had gone down in that storm. Effects of blowdowns last for years. New forest reproduction allows deer to increase dramatically in some places, starve out in other areas where fallen trees severely hamper movement. The lumber companies lose heavily, although they attempt to draw out whatever timber can be salvaged before decay spoils the wood. Hikers and campers find trails and campsites destroyed or blocked. Fire crews face new hazards as downed trees die and dry out.

It seems curious that I was not at all frightened *then* to be walking in the forest during those high winds, while *today* I am filled with apprehension about falling trees. It runs a close second to my preoccupation with fire. However, I've taken a deliberate gamble. Esthetically, it is more essential to me to see the Four Sisters swaying against the stars on a windy night than to cut a safety space all around the cabin. It is more important to have the huge curved spruce artistically jutting out from under my sun deck than to fell it and clear out a nice secure lawn instead. Despite this decision, I still don't sleep well on nights when the wind is high. I picture a great trunk toppling against a wall and scattering books, logs, and chinking into every corner. I lie awake imagining a great mass of branches plummeting onto my ridge-

Very few giant white pines are left in the Northea
This one, close to 300 years old, has a circumference of over ten fe

pole, poking through the metal sheets and roof boards, and impaling me in bed.

Only once have I had a close call. An exceptionally strong winter cold front swept through from the north and snapped the living top off my splendid curved spruce. It was blown 20 feet through the air. It sailed over the cabin ridge, slid down the back side, and crashed to earth with just its 15-inch butt nudging into the edge of the woodshed roof. Even this close call has not changed my decision to gamble, nor my original vow to protect the trees. I still cut only those which are dead.

In getting to know my trees, an exceptional event occurred. On my trips back and forth to the outhouse, I took more and more enjoyment from touching the great white pine. One morning, with my arms wrapped around the trunk, I began to feel a sense of peace and well-being. I held on for over fifteen minutes, chasing extraneous thoughts from my mind. The rough bark was pressed hard against my skin. It was as though the tree was pouring its life-force into my body. When I stepped away from the white pine, I had the definite feeling that we had exchanged some form of life energy. This feeling seemed concentrated between my belly and breasts. In later readings, I found the explanation in Carlos Casteneda's *Conversations with Don Juan* and Michael Serano's *Serpent of Serpico*. Mention is made that the area of the navel and solar plexus is considered the main point of energy in the human body. From here, "fibers" or "rays" of life-force radiate. I have also seen the energy coronas around fingertips in Kerlian photography and the results registered by polygraphs hooked up to plants reacting to stimuli. All these phenomena point to the presence of a pervading life-force, one which I miraculously tuned into by getting to know the trees at my cabin.

I feel this communion, this strange attunement, most readily with large white pines, a little less with big spruces, sugar maples, beeches, or oaks. Clearly white pines and I are on the same wavelength. What I give back to the trees I cannot imagine. I hope they receive something, because trees are among my closest friends.

# 5

# Inca—Mapuche—Pitzi

I wanted an animal to love, to caress, to play with at the cabin, and to take with me on trips. True, I had hundreds of trees as companions, and plenty of wild animals as company. Chipmunks clustered at my back porch begging for peanuts. Nuthatches, chickadees, jays, juncoes, and woodpeckers fed unabashedly at my feeder. Each evening, a button-eyed flying squirrel landed beside the kitchen window with a soft thump. She proceeded to nibble at the peanut butter I occasionally put out for her supper. Once in a while, she allowed me to stroke her silky back before springing into the air, sailing over the porch railing, and spread-eagling on a nearby tree flat as a furry pancake.

All these animals tolerated me because of free food, but not because of any innate affection. However, I did not wish these wild creatures to become pets. I believe that wildlife loses its dignity and, more importantly its ability to survive in the natural environment when it becomes tame enough to accept food or anything else from people. My land was to offer a sanctuary to wild animals, not a soup kitchen. And so it seemed reasonable to find a domestic pet.

My second summer at the cabin, I acquired an ebony black kitten with jade-green eyes. I promptly named her "Inca." The kitten quickly took to life in a log cabin. Inca swung on the curtains and knocked books off shelves. Inca caught mice and chased chipmunks. She dragged my socks into the woods and boxed with my boots. She tapped pencils off the desk and pushed down keys on my typewriter. Her favorite trick was to leap from log to log and pull the fiberglass insulation out of the cracks.

I found Inca's behavior amusing, until it came time to leave for a few days. It was impossible to put her on a leash or carry her under my arm. She turned into a mad demon when placed in the boat, jumping into the water and nearly drowning every time. Finally I stuffed the cat into a knapsack and drew the top tight with a rope. Then I slung it on my back or set it in the bottom of the boat. But regardless of whether I hiked out through the woods, used the boat, or trekked in snowshoes on the ice, Inca kept up a devilish howling, scratching, and scrambling inside the pack.

The cat's residence at the cabin was short. Despite all my cuddling and cajoling, she grew wilder and wilder. Some evenings Inca dashed around the cabin as if it was a mixing bowl and she was the electric beater. Then suddenly she would leap onto my desk, fix me with those clear jade eyes, and sit still as a statue. But the minute I began writing, she pounced on my hand. It was impossible to work with her around. When she attacked the flying squirrel and began stalking birds at the feeder, I decided she was not the proper pet for my cabin. I had Inca spayed and gave her to a cheerful old lady on a 300-acre farm outside the Adirondacks. She could roam and hunt to her heart's content there and curl up beside a chunk stove at night with three other cats and a doting mistress.

Between 1967 and 1969, I spent two winters in residence at a university working on my doctor's degree in wildlife ecology. Our wildlife diseases class met at the veterinary college. Here they were conducting an experimental rabies program, using

wild foxes as the control animals. One day I happened to pass
the pens and saw a young male silver fox staked out in the snow.
His coat was full and shiny, and his tail brilliant and bushy. We
stood gazing at each other—he with slanted yellow eyes as wild
as the day he was born—mine full of an immediate affection and
admiration. By changing my usual route to classes, I was able to
see this fox several times a week. A name came to mind, recalled
from a course on South American native peoples. It was "Mapuche," name of an invincible tribe of Indians in southern Chile,
as invincible as this fox's eyes.

One day I heard that many of the control foxes were no
longer needed in the program and would probably be destroyed.
I checked with one of the vet professors to learn if my fox friend
was one of these. Already I was thinking what a magnificent pet
Mapuche would make and how free he would feel at the cabin.
Before the week was out, I had acquired the silver fox, but no
place to keep it.

Since I spent most weekends at the cabin, I had only rented a
small room in a graduate student dormitory. No pets allowed.
Most of my friends lived in rental rooms or apartments where
similar rules applied. My professors had homes full of children,
cats, dogs, parakeets, and other pets. After a frantic search, I
finally found a very large empty wire cage outside an ornithology
laboratory. On one side a group of wild turkeys gobbled; on the
other a pair of rare Japanese cranes preened. It would be a tan-
talizing, if not appetizing, home for Mapuche. And, it was only
temporary.

I moved my silver fox there in February. Now began the most
discouraging days I have ever spent with an animal. Mapuche refused to let me near him. As soon as he heard my truck approach,
he cowered in a corner. The minute I came through the tiny
door, he curled his lips and bared his teeth. When I offered him
fresh water, horsemeat, or bones, he hissed and snarled. The pen
reeked of rank urine and musk sprayed by the fox. My clothes
and boots stank so badly that I had to keep a separate set just to

wear when I came to his pen. Otherwise my roommates would not tolerate me around the dorm.

This awful behavior continued all through a cold and snowy March. I would stay shivering as long as I could in the pen, hands turning stiff with cold inside my heavy gloves, hoping that the fox would relent and make his first tentative gesture of friendship. Yet day after day, he only glared, snarled, and cowered in the corner.

April came and with it warmer weather. One afternoon I was able to visit Mapuche without gloves or heavy jacket. The sun felt so warm that I lay down for a few minutes on a big log in the pen and closed my eyes. Suddenly something pulled my ponytail. I moved my head slightly and opened one eye cautiously. Mapuche was standing behind me, one paw lifted, poised for retreat. His jaws were closed and his ears erect. His white-tipped tail stood out straight as a pointer. This was not the posture of a vicious or frightened animal. I lay very still. Minutes later, I felt another tug on my hair. I opened both eyes and gazed into the fox's. His met mine unflinchingly, yet with a new expression—mischievousness. Astonished, I watched Mapuche edge forward, take the tip of my ponytail between his front teeth, and gently tug. Mapuche was trying to play!

Ever so slowly, I reached out my bare hand to him. After what seemed hours, my finger tips finally touched the fox. Instinctively, I touched him under the chin, palm up, as one does with a strange dog. But this left my wrist completely unprotected. Would Mapuche slash at my veins with those razor-sharp teeth?

He trembled slightly. I began rubbing his chin, then his throat, and around back toward his ears and neck. A remarkable transformation occurred. The fox's trembling stopped, and those wild yellow eyes gentled and half closed. His ears ceased wiggling back and forth like nervous antennae. His fur smoothed down. Mapuche stood as still as a house dog while I gave him the first human affection and attention he had probably ever known.

Certainly it was the first physical contact he and I had shared in six weeks.

Mapuche's overall behavior changed dramatically. Now when the truck drove up, he leaped against the wire walls eagerly, paws clinging like a cat, tail wagging like a dog. Instead of snarling, he was *grinning* when I came through the door. He accepted meat and bones from my hand. He used his teeth only to tug at my jacket, trouser legs, or hair in play. The fox showed off by bouncing on and off the cage sides, much as Inca had done on the cabin walls. Best of all, the pen no longer reeked of that rank scent born of fear and anxiety. We spent enchanting hours together.

That spring I learned an amazing bit of information at the vet college. Mapuche had been dragged from his den as a tiny kit by a man with heavy gloves and had been handled in the laboratory

Mapuche, my pet silver fox, playing with me before I took him to the cabin.

by students and scientists also wearing gloves. That had been my first mistake—to wear gloves when visiting the fox. My second mistake had been to spend too little time with him. But the bitter winter weather had dictated both actions.

Now Mapuche's whole being was directed toward me, and his day consisted of waiting for my visit. The fox was a curious combination of feline and canine traits. He was fast as quicksilver and smarter than any dog I'd ever known. By mid-May, Mapuche was going for walks with me on a leash! By the end of May and the close of classes, I felt sure he was ready to go to the cabin.

I packed up my books and belongings, borrowed a small cage, slipped him a tranquilizer, and drove back to Black Bear Lake. It was a clear, warm spring day when we arrived. I piled gear in the boat, trying to handle Mapuche's cage as gently and quietly as possible. His eyes glazed in fear when he heard the outboard engine start and water splash on the bow of the boat. Once again I smelled that familiar, gagging odor of his musk.

At the cabin, I immediately tied him to my huge curved spruce tree. Mapuche sniffed the pine-scented air, dug briefly in the damp duff. Here was no smell of turkeys, cranes, car exhausts, or stale excrement. This was the natural world he had been born into. Again a beautiful transformation took place. I watched his silvery coat flatten and blend into the dappled shadows under the firs. His motions grew calmer, surer. He scratched a little hollow to lie down in. Only his two points of clear amber remained alert, questioning, cautious.

Mapuche discovered red squirrels, new birds, black bears, wild foxes, beavers, chipmunks, and deer. All day his ears, eyes, and nose scanned the air for information like radar screens. I kept the fox on a chain, moving him around the cabin from tree to tree. At night he slept under a little A-frame shelter. My plan was to let him become accustomed to the Adirondack environment, take him walking, and then free him each evening so he could learn to hunt. My hope was that he would still return to me for companionship, yet build up sufficient independence to fend for himself in the wild. By September the fox was running free each evening for several hours, yet coming back to the cabin before morning.

One day Mapuche did not return. I waited for three days. Had he succumbed to the "call of the wild" or was he in trouble? It was pointless to roam the woods blowing a whistle or calling his name. The answer came in the form of his luxurious pelt dangling from the hands of a state trooper.

"I knew you had a silver fox," he began, embarrassed. "And I think this may be yours."

A sudden rush of tears blurred my eyes, and my hands felt cold.

"Some people over in Hawk Hill shot it two nights ago," he continued. "They said the fox was bothering a pen of rabbits they kept for the kids. They said he acted funny, as if he wasn't afraid of people. They were afraid he might be rabid, so they called me."

"No, he wasn't afraid of people," I whispered, remembering how his thick, silky fur felt in my fingers, how delicate and elastic his bones and muscles seemed between my hands.

"He wasn't rabid," I added, as an afterthought, thinking that this was the ultimate irony. From babyhood to death, Mapuche's life had revolved around rabies. He had never had it; yet the disease had meant his original capture and his ultimate demise.

The trooper stood quietly, noting the tears in my eyes. "Look," he said, "I *had* to have an examination made for rabies. I *had* to send the head to Albany to the wildlife disease lab."

He stopped a moment, then painfully went on, "The fox was so beautiful that I couldn't bring myself to bury the body. So I skinned it out. I thought maybe you'd like to have the pelt tanned and keep it as a remembrance of your pet."

My brain whirled. I was both revulsed and grateful. Part of me wanted the fox gone forever so that my grief would be shortlived. And part of me now understood how certain cultures can treasure scalps, skulls, furs, even shrunken heads, ashes, and other parts of departed human or animal bodies. It is an attempt to keep and cherish certain characteristics of the object which they once loved or admired. I wanted part of Mapuche at the cabin with me. Blinded by tears, I accepted the skin.

Mapuche's pelt now hangs beside my desk. His tail trails over the arm of my chair. From time to time I reach up and run my fingers through the silvery, glossy fur. It's almost as if he's still there, except his faintly pungent fox smell and those wild amber eyes no longer greet my senses.

The eyes that gaze up at me these days are also amber clear and proud, but they are mild and affectionate. They belong to an enormous German shepherd called "Pitzi." Pitzi means "little puppy" in Cachiquel Mayan language. Pitzi *was* a little puppy when I found him beside a lake in highland Guatemala. He and four other puppies nuzzled their mother, a small, pale-gray, sweet-tempered shepherd. Two years of my doctoral research had been done at this lake. I had passed this house daily to reach my boat, and its occupants were good friends. Pitzi's father, a stocky, black and tan registered shepherd had often accompanied me during my work on the lake. Now the two had produced a litter, and it was time for me to leave Guatemala.

"*Llevese un perito*," offered Don Carlos, the dogs' owner, graciously, "*como un recuerdo de Guatemala.*"

I considered his offer. How could I take a puppy, as a remembrance, on three airplanes, pass migration and custom officials, and carry twelve pieces of luggage and scientific equipment a distance of 2,000 miles?

"*Si Dios quiere, tu puedes*," shrugged the owner. If God so willed, I could do it. He *must* have thought it possible, because on impulse I picked out the single puppy with a white spot on his chin. Snuggling him down in my Indian shoulder bag, called a *morral*, I thanked Don Carlos profusely in Spanish.

My first attempt as a smuggler almost failed. As we stood in line at Miami migration counters, Pitzi awoke. He poked his small head out of the bag and began nuzzling an American flag that hung at the entrance. No sooner did I stuff him back in than he peeked back out. Juggling passport, health card, morral, binoculars, cameras, and Pitzi, I managed to get past the customs agent during the moment the puppy stayed inside the bag. And so it went, in and out, the whole trip. The only time he was discovered was on the last leg of my flight to New York State. The puppy crept out of the bag and went scampering up the aisle. He almost collided with a stewardess. She grabbed him and came back to me with a frown.

"You know it's against the rules to carry a dog loose on a plane," she began sternly. "He has to be in a cage and his passage paid. I'm supposed to report this to the captain."

I envisioned lengthy delays with the airlines and arguments with quarantine officials over the necessary papers and inoculations. I even imagined the puppy being burned up along with other confiscated items—foreign fruits, seeds, flowers, insects, and animals which might pose a threat to America's crops, forests, and livestock.

Then Pitzi saved the day. Giving a short yawn which showed his tiny pink tongue curled above pearly nubbins of teeth, he stretched out in the stewardess's arms and began sucking on her thumb. Charmed, she tickled his tummy, then passed him back to me. Minutes later, she brought a saucer of milk, scraps from chicken sandwiches, and a tiny bit of Dramamine to help him sleep. Pitzi arrived at Black Bear Lake still groggy, but safe. I bundled him in a baby's red wool sweater against the cold and carried my smuggled goods to the cabin.

My dog quickly outgrew the sweater. His paws spread like spatulas. I should have been warned by their size. Before he was nine months old, Pitzi was bigger than his mother; at twelve months, larger than his father. At eighteen months, he could stand on his hind feet, put his front paws on my shoulders, and look me straight in the eyes. When Pitzi sat beside me in the truck, drivers turned to stare; on the street, pedestrians crossed

to the other side. From a distance, Pitzi looked ferocious; but closeup, his true personality shone from warm brown eyes. Pitzi was a people-lover. He would press against people's legs, hoping for a scratch behind the ears, but often pushing them right over because of his weight. His right ear always flopped forward, except when he chased bears or stalked squirrels, giving him a rakish air. Part of Pitzi never grew up. He always remained a "little puppy."

Much as he loved to play, I soon taught my dog to work around the cabin. In summertime, my mail is delivered by boat—one of several still operating on Adirondack lakes. Pitzi runs down to the dock with my outgoing canvas mailbag in his mouth. Greeting the mailman wildly, he is given the incoming mailbag. Pitzi prances back to the cabin, lifting his paws with all the pride of a Lipitzanner stallion. Usually he brings the mail right in to my desk where I wait with a cookie. But on occasion, Pitzi has been known to see a squirrel first and drop the bag in hot pur-

*Opposite page:* Pitzi at the cabin at the age of two months. *Below:* Pitzi proudly delivers my bag of outgoing mail to the mail boat.

suit. Once he even buried it (with two checks totalling $75) in the woods. Now I keep a close eye on his movements during mailtime.

In the fall, Pitzi helps me carry firewood to the woodshed. He carries small branches, used for kindling, in his mouth and waits for a cookie by the woodpile as I trudged in with my tumpline full of logs. Wearing a pair of dog's saddlebags, he also helps carry supplies in and out during freeze-up and breakup.

Pitzi developed another useful trick in the lake. Everytime I went swimming, I urged him into the water. Soon he was jumping off the dock in a true bellyflop and splashing out to me. After a complete circle, nipping and barking, he would head back for shore. Then I grabbed his tail for a free tow to the dock. Now it's a ritual water game; but, someday it might save my life.

Pitzi loves boats. He adores riding up and down the lake in a motorboat, his floppy ear straightened up by the wind. He even enjoys clinging to my sailboat, hunched down under the boom, careful not to get tangled up in the lines. Once we tip over, though, he heads for shore under his own power. Most of all my dog loves canoeing. I center him in the area just behind the bow seat. His 100 pounds help to steady the canoe in wind and waves as I paddle. Even though we glide past beaver houses, often beaver themselves, Pitzi has never upset the craft, although he trembles from head to toe.

Another vehicle he enjoys riding is a snowmobile. After a couple of winters trudging up and down Black Bear Lake on snowshoes and trying to teach Pitzi to pull a toboggan, I despaired of ever making him a sled dog. He sat down a great deal and shivered constantly. Finally I bought a snowmobile. It didn't take Pitzi long to learn to stretch right out on the seat, tail hanging over the back and nose practically in the carburetor. I would straddle him with my feet on the running boards and hands on the steering bars. When he isn't riding the snowmachine, he's biting the front skiis.

This fascination with moving parts extends to all forms of

transportation. Pitzi nips at snowshoe and cross-country ski tips, the bows of my sailboat, motorboat, and canoe, even truck and car tires. One summer weekend, I invited a young professor to the cabin. Pitzi started our visit off by biting through the right front tire of his sports car! My friend was highly intellectual, but not at all mechanically inclined. He had no tools or spare tire. He ended up spending over $50 for a new tire and a service station man who drove 50 miles round trip to help change the tires.

Such incidents are rare, however. In almost every aspect, Pitzi is a tremendous companion and protector. He has a series of barks which inform me precisely whether the mailboat or a canoe, hiker, red squirrel, deer, or rabbit is passing by. Yet, one fall afternoon, I heard him give a new and frenetic bark off in the woods. At first I thought he had cornered a squirrel and was

Relishing soapsuds, Pitzi licks shampoo off my head whenever I wash my hair in the lake.

wildly excited. But the barks continued and held a note of warning. I ambled back through my fir forest to investigate. There, against a large dark hemlock, my dog was trying to climb up and a young black bear was trying to climb down. Pitzi had treed a bear and was not about to let him go. Dog and bear were at a precarious pass. Once it decided to descend, Pitzi's life would be in jeopardy. One swipe of the bear's paw in the right place could kill him outright.

I recognized the bear as a two-year-old male that had been seen several times around the lake that summer. He had stolen hamburgers from a neighbor's barbecue, ripped screening off kitchen windows, and tipped over garbage pails at camps. This bear was used to people and to scavenging for his food. Hunting season was due to start in three weeks, and undoubtedly such a semitame creature would fall before the first hunter's rifle.

I ran for my .300 Savage. When I got back to the tree, the bear was dangerously lower. It was clear from his actions and growls that he longed to climb down and run into the forest. Pitzi was frantically clawing at the tree and yelping. I had no time to decide. It was bear or dog. I aimed up the tree, right behind the eyes, and dropped the bear almost at Pitzi's feet. It died instantly.

With considerable difficulty, I dragged the 150-pound animal back to the cabin while Pitzi sniffed it all over. I tied a stout rope around the hind feet, threw the line over a branch, and hauled the bear up in the air. Then I cut the throat to bleed it. Next day a very curious dog watched while I skinned out the bear. Nothing was wasted. The skin went to the same tanner who had prepared Mapuche's pelt. It now warms the back of my desk chair. The claws were saved for a necklace. The skull I buried for several months, then dug it up clean and white and tacked it to my cabin wall. Best of all, Pitzi and I enjoyed many delicious meals of black bear steaks and stews. Friends who shared supper with me marveled at the fine "roast beef."

I found it emotionally difficult to dissect this young bear into cuts of meat because once shed of its rich black fur coat, the bear's body looked amazingly like a human being. Yet I knew I had done the right thing. I had saved my dog's life and saved the bear from a possible disabling wound. Most bear hunters in the Adirondacks shoot only for "sport" and leave the body, meat and fur, in the woods. In my hands, everything was salvaged and the bear died without pain or fear.

While this bear might have been Pitzi's most dangerous, *direct* adversary, there was another animal in our woods which *indirectly* was just as lethal. Porcupine! Pitzi's encounters with porcupines were perilous and have become legendary around Black Bear Lake. He has so far tangled with five and still not learned to leave them alone.

Almost every winter a porcupine crawls under the cabin to sleep beneath old lumber. Isolated buildings are favored winter retreats. And every spring when they waddle out, Pitzi is waiting to molest them. On his first encounter with a "quill-pig," he received a tail right smack in his face. I counted seventy-two quills in his nose, gums, tongue, roof of mouth, chin, and cheeks. Miraculously they missed his eyes. Pitzi looked like a grizzled old woodsman who hadn't shaved for months. His screams were those of an old-time movie actress in distress. He pawed madly at his face. The closest veterinary was about 50 miles away. I rushed down the lake by boat looking for a friend to help. First we wrapped the dog in a large, thick blanket and hog-tied his legs together. Next we stuck a round, smooth stick of wood between his jaws. While I straddled Pitzi and held his mouth tight on the stick, my companion began to jerk out quills with a pliers. Poor Pitzi moaned piteously. It took all my strength to hold him down and not let him bite us. He was literally out of his mind for a few moments. Seventy-two quills later, we released the dog and drew back apprehensively. He gave a shake, loped to the lake for a drink, and came back wagging his tail. Nothing more happened. In spite of vets, anesthetics, advice to clip quill tips or soften them with vinegar, I firmly believe that the best method is to pull out the barbed quills as soon as possible and relieve the animal of its tension and pain. Now I carry a pair of pliers and a length of rope on all camping and backpacking trips, for Pitzi continues to court disaster whenever he spies a porky.

If Pitzi could talk about his unusual life in an Adirondack log cabin, so far from his native home in Guatemala, I think he'd say, "The best times are when I'm sitting in the front of our canoe, and She's paddling. We go past a beaver's house and I hear mewing inside. Then I smell a big buck browsing along the shoreline. I'd like to jump in but She won't let me. And then we go home and She gives me a big dinner of venison scraps. I curl up on the bearskin rug by the fireplace and doze while She reads in the rocking chair. I have to be careful not to let my tail slip under the rocker while I'm dreaming. That hurts. Sometimes She leans over and scratches my belly. That feels good."

And I'd have to agree with the dog in my life. Those really are some of the best times.

## 6

# Becoming a Woodswoman

My very first glimpse over the folds of Adirondack wilderness came on a June day when I stepped down to the shore of Lake Serene. Hill after hill lapped away in lightening shades of blue-green. The clear lake was ringed with dense forest, summer camps, and a few small hotels. I had never seen anything so beautiful or primitive in my travels. The live scene was better than any nature poem or photo I'd admired. Bemused, I intuitively realized that I had found what I'd longed for all my life. I had come, like hundreds of other young, needy college students, to work at an Adirondack summer resort, saving salary and tips for tuition and books.

My handsome new boss suddenly appeared beside me. "How do you like the view?" he asked, stopping to gaze over the lake. "Think you'll enjoy spending a summer so far from the suburbs of New York City?"

Could he detect the delight on my face? Did he sense the growing joy within me?

"Mr. Brown, are those hills really wild out there?" I asked seriously. "I mean no houses, no farms, no roads in between them?"

"Yes, they are," he replied, his brown eyes crinkling with a smile. "All that country you see, and a lot more, is state land. It belongs to you and me and about 20 million other New Yorkers. Up at the far end of this lake, 6 miles from this hotel, there's a big marsh and thousands of acres of state land and lakes stretching north and east. Anyone can camp on the Forest Preserve."

"You mean all those hills and lakes are free for hiking and camping?" I asked incredulously.

"Yes. Are you thinking of trying it?"

"Oh, I'd like to," I said eagerly. "I never have, though. I mean there was no place to go around the city. And my mother wouldn't let me besides," I muttered as an afterthought. "But I sure am going to try it now!" I declared loudly with all the new-found independence of eighteen years, college, *and* a summer job.

"Well, you work hard this summer," said Mr. Brown, "and I'll see if you can find a couple of slack days when you can get off into the woods."

A flood of gratitude swept through me, especially since one of the principal conditions to working at this hotel was NO DAYS OFF between July 4 and Labor Day. My job of caring for four horses, teaching riding, laying out and maintaining nature trails, and pinch-hitting as an extra waitress when the hotel was full, promised to keep me busy every day.

Mr. Brown stood a moment longer looking out over the lake from under the tall spruce trees. He tapped a pipe wrench absently against his calloused palm. I shifted uneasily, not knowing what to say to him. Then, almost to himself, he murmured, "The last two lines of Joseph F. Grady's book, *The Adirondacks*, say it all. His tall, gaunt old woodsman ends by saying, 'It's 55 years since I first came here, and the woods are as beautiful today as they were then. God, it's a wonderful country!' " And he continued to stand there, musing. "I'm only thirty-five," he said, "but I feel just the same way about these mountains."

I stared at him, feeling the nudge of a bond beginning between us despite our age difference, a bond of nature. It was the only time I would see Morgan Brown relax for the rest of the summer. A moment later he strode off, pipe wrench swinging. Little did I imagine then that my first—scariest—funniest—and most romantic camping experiences were to take place right here in the Adirondacks over the years to follow. And that the best would be with Morgan Brown, the man who would one day be my husband.

My boss kept his promise. The week before Labor Day there was a period when all the hotel guests were either elderly or uninterested in riding. On a Monday night, Mr. Brown announced to me, "You can have off from Tuesday afternoon to Thursday evening if you still want to go camping. Take one of the hotel canoes and ask the chef for some grub."

I stared at him in astonishment. "But the horses," I began. "Who'll feed and water them, or clean their stalls?"

"Leave 'em up in the pasture," answered my boss. "The rest will do them good. They're getting worn down from so many riders this summer. If you're going to go, this is the only time I can spare you."

I scrambled into action. I borrowed an old tarp that covered hay bales from the stable to use as a ground cloth. Two flannel blankets and a dozen safety pins formed my sleeping bag. A small canvas Boy Scout knapsack carried my gear—matches, extra shirt, flashlight, and food. The French chef, however, was uncooperative.

"With fifty-five guests to feed and a staff of fifteen, you want me to prepare a menu for a three-day camping trip?" he snapped sarcastically. "Jesus Maria! Go down to the stock room, take some tin cans, and get the hell out of my kitchen!"

Most of the cans were large number 10s. There was no way I could lug a gallon of stew or corn beef hash. Finally, I settled on seven small cans of Campbell's soup, one for each meal. I figured they could be eaten concentrated right out of the can, without bothering to mix and heat soup. That should be nutritious and filling.

When I left the hotel dock at three the next afternoon, I was tingling with anticipation and anxiety. Off to brave the Adirondack wilderness alone for three days with no radio, phone, or any other form of communication. It would be the first time in my life to be so long without contact with the human race. What if I met some bad men in the woods? What if I fell and got hurt? Or if I tipped over and drowned?

My nightmare reverie was interrupted by Mr. Brown's cheery, "Well, if you're not back by Thursday night, we'll send out a search party. Got your compass, map, knife, and matches?"

Nodding in what I hoped seemed a nonchalant way, I pushed off from the dock. The red Old Town canoe slapped lightly against the waves.

"You going down to the marshes and explore that area?" asked my boss casually. "I'd just like to know where to look for your bones."

"I'm planning to go there first," I answered, "look around, then bushwack back to Sea Gull Lake, Balsam Pond, William's Creek, and Terror Lake." (The very name sent a shiver down my spine.)

Mr. Brown nodded and cocked his curly brown-haired head to one side. In what seemed to me a somewhat sceptical tone, he called, "Well, that's quite a schedule, Daniel Boone. Have fun!"

I dug in my paddle determinedly and soon was out of shouting distance. Heading up Lake Serene, I rode a west wind and waves for three hours. Toward evening, I came to the narrow entrance of the marshes. It was actually the lake's inlet, but the current was sluggish. I slipped into calm waters. The inlet widened into a huge shallow swamp. White water and yellow cow lilies tickled the bottom of my canoe. Blue pickerelweed brushed its sides. The water was brown as tea, stained with tannic acid from the white cedars and tamaracks which fringed the shores.

I yearned to see a bull moose knee-deep in water, browsing on the aquatic vegetation. It looked like splendid habitat for moose; yet I knew that the last animals had been shot in the Adirondacks in the late 1800s. Their decline was due in part to overzealous hunters and in part to the highly fatal "moose disease." This is caused by a nematode parasite (*Pneumostrongylus tenuis*), or brain worm. The worms also infect white-tailed deer, but are relatively harmless to them. But moose can get it from deer. In them, it becomes a lethal brain infection. As deer increased in the Adirondacks near the turn of the century, they put the moose on the decline and eventually toward extirpation.

Here and there beaver houses decorated the banks like huge beehives. Suddenly a heavy splash shattered the still surface of the marshes. I practically leapt off the seat before realizing it was only a beaver warning its clan about the intrusion of my bright red canoe. The beaver and the wildness of the scene made me feel as though I was in the farthest reaches of Saskatchewan. I gave a great sigh of contentment and suspense. Alone at last in the Adirondacks!

Shadows were deepening along the shoreline as I paddled toward land to find a campsite. I discovered at once that the Adirondack forest darkens quickly. Even though a golden sun still gilded the lilies in the swamp, the woods were ghostly dim. There was no time to walk back in and find a campsite that evening.

I located the first level spot in sight and carried my camping equipment up from the canoe. Awkwardly, I began to set up my first campsite and campfire. It was almost dark by the time I finished. Already I had learned important lessons about camping in comfort in the Adirondacks. Mosquitoes and punkies are murderously plentiful around swampy places. Swamp water looks bad and tastes worse. Ground under low balsams and tamaracks is damp. Dry twigs of evergreens burn much faster than branches of hardwoods such as birch, beech, or maple.

I huddled closer to the fire. It seemed to burn with a ferocity of its own, devouring my meager pile of firewood. It was almost gone. I groped inside the pack for a flashlight, resolving to gather a few more pieces of wood before rolling up in my sleeping bag. I discovered that the switch had been pushed on during my trip and only the feeblest glow remained. Next time I would turn the batteries upside down to protect them. But for now, nothing could entice me into that pitch-black forest without a light.

I resigned myself to night. In the last lingering light of ruby embers, I opened a can of black bean soup and gulped it down in thick spoonfuls without water. Wrapped in flannel blankets, smeared with insect repellent, without the comforting crackle of a fire, I began to hear the noises of the night. They intruded on me in a menacing way. Some large creature was rustling through the bushes about 200 feet away. A deer? A bear? A beaver slapped its tail out in the marshes. Could a canoe be coming? A Barred Owl began its fanatical screeching across the swamp. Its mate answered right above my head. Mysterious soft murmurs, sighs, scufflings, squeaks, clawings, and scratchings filled the forest as mice, voles, hares, owls, foxes, flying squirrels, shrews, moles, bats, and insects fled and fed upon each other in the eternal struggle for life. I was scared out of my wits!

Then thirst hit. Condensed black bean soup is the worst possible thing to eat next to a swamp. I dared not walk down to the shore for a drink; I dared not drink the dark stagnant swamp water. A bad combination!

All told, it was the most educational night of my camping career. Of course, I survived until morning and woke with the firm resolve to camp hereafter on high, dry ground, near a clear creek, with a tall stack of firewood, extra flashlight batteries, and nonsalty food on hand—and plenty of daylight for pitching camp. The rest of the trip went well. I didn't get to all the places I'd planned, but I did enough to gain an initial courage and enjoyment toward camping. When the red canoe returned to the hotel dock at dusk Thursday evening, I felt in some subtle way like a different person.

"Give me a hand with the dishwasher, Daniel Boone!" ordered my boss when I encountered him in the kitchen. As we were briskly scraping and stacking dirty dishes, he asked, "How'd you like it?"

"Oh, it was *wonderful*. I really love camping," I said inadequately, but the inner glow must have shone on my face.

"Good!" he said reassured yet amused, noting the mosquito bites, dirty fingernails, and smoky scent. "You're unusual, you know. Not many girls would take off into the woods alone like that. I'll have to find you some better equipment and get you back into a real wilderness area."

I continued stacking in disbelief. My boss was an expert woodsman by reputation. The hotel attic was piled high with his outdoor gear, skiis, sleeping bags, tents, parkas, mosquito netting, army hammocks, ground cloths, cook sets. What an experience it would be to go camping with him!

Then the rush of Labor Day business, my return to college, and the start of new classes obscured all thoughts of further outings. Weekends, however, I'd hitchhike back to the Adirondacks and help out at the hotel. There was always a crowd of hikers, photographers, riders, and nature lovers enjoying the fall foliage. One weekend in early October Mr. Brown faced me across the stable railing. "Can you cut classes a couple of days next week?" he asked, brown eyes asparkle. "I'm closing the lodge Sunday night. Everyone leaves that afternoon. I thought we could charter a seaplane and fly back to a remote lake, camp Monday and Tuesday, and I'll drive you back in time for classes Wednesday morning."

Thus began the most beautiful camping trip of my life. A Cessna 170 on floats buzzed the empty hotel early Monday morning. Already a pile of camping gear sat on the dock in pack baskets. We'd been up since dawn sorting equipment up in the attic. My boss had generously given me a lightweight mummy bag, ground cloth, and old canvas hunting jacket. A food chest held rich spoils from the hotel kitchen—rare roast beef, creamy potato salad, a homemade pie, pure Adirondack maple syrup, flapjack mix, milk, butter, cocoa, cold cuts, and freshly baked bread. It was a far cry from the Spartan menu of my first camping trip.

We loaded everything into the seaplane, including an iron skillet and grill, and belted ourselves in beside the bush pilot. Mike was in his fifties, renowned in the mountains for his years of skillful "seat-of-the-pants" flying. His weathered face cracked into a grin as he pushed forward on the throttle and skimmed smoothly over Lake Serene.

"Taking a vacation for a change, eh, Morgan?" he asked. "Well, you earned it all right."

I suddenly realized that this probably was the first free day my boss had had since he opened his lodge in early June. He had been on constant call to fix this, repair that, decide everything, satisfy the guests, and direct the staff for four solid months. It must indeed be a holiday for him. Glancing at Morgan's tanned face, I realized he looked more relaxed than I'd ever seen him.

"Back to Deep Lake?" asked the bush pilot, adjusting the trim tabs as the plane rose gracefully above the shoreline.

"Yes," answered Morgan. "You can drop us on that rocky point off the south shore. Anne and I will carry our gear back to that old campsite under the big pines. We'll be more shelteerd from the wind that way."

"Smart idea," said Mike. "Barometer's going down and my broken collarbone aches, so I wouldn't be surprised one of those cold autumn fronts is moving in. When you coming out?"

"Tomorrow afternoon. Could you pick us up about four? This young lady has to get back to school, and I have a hotel to close up."

The plane droned over a kaleidoscope of colors for miles—red and scarlet hardwood forests, tawny beaver meadows, green-gold swamps, blue lakes and ponds, gray rocky ridges, dark evergreen patches. I was amazed by the sweep of land unmarred by roads, hamlets, towns, factories, or shopping centers.

Dipping in a wide arc, the seaplane drifted down to Deep Lake. We slid into a roaring glissade over the black water. Minutes later Morgan and I were standing on the point, surrounded by gear, saying goodbye to Mike.

"If the weather really socks in tomorrow," he yelled from the floats, "you better plan on walking out. I'll come back for the equipment some other time. But as long as there are any breaks in the clouds, I'll be in to get you. Have a nice time."

He hauled himself into the cockpit, slammed the door, and waved. Mr. Brown grabbed a wing tip and pushed him into deeper water. I heard the mounting roar of the single engine, water rushing over the floats, and wind sweeping across the wings. Then the little plane sprang clear of the lake, leaving two silvery streams of water falling through the air from its pontoon tips like pearl necklaces. The plane soared like a seagull over a low hill and disappeared. Its roar faded rapidly.

Seaplanes provide access to many remote Adirondack lakes.

Just as rapidly I was flooded with the enormity of my situation. I was all alone with "an older single man" on a remote Adirondack lake, completely dependent on him for my survival. I hadn't the slightest idea where I was or what to do next. A peculiar tremor ran through my body compounded of the anticipation of camping, the threat of a possible storm, the actual physical presence of my much-admired boss, and my new role as a partner, not an employee.

Morgan was already shouldering two pack baskets, one in each hand, muscles bulging under his plaid flannel shirt. He seemed oblivious to my confusion.

"Grab some gear," he said in a businesslike tone, moving toward the white pines. "I'll show you how to set up camp. Mind you, we wouldn't camp under these pines in summertime. We'd want the breeze on the point to keep away bugs. Besides, these tall pines can be dangerous in a thunderstorm by attracting lightning."

We worked all afternoon, cutting poles, setting up little benches and a rustic table, hanging bags and clothes on a line to air, collecting firewood. Morgan advised me to stow dry bark and twigs inside the tent in case it rained. A tiny spring bubbled nearby so we filled all our pots with water. By 6 P.M. the camp was shipshape and twilight was settling over the lake.

I retreated for a moment and modestly laid out my mummy bag and ground cloth under a huge pine. It never occurred to me to sleep in the same tent with my boss.

"You're going to be a little chilly out there in that sack," warned Morgan. "It's only a summer bag and we're liable to get some cold wind or rain tonight."

"Oh, I'll be OK," I said embarrassed. (I'd never slept alone with a man, much less with an *employer*, in a tent or anywhere else.)

"You know you *can* sleep in the tent," he continued, as if sensing my thoughts. "Campers share their shelters. In the state lean-tos up here, woodsman's etiquette demands that every hiker, male or female, be given shelter unless it's too crowded."

"No, it's all right," I insisted steadfastly. "I don't get cold at night."

"Have it your way, Daniel Boone," he said and smiled. "But just remember the tent's here if you need it. Come on, let's get some supper cooking."

A spectacular sunset glowed across Deep Lake, reflected in ebony waters. Saffron, scarlet, salmon ribbons alternated with long strips of gray clouds. A fitful breeze shook the hardwoods, shaking leaves down through the branches with a rustle. Morgan laid roast beef slabs over the grill beside a roaring fire. A large enamel pot bubbled. Aluminum plates, cups, and utensils appeared. The temperature was dropping steadily. Again that curious tremor shook my body. I shifted closer to the fire.

We ate a hearty meal, taking our time. No temperamental French chef was calling out orders in the kitchen, no waitresses fluttering around like panicked quail under his scowl. There were no dirty dishes waiting in a stack beside the steamy dishwasher. By the time we finished, the autumn stars were blazing above the white pines. There was no moon. Now and again a thin veil of cloud slid across the sky, pushed by some unfelt, high, and distant wind. Compared to my first night of camping beside the marshes, here all was deathly silent. Only one lone cricket chirped behind the trunk of an enormous pine.

I shivered again inside my canvas shirt. Morgan took off his heavy wool jacket and placed it gently over my shoulders. "Would you play me a song, Anne?" he asked, pulling an old guitar from his pack basket.

"How did you know I played?" I questioned, still unable to speak his first name.

"I've been watching you all summer," he said candidly. "Like I said before, you're quite a girl. Different from most who come to work at my hotel. You really love nature and that's a nice trait to find in a woman."

I plucked a string nervously, wondering if my blush showed

in the firelight. All summer *I* had been watching Mr. Brown, enamored by his easy competence, physical strength, good humor, and firm character. But never had I dreamed that he noticed me among the dozen girls working at the inn. I was tongue-tied. No way I could sing.

Morgan must have noticed my discomfiture, because he began talking then, arms wrapped about his knees, eyes riveted on the fire. He talked about his first camping trip as a boy, hunting sprees with his father, when he came to the Adirondacks, and how he acquired the hotel. Gradually I relaxed. Now I saw my employer as a *person*, a man with a great love for these mountains and for the independence which they allowed in life-style.

Close to midnight a light wind sprang up and a plume of sparks swayed up into the night sky. Looking up, I noticed that the entire sky had blacked out. A lapping began out on the point.

"Time to turn in," said Morgan, laying an arm across my shoulder. "You can still change your mind and move in the tent."

I rose stiffly, trembling more than ever. But now I knew it was not just cold and anticipation of a storm, but the awareness of a deep affection for this man. Shyly, I shook my head, slipped his jacket off my back, and handed it to him. He took the shirt slowly, then, to my total bewilderment, he brushed my forehead with his lips and whispered, "Sleep well, Daniel Boone."

I didn't. At 3 A.M., a penetrating drizzle began seeping through the pine trees. By 4 A.M., my mummy bag was damp and I was shaking with cold. Waves were dashing on the rocks of the point. I crawled out of the bag and stiffly dragged it over to the tent. I unzipped the flap quietly, hoping not to wake Morgan. But he sat up immediately and helped pull the sleeping bag inside.

"I thought you might be coming over any time now," he chuckled. "Poor baby, you're shaking like a leaf."

Very calmly, he unzipped his large down-filled bag; very gently, he pushed me down by his side; very naturally, he pulled me into the warm hollow of his body and drew the dry bag over my damp clothes.

"There," he said quietly, "you'll dry out quickly. Now sleep. The way this rain is moving in we may have a long, wet walk out tomorrow. We'll need our energy."

Of course, neither of us slept much, suddenly acutely aware of one another's body, breath, smell, texture. But even as I lay in a pretense of sleep, I was savoring the wild Adirondack night, the pelting rain on our tent, the wind moaning through the pines, the waves in the distance, the stalwart arms around me. Never had I felt so sheltered, safe, and happy with anyone in my life. Gradually my trembling stopped. By first gray light we were sound asleep.

We were awakened with the crash of a branch nearby. The difficulty of our situation presented itself. A rough autumn storm was blowing. Morgan looked up at the turbulent sky and doubted that Mike could fly through it to pick us up. We had brought in so much gear that the two of us could never carry it out. Yet I had to be back at the university next day for an exam. We discussed the situation and decided on a compromise. I would walk out alone by trail and hitchhike back to the hotel. Morgan would wait at Deep Lake, hoping the plane would make it and get everything out in one trip. If he didn't show up, I was to borrow Morgan's car and drive back to school, returning the following weekend. If he *did* make it, we should arrive at about the same time at the hotel. He could still drive me down. It was a painful leave-taking so soon after our newfound closeness. Only five hours of daylight remained.

Morgan walked with me to the start of the state trail. "You can't possibly get lost," he said reassuringly. "The path is old, well-tramped, and marked with red markers every few hundred feet. You'll have 5 miles of trail," he explained, drawing a map with a stick on the ground, "so you should be out to the dirt road by 4 P.M. latest. Turn right and walk half a mile to the paved state highway. Head south and start hitching. I don't worry about you getting a ride this time of year with a stranger. They're all "natives" and will be glad to give you a lift. If you get to the road by 5 P.M., men will be driving home from work so you should be back at the lodge no later than six." He gave me a sandwich, apple, and candy bar wrapped in aluminum foil. "If Mike makes it, I'll be at the hotel dock just before dark."

He kissed me goodbye, and I began gingerly picking my way through a tamarack swamp. "Take care, Daniel Boone," I heard as I rounded a bend in the trail. In my state of heady exhilaration, every color, every scent, every sound seemed intense and beautiful even in the pouring rain. Fallen leaves formed a carpet as polychromatic as a Persian rug—colors as warm, wet, and rich as finest wines and brandies—burgundies, clarets, and rosés, peach, apricot and plum. Gusts of chill wind rattled the trees, causing fresh showers of bright leaves to deepen the pile beneath my boots.

A bold Canada Jay or "whisky jack" darted across the path and began a raucous mewing. A bevy of chickadees browsed and chirped inside a balsam stand. A red squirrel debated passage with me. The air held that pungency and integrity of odor one enjoys on first opening a can of ground coffee or a fresh packet of pipe tobacco.

I hummed and skipped over those 5 enchanting miles, soaked to the skin but glowing warm, in love with the woods, with life, with Morgan. Two French Canadian lumberjacks gave me a ride to the hotel, and I went in to towel myself dry and pack. As dusk descended, a faint drone sent me dashing to the dock. There, through a break in the dismal scud overhead, appeared the silver Cessna bounding around on the strong winds.

Mike never even shut down the engine as Morgan leaped ashore. I grabbed a wing tip as I'd seen him do the day before and held the plane off from the dock. Camping gear was flung precariously out the door.

"Got to get back up through that break," yelled Mike, pointing toward a pearly-gray section of sky. He slammed the door shut. We both pushed him off and the plane's prop spat rain and water back into our faces. The plane raced over the lake's stormy surface, bucked into the air, and disappeared through the slot in the clouds. I was reunited with my beloved camping companion.

Over the next couple of years as I continued to work at the hotel summers and finish college winters, new camping experiences took place. The very name of Terror Lake, its size and shape on the map, intrigued me more and more. The lake was 6 miles back in, but the trail had been obliterated by the blowdown of 1954. I could find no one who had been there within the past five or six years. Morgan was too busy to leave the inn, so I decided to try for Terror Lake with my best girl friend, Betsy. A physical education major, Betsy was robust, good-natured, and full of common sense. We managed to get three days off from hotel duties and borrow the same red canoe. Betsy worked as a waitress and Morgan impressed upon her the importance of being back in time for the Friday evening weekend crowd.

Our jumping-off place lay at the upper end of the marshes. We plotted our course on the topographic map—along Catamount Creek for about 3 miles, then across a long beaver meadow, through a low notch between Jagged Mountain and another nameless peak, and across a mile of woods down to the shore of Terror Lake. It looked easy. We planned to be there by dark and camp at the narrows.

At first the going was good, but then we hit low, damp flats where thickets of balsams and spruces formed a prickly barrier to our progress. Perspiring under our packs, we stopped by a tiny stream for a drink and a candy bar. Unaware, I dropped the wrapper as I leaned forward to scoop water into my mouth. After two hours of battling through the balsams, Betsy and I decided to take a detour and cut right over the top of Jagged Mountain. To our dismay, the blowdown had hit hard on that side. We found ourselves crawling under, leaping over, tightrope walking huge logs and dead tops. To add to our problems, a late afternoon thundershower drenched us. As we neared the summit, we were surprised to find that a swamp, freshly made by beavers, blocked the way. Twilight was coming so we backtracked looking for a level, open spot of ground. Nothing.

After thrashing around for twenty minutes, we decided in desperation on a sloping shelf of rock about 6 feet wide and 7 feet long, covered with patches of soaking moss. We were hemmed in on every side by downed timber. The one advantage here was that our fire could not burn into the duff or catch the overhanging branches on fire. The only thing worse we could imagine than sleeping on stone was having a forest fire burn us up in the middle of the night.

Betsy and I spent a wretched evening. It took us forty-five minutes to get a fire started, and then we burned out the toes of our wet socks by hanging them too near to dry. There was no sweet spring at hand, only sour swamp water. Without room to pitch a tent, we lay down our sleeping bags on a poncho and hoped it wouldn't rain any more. To sleep on a slant on bare rock is a miserable way to spend the night. To slip two wet boots over half-burned-up socks is not a happy way to start the day. The swamp defeated us. After two hours of trying to cross it, we gave up. We had reached the halfway point in time. Our hotel duties were waiting for us next evening, so we started back to Lake Serene. Terror Lake would have to wait for another day.

Starting back through the blowdown, Betsy and I were often completely out of sight from one another though only 10 feet apart. So thickly had the young spruces grown up in the openings made by the windstorm that they formed an almost impenetrable tangle. In this maze we lost our sense of direction. By the time we emerged at the foot of the mountain, we were completely lost. To add to our confusion, the sky was an overcast gray, obliterating all sense of direction.

For the first time in my life, an unreasonable panic struck and

I wanted to run at full speed to some place I recognized. Only my wet leather boots rubbing on blistered toes, and my friend, Betsy, held me back. She caught my arm.

"We musn't panic," she stammered. "We must follow a stream. Always follow water downhill," she recited in a monotone as if from rote memory.

"But there *is* no stream here," I protested. "Only these blasted balsam flats."

"Then let's use our compasses and walk in squares. If we make 90-degree turns at each corner and keep looking, we're bound to find water."

We began tearing our way through the dense stands of trees with our packs catching over and over again on snags. Soon we found ourselves veering right into circles. The balsam trees all looked alike, same age, same height. Before long we were exhausted and desperate.

"This is no good," I moaned, still fighting the urge to bolt. "Let's go in a straight line. You stay here and direct me with the compass until you almost can't see me anymore. Then I'll blaze a tree and wait for you to catch up."

We tried this and eventually worked our way into more open hardwood forest.

"Listen! Water!" cried Betsy.

We rushed toward the sound and found a small, clear creek. Throwing off our packs, we drank deeply. As I rose, my eye caught the glint of red paper. I reached down wonderingly and picked up a candy wrapper.

"Do you suppose . . . ?" I began.

Betsy interrupted in joyous relief, "Look, here are our footprints. My boots! Oh, we're not lost. At least we know where we *were*."

We got back to the red canoe by late afternoon and arrived at the hotel just before dark. The two of us paddled furiously, knowing we had missed our evening chores. Paddling helped work off the great surge of adrenaline which had infused our bodies from fear. Although our total time lost had been only four hours, we had been thoroughly shaken. I could empathize with the feelings I had read about, the panic, lack of orientation, blind fear, irrational actions on finding oneself lost in the woods.

"Let's not tell anyone we got lost," whispered Betsy as we unloaded the canoe.

"But they'll want to know why we are late, and about Terror Lake, how it looks, what we did. Remember we might have been the first people to reach there in years."

"Yeah, and now we know why no one else made it either!" laughed Betsy.

Our quandary of what to say was solved for the moment when Morgan Brown saw us.

"You're late!" he snapped. "We've got a full house tonight and the dining room is shorthanded. Betsy, see if you can help the waitresses cleaning up," he ordered. "And, Anne, you give me a hand with these dishes." He slammed down the dishwasher cover and handed me a scraper. We scraped, stacked, and washed dishes furiously for an hour. Then, as we piled the last of the dinner plates behind the range, Morgan gave me a wink and said, "How was it, Daniel Boone?"

I paused before answering. The kitchen was empty. My still damp boots grated painfully on ten raw toes. The still hot plates stung new blisters on my palms from the paddle. "It was *awful*," I sputtered, as much dismayed by our terrible camping experience as by Morgan's anger at us. Tears welled up.

"Did you get lost?" he asked mildly.

"*Yes, yes* we did! We never got to Terror Lake at all."

"Good!" exclaimed my enigmatic boss. "Now you're no longer a novice. You're on your way to becoming a real woodswoman. From now on you'll respect the woods, you'll take fewer chances, and calculate your risks. And you know what? You'll enjoy camping more than ever."

Reaching over, he wiped a lone tear from my eyelid. "Know what else?" he asked quietly. "I missed you and worried about you." Then he enfolded me in a deep bear hug which miraculously erased the exhaustion, frustration, and pain.

How right Morgan was. Camping has become one of my most beloved pastimes. I take a fierce delight in swinging a pack on my back or into a canoe and heading for the hills or lakes. In my opinion, camping can be the greatest expression of free will, personal independence, innate ability, and resourcefulness possible today in our industrialized, urbanized existence. Regardless of how miserable or how splendid the circumstances, the sheer experience of camping seems a total justification for doing it.

# 7

---

# Becoming
# an Adirondack Guide

One chilly fall afternoon I was coming back alone on the faint trail from Roundhouse Pond, a small, wild lake near Hawk Hill, when I met a man. It was the first time I'd ever encountered another single individual back in the woods. I was startled. So was he. What to do? Stop? Stare? Run? Pass by with a nod? Stand still for a chat? A delicate situation in woodland etiquette when you are the only two strangers within a 2-mile radius.

We both stopped. We both eyed each other carefully. I saw a wiry, short, blue-eyed gentleman in his fifties, wearing a patched plaid shirt and a sweat-stained hat with a licensed guide's badge pinned to the side. His face was weatherbeaten, clean-shaven, and ruddy-hued.

"Well, well, well," he said with a wide smile. "Fancy meeting anyone back here. How's everything up at Roundhouse Pond?"

"Oh, it's nice there," I replied, smiling back. "I saw three mergansers and a lot of deer tracks."

"Mergansers, eh? Moving south already. This your first time up to the pond?" he inquired, resting his hip against a short hiking pole he had planted in the trail bed.

"Yes, my first time," I answered, leaning in turn against a tree.

"On nice days like this, I take some time to go exploring around Hawk Hill."

"You wouldn't by any chance be the girl who built her own log cabin up at Black Bear Lake?" said the hiker, face suddenly brightening.

"That's me. Anne is my name," I responded.

"Well, well, well. That's quite a feat. I've been wanting to meet you. Heard you knew a lot about wildlife and loved the woods. So do I. I used to be a factory supervisor in a big city, but soon as I could I retired and came to live in the Adirondacks. I've hunted and fished this country since I was a boy. Rob's the name."

We shook hands awkwardly, then relaxed.

"How long have you been a guide?" I asked, pointing to his badge.

"About ten or twelve years," said Rob.

"Is it hard to become one?"

"Well, it takes a little time. You have to know a certain section of woods pretty well, most of a topographic map quadrangle. A licensed guide must vouch for you, and then a state game warden must sign your application. Both swear that you know your way around the woods. Then the Department of Environmental Conservation reviews the form. If they decide you are competent, they grant you a guide's license."

"I'd love to be an Adirondack guide," I said wistfully, thinking of the mystique and prestige associated with the badge, "but I really haven't hiked all that much around here."

"Well, well, well. You could certainly learn the country. Anytime you want to go into the woods, I'd be glad for the company. I'm out all year, hiking in summer, mink trapping in fall, snowshoeing in winter, fishing in spring. My wife's always worrying that I'll meet a 'widow-maker' when I'm alone."

"What's a widow-maker?" I asked, perplexed.

"It's a limb or tree that falls on a person back in the woods and makes a widow out of your wife," Rob explained.

"I'd love to go with you sometime, Rob. Why don't I stop by your house and we'll plan a trip," I said, shivering now from the autumn chill. We said goodbye and each went our way along the trail.

Bad weather, my writing commitments, and Rob's mink-trapping season intervened. It was not until mid-November that Rob and I found a free day for our first hike. Only it would have to be made on snowshoes. Fourteen inches of fresh snow lay on the ground.

"We're going back to check on Kelly," announced Rob as we looked over our snowshoe harnesses beside his kitchen stove.

"Who's Kelly?" I asked, boring a new hole into a strap with an awl.

"Kelly's a real, honest-to-goodness hermit who lives back at Buck Pond most of the year. He comes out once a month for his social security check and some grub. It's been over five weeks since I saw him, though, and I'm a little worried. Maybe this new snow held him back, but we'll go and see, OK? You'll see some nice wild country back there. Think you can snowshoe 10 or 11 miles?"

"Probably," I said warily. (The most I'd ever done was about 8 miles.)

"It's pretty flat most of the way," said Rob, "and the snow's not too soft. We should have good going."

It *was* good going *and* wild country. We moved at a steady pace, stopping now and then to chat or knock snow chunks from the webbing. As we approached Kelly's cabin we smelled the sweet smoke of burning yellow birch in the air.

"He must be alive if he's got a fire going," commented Rob dryly.

We came through a fringe of firs into a clearing beside a shallow pond. A crooked stovepipe protruded from a gray ramshackle shack. Smoke oozed from each joint and out the top. An axe-scarred wood rack stood beside the door and yellow splinters of wood lay scattered all over the snow. The windows were covered with sheets of plastic and wire. The door eased open a notch and a white-haired man peered out.

"Hi, Kelly," shouted Rob, unslinging one strap of the pack basket from his shoulder. "Brought you some newspapers and grub. Figured you must be running low by now."

"Why, I'll say so, Rob," answered Kelly in a querulous voice. "Only have three cans of beans left and a little catsup. I was figuring on coming out in a day or two. I was kind of waiting for this snow to settle." He kept staring out the door at me.

"This here is Anne," explained Rob, pointing at me, even though there wasn't another woman within 5 miles of Buck Pond. "She's getting to learn the woods so I brought her back here to see this part of the country."

The door opened wider now. "Well, come in," said Kelly cautiously. "Don't remember as how I ever had a woman back in here before."

Before long though, the old Swedish lumberjack had relaxed and we were munching sandwiches and talking alongside the rusty 55-gallon oil drum which served as stove. Kelly hadn't shaved for days and his skin was blotched from lack of vitamins and fresh foods. Yet his eyes twinkled mildly and his gnarled hands were gentle as he cleared a spot on the bench for me.

I gazed around the hermit's one-room hut in fascination. Beside the stove and rough-hewn plank table, the only other objects in the room were a dingy, saggy bed, the bench we were sitting upon, an old sink with hand pump, two pails, and a few dishes. A pipe, tobacco, and scattered newspapers seemed the hermit's only sources of entertainment. I sensed that here was a man who had passively retreated from the world. Torpid as a woodchuck in winter, Kelly was content to sit by his stove at Buck Pond. He roused from his inertia once a month to walk out to Hawk Hill for food and money. Once a year he hitchhiked to Lake Serene and stayed a few days to see the World Series games on television.

Rob and I traveled many miles together in the following

months. The next two summers we walked to no less than thirty different lakes and ponds in the 10-by-15-mile rectangle that comprised the Hawk Hill topographic quadrangle. We averaged about 150 miles per summer. By the third autumn after I had met Rob on the little trail to Roundhouse Pond, I was ready to apply for my guide's license. Rob vouched for me, as did the local Environmental Conservation officer.

I got my license and guide's badge that winter. I am one of about 250 guides registered with the Department of Environmental Conservation as capable of leading people in the woods for recreation, hunting, fishing, or on searches and rescues. Of these guides, about 85 percent operate in the Adirondacks. Only two or three are women.

None of us could hope to make a living entirely from guiding today, since few clients wish to pay the $25 to $50 daily fee required to break even. Each guide more or less has his or her specialty and particular section of the woods. Rob takes out trout fishermen, but only a trusted coterie. He walks in to ponds and streams where big brookies lie, and whose names and locations shall remain forever unspoken. Another friend, a survival expert, guides only serious deer and bear hunters. I cater to families who like camping, canoeing, and backpacking, and students with an interest in natural history. And once I took a Hollywood screen writer out for a day—and earned $100! Most of us guide because we take pride in the badge and license, find pleasure sharing the Adirondacks with outsiders, and probably secretly wish we had been born a hundred years earlier when guiding was a fulltime profession.

In the old times, men came and stayed to hunt for days in the Adirondacks. Fashionable city "sports" would hire local woodsmen for from $5 to $8 per day. Their services included everything from leading the way into camp, carrying all the supplies plus a guideboat if needed, making the fire, setting up tents or arranging the bedding inside an Adirondack lean-to, cooking the meals, heating shaving water, often shooting the deer or bear for the city hunter, and always gutting it and packing it out of the woods.

The Adirondack guide was immortalized in Winslow Homer's paintings. In fact one of his most famous is entitled "Adirondack Guide." Old felt hat, scarred leather boots, baggy wool trousers with suspenders, an Adirondack pack basket, and enormous strength characterized these men. Good guides were legendary and in great demand. Names of notables are still mentioned with respect bordering on hero worship in various parts of the mountains—Mitchell Sabattis, Chris Crandell, Artie Church, Andy Carmen, Frank Baker, Lou Hathaway, Ira Parsons, Mike Cronin, and so on. Theodore Roosevelt was in company of his guide, Mike Cronin, in the High Peaks country when the news reached him of President McKinley's assassination in Buffalo, N.Y. But most of this old breed is gone.

As my confidence and prowess as a woodswoman increased, my camping and backpacking equipment improved. I have to laugh at the comparison between what I carried on my first camping trip to the marshes and what I carry now. A Kelty-style aluminum-frame backpack holds most of my gear rather than a canvas scout knapsack. I still use an Adirondack pack basket for canoe camping or for carrying large objects in the woods. By slipping a large plastic garbage bag over the top, the pack stays dry in any rain.

For sleeping, I use a duck-down, 3½-pound, "Icelandic Special" sleeping bag (good to 32 degrees) in summer; a goose-down, 5-pound, Eddie Bauer bag (good to zero degree) in winter. Putting the two together will protect me well into sub-zero temperatures. No more flannel blankets pinned together on the sides! I sleep on foam rubber pads, a short one for backpacking, a full-length for boat or car camping. Air mattresses or balsam boughs will not suffice—I want a smooth, hard, flat surface. A good night's sleep is too important when in the woods. I also allow myself the luxury of a soft down pillow. It keeps my neck warm and allows me to stuff it in my ears or over my eyes if the surroundings are noisy or bright. This also helps me sleep better.

In my pack I always carry a space blanket or a lightweight, large poncho to serve as ground cloth. My tent is a 4-pound, orange "Mt. Marcy" with a 1½-pound rain fly. It shows up beautifully in color photos, and in an emergency would be readily visible from search planes. However, this tent is not suitable for winter or high mountain tenting. For boat or canoe camping, I prefer a "pop-up" tent which needs no stakes or guy lines. I have a three-man, 9-pound model which is perfect on the beach. All my tents have extra-fine mesh netting to prevent entry of those noxious "no-see-ums" (close relative to the sand fly), and sewn-in floors. I always carry an extra piece of netting plus a needle and thread in case something tears or gets burned.

My food has also come a long way from those seven Campbell soup cans. Now it's all freeze-dry or high-energy concentrates. I carry only one lightweight, 1½-quart aluminum pot to cook in and one empty coffee can (it can be thrown away when rusty) to brew in. One tablespoon, one hunting knife, one tin cup (the 2-cup measuring type), and an aluminum pie plate for the dog are all my utensils. Whenever possible, I cook on a wood fire, being partial to the sound, sight, smell, and taste of it. (For emergencies, I carry a tiny butane gas stove.) My pot stays black from the start of one camping season to its close. Scrubbing blackened cookware is a waste of time, especially if the pot goes back on the fire again in just a few hours. I merely put the sooty pan in a heavy plastic bag between meals. A lightweight, 1-quart, wide-mouthed plastic bottle serves better than a narrow-necked, metal canteen. It can be filled easily in a brook and powdered drink mixes can be poured right in.

The pockets of my pack hold the various items necessary to survival, usually *two* of most things. I carry two small flashlights, one sealed disposable unit, the other a penlight with extra batteries and bulb. You can walk a long way at night with just a penlight. Book matches are carefully wrapped in plastic bags, and several kitchen matches are coated in candle wax to protect them from moisture. There's one pen and one pencil, some writing paper, Kleenex, two candles, a tiny bottle of lighter fluid for starting fires on miserable days, maps, rope, two compasses, and extra shoelaces. In a waterproof bag, I carry essential medicines, including a few morphine and Demarol tablets for severe pain and injury. This bag also contains a snakebite kit, elasticized bandage, a mirror to help in getting particles out of eyes, tweezers for extracting splinters from skin, and a needle for treating blisters. Two more luxuries which I carry are a good pocket book to read on rainy days and some sleeping pills for nights when I am so exhausted that sleep won't come.

All my equipment has been tested, retested, simplified, and refined with every camping and backpacking trip. The pack weighs in at about 38 pounds with seven-days supply of food. Pitzi's saddlebags weigh about 10 pounds with his food, pliers for porcupines, his plate, and a thin rubber mat for sleeping. This keeps him from getting too cold at night on the tent floor. If I add camera equipment, the weight jumps to 45 pounds. Pitzi may even be pressed into carrying some of it. The minimum I can work with is two Nikormat cameras, an extra telephoto lens, a light meter, and aluminum tripod. Usually I sling each camera from the posts of my pack with rawhide straps. I wrap the lenses in a plastic bag with a rubber band. If it rains, the entire camera can be protected; if fair, just the lens is shielded from dirt or scratches. Film, extra lens, and meter go in a "fanny pack" which I wear (in reverse) across my belly, zipper side up.

The most critical evaluation of my equipment and ability came in the summer of 1973 when I took the Northville–Lake Placid Trail across the Adirondack State Park for an article I was writing for *National Geographic* magazine. It is like a short version of the Appalachian Trail, running from the southern portion of the mountains through the High Peaks up to the northern edge. It links lonely lake to lonely lake, crosses two major wilderness tracts, and winds among trailless peaks. All the trails I had trod with Rob were good training for this 113-mile footpath

With loaded packs, Pitzi and I set out on the 113-mile Northville–Lake Placid Trail.

which runs from Upper Benson (near Northville) to Averyville (near Lake Placid).

Pitzi and I began the trip with 10-pound saddlebags and 45-pound backpack. He was dismayed from the start about carrying his "doggie pack." I had to coax him into it like a stubborn horse into a bridle. Traveling alone, I felt much the same apprehensions which had plagued me before starting on my very first camping trip at Lake Serene. Once I entered that tunnel of trees I would be committed to carry my entire life-support system for several days until coming out at the far end. (There are only four crossings along the NLP Trail on which a traveler can emerge to civilization.) What if I fell and broke a leg? Or met rough kids on drugs? Worse, a criminal?

To bolster my courage, I asked Ted, a policeman-friend, to see me off and watch for my appearance on a dirt road crossing in about seven days. His last words of advice, after adding a small pistol to my already staggering load, were, "If you meet anyone who arouses your suspicions, tell them your husband is downtrail looking for birds. Then scoot!" Turning to go, he muttered chillingly, "If anyone harms you, I'll be looking for them with the crosshairs of a rifle." I felt safer.

I soon lost my fear because the trail offered so many diversions. That night Pitzi and I camped at Silver Lake as a salmon sunset glowed above blueberry-dark hills. Loons were calling. The moon was full. Luckily the state lean-to was empty so I didn't bother to set up the tent. Next day we passed through stands of magnificent timber, saw tranquil lakes reflecting ivory thunderheads, hopscotched through swarms of tiny toads and scarlet salamanders on the moist trail, prowled around old lumberjack camps, and sniffed wildflowers. Wherever water was deep enough to swim, Pitzi and I jumped in to refresh ourselves. And, of course, we drank from any river or rill, so pure are our mountain waters.

Every 5 or 6 miles along the trail we came to state lean-tos. The famous three-sided log shelter offers protection from rain and wind, facing its fourth side toward a large stone fireplace. However, lean-tos do not always provide a sound night's rest. Pitzi's nocturnal chases of rummaging porcupines, raccoons, and mice, plus the snores of whatever transient backpacker happened to be sharing the shelter, kept me awake most of the night. By state law, lean-tos are open to the public for three days without a permit. Every occupant is obliged to share it with others.

Actually my dog and I rested better in my snug orange mountain tent pitched on a woodland flat or sandy beach where the only interlopers were a red fox slipping past or the plop of a frog.

The lean-tos we passed were replete with graffiti. Some had obviously been written by bored campers on rainy days; others by proud woodsmen after feats of great endurance; still others by humorists of the century. The Miller's Falls and Moose Pond shelters especially were museums of woodland witticisms. Written with charcoal chunks, lipstick, and pencil stubs, they read: "John was here for a short time, but had to go back to the meter to insert a dime." (This was 5 miles from the nearest road.) "Bugs! Bugs! Bugs! Help! Man-eating Piranha Bugs. I am being eaten alive." Or, "Jack cut the wrong kind of meat. Saturday, 11 A.M., had to go out to Drs. in Saranac Lake for emergency surgery. Nine stitches. Come back in with flashlight Saturday night." Then there was, "Gary was here. Joanne wasn't. Darn!" And, "Corky says he ain't cumming back here in the dark or rain or ANYTIME!"

Graffiti tells of the trials of the trail—the insects, the injuries, the inclemencies of weather, the cravings and yearnings, the loneliness. Oddly enough, I never read any extolling the *beauties* of the trail.

At West Canada Lake, long noted for being one of the highest and wildest Adirondack lakes (2,368 feet), I encountered a state outpost headquarters. After four days alone, it was good to talk with someone and to know that emergency facilities were available. I continued to be preoccupied over the fear of a broken limb and agonizing hours of waiting alone for help.

At every opportunity, my dog and I swam in the cold, clear waters of the Sacondoga River along the Northville–Lake Placid Trail

Earl Overacres, park superintendent, and his wife, Thelma, first came to West Canada as honeymooners. They loved the place. Work and a growing family kept them living "outside" near the city of Rochester, but every vacation time they'd head for West Canada. Then, twenty years later, Earl received a phone call from the Department of Environmental Conservation asking if he'd like a job living "way back in." Earl and Thelma made an instant decision. Yes! Two hours later, they were on their way to the Adirondack wilderness to inspect their new home.

"This is where we always wanted to be," said Thelma, smiling as she invited me into their rugged log station house. "I still commute between Rochester and West Canada," she continued, " 'cause I still work as a secretary. But every weekend, I join Earl here, traveling by station wagon and seaplane or on foot." A cheerful, silvery-haired lady, she served me ice-cold rootbeer and BLT's made with fresh-baked bread and homegrown lettuce. Pitzi lapped up the bacon fat and collapsed on the cool stone hearth of their fireplace.

Nearby are the remains of another, older stone fireplace preserved as a monument to French Louie. This famous hermit trapped, hunted, and fished the West Canada lakes for over thirty years (1878–1915). Louie was a French Canadian with a touch of Irish and Algonquin Indian. He is described as "hard as Laurentian granite and tough as Adirondack spruce." Renowned as a guide and expert woodsman, Louie would have chuckled at my following the carefully marked Northville–Lake Placid Trail, carrying the hikers' "bible," *Guide to Adirondack Trails*, and a compass. He was a man who strode through the woods like a bear making straight for a scratching tree.

Louie was already dead when this footpath was created by the Adirondack Mountain Club (ADK) in 1922. The work was done mostly by two members, Edwin M. Noyes and Howard Rowe, over a two-year period. They laid out an 18-inch path along an 8-foot cleared right-of-way. The two men did not hand-

Pure streams and lakes provide drinking wate
for hikers in the Adirondack

carve the entire 113 miles. Twenty-five percent was new trail; the rest, connections between Indian trails, animal tracks, old military and logging roads, and fishing paths which ran in the right direction. In those days, a railroad served both ends. From station to station, the entire trail was 133 miles long. Today, most hikers cut 10 miles of country road off either end, driving directly to the actual footpath.

During my first week on the trail, I met twenty-eight people, plus two packs of Boy Scouts. Pitzi confronted them boldly. They passed us shouting and puffing like little beagles on the track of a 'coon. Most other hikers were teenage boys or families of four or five. At Mud Pond lean-to, I met a friendly farmer with handlebar moustache and his four, blue-eyed, blond boys. They tumbled around their father like baby foxes. Their love for one another was touching. Over a cup of tea, I learned that this was a very special vacation. The rest of the year, the boys were in custody of their mother in some distant city.

At Cedar Lakes, I met John Remius, another outpost ranger, who was equally hospitable and helpful. I also encountered two "hippies." They carried a guitar, Chinese philosophy books, crunchy granola, no bathing suits, and a road map for orientation. Wandering a leisurely 3 miles a day, the pretty girl with long braids drawled, "Our home is where our packs are."

I found useful booty along the trail—three bars of soap, a can of tunafish, a lens cap for my camera, one red, size 48, windbreaker, a pair of purple jeans which fit perfectly, and an exquisitely tied trout fly. Our packs grew heavier rather than lighter. On the sixth evening, Pitzi compounded the problem of weight.

We were camped on the Cedar River Flow. The night was hot and muggy with plenty of mosquitoes whining around. The fire was burning low just before bedtime when Pitzi dashed into the lake to chase a beaver. He returned to the tent soaking wet. I let him in to escape the mosquitoes and by midnight the tent had turned into a steam bath. The walls were dripping and the sleeping bag was soggy. The dog further disgraced himself by eating quantities of woodsgrass, then scaring both himself and me by barking every time his stomach growled during the night. Our gear weighed more than ever come morning.

We reached the dirt crossroad at the Moose River Plains Primitive Area next morning. We were tired after seven days on the trail, averaging 8 miles a day with numerous stops for photography. Our food was gone. Pitzi had lost 6 pounds; I, 5. It was time to meet my friend, rest, and restock our packs.

Ted met me with*out* his usual happy-go-lucky expression. "I want you to go home and stay out of the woods for a while," he began. "There's a murderer on the loose!"

I was astounded. The Adirondacks are probably one of the safest places in the East. There are rarely murders in our mountains. The last one had been twenty years or more ago when a policeman was shot in Lake Placid. Yet, unbelievable as it sounded, the villain was a mere 15 miles away from where I had camped the night before. A 300-man hunt was underway, using state troopers, Conservation officers, Search and Rescue team members, and bloodhounds. The murderer might well be headed this way. Robert Garrow had already killed twice, two known victims, using a knife. The event held the area in a state of shock and terror for twelve days while the criminal hid out in the woods, moving undercover. I went back to my cabin, passing through seven road blocks on the way, and waited. Finally the man was caught near Lake Champlain.

Resuming the Northville–Lake Placid Trail where I had left off, as autumn approached, I found days were cooler, bugs less numerous, and scenery more rugged. Pitzi and I trod past lovely Tirrell Pond, skirted cedar-edged coves at Long Lake, whispered over white pine needles on old tote roads, and climbed abandoned fire towers for sweeping views of the approaching High Peaks. On a rainy morning, we squished into the neat meadows of Shattuck Clearing. Andy Blanchette, the outpost's bachelor caretaker, smiled whimsically when I asked what he did in his spare time.

"I just look around," he said softly. "I see a new challenge every time I look up at the Seward Range."

Andy couldn't have *too* much spare time, judging from the immaculate condition of his station. Bright flowers clustered in window boxes below sparkling window panes. His horses, love of his life, were well-groomed and shod. From time to time, Andy rode them over the fire trails and tote roads which skirt the Cold River. I left the mist-shrouded meadows with regret.

Pitzi and I trudged on through ever more drenching rain. We spent a chilly night on the sand floor of old Seward lean-to. I'm eternally grateful to the anonymous camper who left dry firewood in a corner. Even with a fire, Pitzi shivered so hard that I opened my sleeping bag and pulled him against my stomach to stop his shudders. Gradually, his trembling stopped, just as mine had quieted years ago at Deep Lake when Morgan drew me next to his warm body.

Next morning we reached the remains of Noah John Rondeau's "Hermitage." One tiny, dilapidated shack still stands high above the Cold River, sad, broken, and blackened. Clayt Seagers, former Director of Conservation Education for the Department of Environmental Conservation, wrote in *The Conservationist* magazine, "Noah occupied a hole in a woodpile way to hell and gone back in the Adirondack wilderness for thirty-three years." The noted hermit maintained two small shacks which he called his Town Hall and Hall of Records, plus several teepees of firewood. These teepees were his invention for instant firewood. By standing 12-foot lengths of partly notched saplings in a wigwam shape, Noah simply had to reach for a long stick, smack it with an axe, and shove the premeasured faggot into the fire. In summer, he actually lived inside his woodpile!

It was 19 long miles, or a fast six-hour walk, from the Hermitage to the nearest town. Apparently Noah liked it that way. In his journal he wrote: "April 29 I walk about my Town Hall and City. Robins and Juncoes, Chipmonks and Sparrows. No gas stations, no dogs on every corner, no church bells in my ears.

What freedom alone in natural primitiveness. . . ."

Except for sorties out for supplies and for his famed public appearance at the National Sportsmen's Show in New York City (for which he was flown out by helicopter as the "Hermit Mayor of Cold River City"—population of one), Rondeau led a simple life of hunting and fishing, growing wildflowers, reading, and writing. As old age and ill health appeared, Noah went to town during the winters. He passed away in Lake Placid in 1967. So far as I know, the only memorial to his name is the Department of Environmental Conservation trail sign at the Cold River Hermitage.

From Rondeau's camp to Duck Hole was a short hike. Duck Hole is called the "crossroads of the Adirondack trail system." The caretaker at this outpost headquarters told me that a busy

The sole remaining building of Noah Rondeau's hermitage near the Cold River.

summer night may see 200 people camped here. Toward dusk, the storm clouds lifted around Mt. McNoughton's shoulders and a flush of pink suffused the ink-black lake and rain-spattered hills. The bridge over the outlet was silhouetted against pearly steam rising from the stream. I could appreciate why many nature enthusiasts consider Duck Hole one of the most scenic spots in the mountains.

As a few leftover raindrops drummed on the lean-to roof that night, I reminisced back on my trail trip. Except for the freak experience of finding a murderer loose in the woods, all my fears had proven groundless. Moreover, I was rich with self-confidence, hardened muscles, new friends, and a deeper love for the Adirondacks. Before I headed out to Lake Placid and ended my trip, I felt a detour should be made into the High Peaks themselves. The saying is, "All trails lead to Mt. Marcy"; so that was where I went.

New York's highest mountain (5,344 feet) is a major attraction. The heavy human use was directly reflected in the condition of the trail I now walked upon. Roots writhed like arthritic fingers, exposed by thousands of pounding boots. The recent rains had made mud holes a foot deep and sometimes 20 feet wide. I got stuck in one and had to yell to a passing backpacker to pull me out. Pitzi was black to his belly. To climb Mt. Marcy, I decided, was an endurance test more difficult than the past 100 miles of the Northville–Lake Placid Trail. I was so busy watching my feet, jumping, slipping, teetering, sliding, clenching, and gripping, that I could not begin to enjoy the mountain until I reached solid rock and alpine meadow above 5,000 feet.

Here, using my imagination, I could have been standing several hundred miles northward on the tundra. Alpine plants grew from crevices and tiny patches of mountain meadow. There were Lapland Rosebay, Mountain Sandwort, Alpine Goldenrod, dwarf birches and firs—all rare or unknown elsewhere in the state. This vegetation is a remnant of the Ice Age, left behind when glaciers retreated about 10,000 years ago. Plants struggle for

Shielding a tiny blaze from the strong winds atop Mt. Marcy,
I prepare a trail lunch.

life up here, surviving some of the coldest temperatures and strongest winds in the nation. At all times, they must wrest nourishment and moisture from the thinnest layer of impoverished soil above this massive mound of bedrock.

The view atop Mt. Marcy was spectacular, looking east into Vermont and west across the rolling lesser peaks; but the sense of wildness which had been with me for so many days now was marred by scores of people. Descending by a different trail to Marcy Dam Ranger Station, I passed lean-tos that were black hovels, fit only for witches or porcupines. Their floors had been chopped out for firewood, their roofs leaked. Torn plastic sheets flapped at the entrances. Outhouse doors had been torn off for kindling wood. Fireplaces had been kicked in, grills knocked topsy-turvy, hearths turned into trash heaps. The ground around these shelters was beaten bare, and parts of the trail were deep ruts where water had cut right down to bedrock.

Down at Marcy Dam, I counted 203 people registered in the trail book as of Friday the past weekend, 427 on Saturday, and 120 as of Sunday. Clearly all trails did lead to Marcy!

I stopped at the ranger station to chat with Allan Jordan. Holding onto his huge St. Bernard while I restrained my German shepherd, the ranger told me that 40,000 people had used the Marcy Dam campsites and trail in 1972.

"How do you keep track?" I asked.

"We have an electric eye counter along the trail," the ranger confided.

Tying Pitzi to a tree and slipping off my pack, I said, "That many people certainly explains the condition of the trails up Marcy and the trash in the woods."

"Yes," replied Jordan. "It used to be that older people did most of the hiking and camping. They enjoyed the woods and kept them clean. Now 50 percent of the people are kids under twenty-five years old. Word's gotten out that Marcy Dam and Lake Colden are 'where the action is.' Kids come to camp for most of the summer, moving from campsite to campsite, so it costs them practically nothing. I spend most of my time just keeping the campsites tidy."

Allan invited me to meet his wife and sit a spell on the steps. The pretty brunette brought us glasses of iced tea while his two little girls peeked around the trees, shy as fawns. Allan continued, "I took 5 *tons* of garbage out from here last Labor Day. Up at the Lake Colden campsites, the trash had to be airlifted out by helicopter!"

"But why?" I demanded. "Why is the public so thoughtless?"

"I figure they probably feel too tired to carry another ounce; or they bury their trash too shallow and the bears and 'coons come along and dig it up; or they just expect someone else will clean up for them. To few abide by the woods' commandment, 'You carry it in, you carry it out.' When the Adirondack Moun-

On the way up the trail to Mt. Marcy, I stopped to see the spectacular view from Marcy Dam.

tain Club held its annual spring clean-up at Raquette Lake in 1970, they hauled *12 tons* of garbage from Big Island to shore by boat!"

"But," I fumed, "the public cannot expect dedicated mountaineers and state employees like yourself, Allan, to act as glorified garbagemen in the woods. There must be some way to educate them." He shook his head resignedly and turned up his palms. "How?"

After a few more moments of commiserating and sipping iced tea, I shouldered my pack again and said goodbye. My plan was to climb Algonquin, second highest peak in New York. I was curious if I would find the same distressing conditions on this new trail, and if the view from the top might be more impressive. On the way, I fell in step with an ADK 46er—an Adirondack Mountain Club Forty-Sixer. He was nattily dressed in Bean's packboots, Pendleton shirt, and a plaid tam-o-shanter over his iron-gray hair. He was one of several hundred hikers who have climbed all forty-six Adirondack mountains over 4,000 feet (though recent measurements indicate four of them may be just a few feet under). The first person to ascend them all did so in 1925.

Still fretting about the deleterious impact of humans on the High Peak country, I shared my concern with this perceptive gentleman.

"I think you'll see some changes in the future," he reasoned. "Something will have to be done to ease the stress on these trails and on our nine fragile alpine summits. You'll find Algonquin almost as bad as Marcy. Its delicate soil and tiny plants have been pounded down by hikers' feet. Parts of this trail have eroded into deep ruts right down to the bedrock."

We walked on awhile in silent mutual concern, feeling the autumn sunshine on our shoulders.

"What sort of changes would work?" I queried.

"Well, people might be allowed into the High Peaks only by permit. They could be forbidden to camp above 3,500 feet.

The state should remove its lean-tos at higher elevations. The cold temperatures and demand for firewood make them pretty vulnerable to unscrupulous campers."

I nodded my head in vigorous agreement, remembering the shelters on Marcy's upper flanks.

"You know, our club probably had a lot to do with starting the stampede to the High Peaks," said the 46er self-consciously. "The area is really stunning, but now people are climbing just to 'bag a peak.' They check off mountains as if they were adding birds to a life list."

We parted company shortly afterward; he to detour up Wright's Peak, and I to climb right up Algonquin. I reached the summit by late afternoon. The sky was entirely clear and faultlessly blue. The view was far better than on Marcy. I could look one way across ranges of purple mountains toward the gentler hills of the western Adirondacks. Turning half a circle, I gazed down to Lake Champlain and its lowlands before lifting my eyes again to the lavender outline of Vermont's Green Mountains. South, I thought I detected the smudge of smog which would be Albany and Hudson River valley towns 100 miles away.

The setting sun was throwing an intense golden glow over the entire mountaintop while the clefts below were darkening with shadows. I began looking for a camping spot, determined to stay right at the top overnight to absorb the beauty of sunset and sunrise. Skirting around gigantic boulders, mounds of bedrock, and clusters of alpine flowers and miniature trees, I tried not to destroy anything. Finally I found a flat patch of moss, lichens, and a creeping shrub which looked large enough to accommodate my tent and offer some cushioning. The guy lines and corners had to be held taut with rocks because the soil was too shallow to hold tent pegs. Here and there pockets in the bedrock held pools of rain water. Enough for Pitzi and me to cook with and drink.

My tent flaps faced west into a glorious sunset. As the swollen sun lowered, its rays turned my tent into a translucent scarlet

Sawing wood for the campfire before the sun sets,

I prepare camp atop Algonquin Mountain.

balloon, my pack into a burnished copper-orange sack. The small campfire flickered with hot orange flames. Now the sun sat on the jagged edge of purple-black mountains. The world was orange and purple for a moment, before the sun was swallowed. I took a last look around the horizon. Never before had I sensed so keenly the immensity, grandeur, and wildness of these mountains. As an early guide remarked, "It makes a man feel what it is to have all creation under his feet."

Suddenly it was twilight and a chill crept into the air. Not a breath of wind. Far off to the south, practically on the rim of the sky, a few thin skeins of cloud turned rosy. A lone jet trail overhead flared crimson for a minute, then turned ghostly gray. I pulled on a down jacket and traded hiking shorts for jeans. Pitzi was already curled up asleep in a little hollow. Yet I stayed up until it was totally dark and watched the night cross the sky and the stars break out in spangles. Not a sound broke the alpine stillness—no planes, no cars, no animals, no trees, no people, no running water. It was an exceptional night on top of the High Peaks, probably 1 out of 300.

Toward dawn, my tent began to flap and quiver in a strange manner. I half woke, listening for wind, imagining how easily one could be blown off this precipitous mountaintop in a gale. I could detect no gusts, so I fell asleep again.

A glance out the tent at dawn showed me why the tent had quivered and the predicament I was in. A front had moved up from the innocent-looking south. I should have paid attention to the smudgelike smog and the wispy cloud strands. A wall of fog and mist was rolling over the mountaintops, descending from the sky, obscuring everything. I crawled out, stood up, and saw a monstrously inflamed red ball poised on the horizon, silhouetting two stunted spruces, no higher than my knee, and probably 150 years old. Then abruptly, the sunrise was snuffed out. Fingers of fog closed over the top of Algonquin like a giant hand enclosing a giant breast. I could see no farther than 50 feet.

Working swiftly, I struck the tent, repacked, saddled the dog with his bags, stamped out the fire remains, and swallowed half a cup of stale cold tea. All the while I kept peering into the gloom, hoping for a break. I began to feel disoriented. I could no longer remember where the first cairn lay which marked the way off the rocky summit. I could find no trace of footsteps or scuffmarks on the smooth stones around me. With a compass, of course, I could always strike out in the general direction I had climbed up from, but if I missed the trail at timberline, the dog and I might spend hours struggling through stunted firs and birches before reaching the more open, taller forests below.

Pitzi and I began our first tentative steps down the summit. The murk swirled about us. I had rapidly learned a new lesson in backpacking and camping: Never camp above timberline! Weather can change dramatically in the Adirondacks. Extremes of temperature and wind are common atop the High Peaks. With luck and an occasional glimpse through the fog, we made it safely down the mountain; and a short time later, safely off the North-ville–Lake Placid Trail.

It had been quite a trip over the years, starting at little Round-house Pond, and leading right up to the top of lofty Algonquin Mountain. I felt I had really earned my guide's license besides picking up much valuable woods experience.

I had lots more to learn, however, in surviving the rough Adirondack winters.

# 8

## My First Winter

### (Or, How To Be Lonely Without Even Trying)

After the November freeze-up covered Black Bear Lake with a sheet of pearly ice stretching uninterrupted from shore to shore, but still of uncertain thickness, I began trekking in and out of the woods. Until freeze-up was over, in about two to three weeks, I would stay off the lake and carry everything on my back through the woods. This included food, milk, mail, garbage, kerosene and supplies. The walk took half an hour without snow, up to an hour in it. Existing during this period was certainly harder and more time consuming than in summer and fall; however, it put me in excellent physical condition and allowed me to become better acquainted with the lakeshore around Black Bear Lake.

One of the funniest things that ever occurred at the cabin took place during freeze-up. A famous magazine was doing an article on the Adirondacks. They decided to send one of their star photographers to take pictures of a "resident writer in a log cabin." A long phone call ensued in which I valiantly tried to convince the photographer that he *had* to walk in by foot. Our conversation went something like this.

"Hello. Look, I'm hiring a helicopter today and I'll be over to shoot you about 11 A.M.," he began energetically.

"There's no place to land it," I advised.

"No place to land it?" he protested. "Aren't there any fields around there?"

"No, only woods."

"Don't you have a front lawn?" he persisted. "Or a back-yard?"

"No, only trees."

"How about a farm? Isn't there a farm around there?"

"No, no farms."

"Well, for heaven's sake, there must be *some* sort of an open-ing. What about the lake. We can land on the ice."

"I'm afraid the ice is only a couple of inches thick so far. Barely safe to walk on, so it wouldn't hold a helicopter."

"We have to figure something out. I can't waste all that time *driving* there."

"The closest clearing I can think of where a helicopter could land is a single tennis court at a hotel about 8 miles away. I could meet you there and drive you to Black Bear Lake. You'll still have to walk a mile and a half to the cabin."

A pause. "Walk? A mile and a half? You mean there's no road to your cabin?"

"No, just to the foot of the lake. We use boats in summer, snowshoes or snowmobiles in winter. But you've come at the worst time of year when you can't use any of them. So, we walk."

"Can we use a snowmobile?" he asked hopefully.

"Only for about a third of a mile. The rest of the trail is too narrow and hilly, and in parts there's no trail at all."

"Well, please get one. It'll save a *little* time."

Money seemed to be no object to him and time appeared to be of the essence. So I rented a snowmobile. In those days the machines were just coming into popularity and I had not yet con-sidered buying one. I met the man, told him to hang on tight, and whisked him and his cameras all of a third of a mile closer to my cabin.

The cameras and equipment were terribly heavy. The photographer was terribly good-looking, but terribly out of shape. Before we even got there he was sweating profusely and panting hard.

"Oh, for a helicopter," he said and winked, then groaned as snow dropped off a balsam and down his neck.

But he was a very good sport. The sight of my rustic home, books, rugs, pelts, and curios from distant travels perked him up. He took a great many pictures in the next two hours and then seemed reluctant to leave. Whether it was because he dreaded the "long walk back," or would have liked to spend a cozy evening by the fire, I'll never know. I think it was both, and I kind of wish he'd stayed.

As soon as a test hole chopped in the ice showed 3-inch thickness, I felt it safe to start walking down the lake. First I cut a straight spruce pole about 8 feet long and hammered a nail through one end. If I fell through, I could lay the pole across the hole to either edge and haul myself out, or drive the nail end into the ice like a long claw to get purchase. The other end of the pole served as a sounding surface. As I walked, I kept tapping the pole ahead of my feet on the ice. Good ice makes a solid resonant thwang; rotten ice, a dull thud; thin ice, a high short tap.

The first week or two I was extremely cautious and leery about walking on ice. Some of my loneliest experiences on Black Bear Lake took place on those blue-gray, chill December evenings when daylight failed at 4:30 P.M. and snow showers sifted down from lowering clouds. I would walk home over gray glare ice with a heavy pack and my pole, wondering if I'd even have a chance for a second breath if I fell through now—or now—or now.

By Christmas, however, snow had blanketed the entire lake and ice had thickened to almost 2 feet. I felt cocky. I used my pole only to tap the frames of my bear paw snowshoes, which now became necessary for travel. Every trip was different and

An early snowstorm coats pines and hardwood branc
as Pitzi and I walk out with the mail during the freeze-

enjoyable. The lake was a wide white canvas upon which I created snowshoe patterns as freely as a finger painter. Sometimes I'd see dainty fox tracks curving around the islands, or a jumble of deer hoofprints around an open spring hole, or the slide of an otter on the bank, or the juxtaposition of hawk wings and hare paws near shore. Rhythmic waves of snow or streaks of glare ice might be sculptured by the wind. A blood-red, setting sun could throw immense blue shadows of pine trees across the pearly snow. Or a brilliant white noonday sun might turn the cover into a vast field of flashing diamonds.

That first winter I perversely spent Christmas Eve alone at the cabin, not having any family to join nor wishing to visit well-meaning friends or neighbors. Temperatures dropped to minus 26 degrees on my back porch. Hawk Hill later reported minus 42 degrees! The moon was full. I stepped out into this glorious night insulated with long johns, three pairs of wool socks, two pairs of mittens, a turtleneck shirt, Icelandic wool sweater, heavy lumberjack pants, and jacket with hood. Strapping bear paws to my boots, I took a short walk through the forest beyond the cabin. Small firs had become marshmallow mounds. The creek had vanished into a musical under-ice rivulet. Drifts were decorated with wedding cake frillery. In the intense cold, my harnesses creaked and my fingers tingled. Snowshoe hares slumbered in shadowy caves beneath snow-laden spruces. The black balsam clumps seemed to shelter hefalumps and other strange snow beasts. Birches and beeches threw parallel shadows on a blue-white snow. Every few minutes, a trunk retorted like a rifle shot in the frigid air due to the awful contractions of wood. Across the bare canopy of the forest, sparkling stars were strung upon brittle branches. It was a magical night—a night fitting to be Christmas Eve.

Next day I decided to go out for dinner. I left the cabin at noon when the temperature stood at minus 22 degrees and a north wind at my back was blowing at 20 miles per hour. This gave a wind chill factor of minus 70 degrees. At the time, I did not realize this placed a person in serious danger of freezing any exposed skin. I put on all the clothes of the night before, plus goggles, scarf, and insulated rubber boots. I started down the lake on snowshoes. None of the summer people had braved a trip up for the holidays. I was alone on the lake. Halfway down, my toes and fingers passed the tingling stage and started getting numb. Stopping a moment, I forced my arms out of the jacket sleeves and stuck a hand under each armpit. But there was no help for my feet. I was afraid to move too fast for fear of freezing my lungs, so I continued trudging along at a fast shuffle. Three-quarters of the way down the lake, my feet were numb to the ankles and my nose felt funny. I couldn't comprehend the speed with which my body was chilling. By the time I reached the parking lot, my legs felt like two stubs, and my fingers could barely move.

As I tried to fit the key into the truck door, I suddenly realized how perilous my situation was. The lock was frozen. Unless I could get into my truck, start the engine, and warm up the cab, I was in danger of freezing. All the camps around Black Bear Lake were locked shut. To turn and walk back *into* that arctic wind, cold as I was, would have been foolhardy. It was 3 miles out over the mountain to Hawk Hill and my nearest neighbors.

I found a matchbook and tried to light one under the key. Either the wind blew it out or my heavily gloved hand dropped it. There was no other way I could heat up the lock. With persistence I finally warmed up the key and it melted its way into the lock. The door opened. I was shivering violently.

Now a new problem emerged. The gearshift was so cold it would not move. That meant I would have to sit with my foot on the clutch pedal until engine and heater warmed the cab—*if* the engine started. I pulled the choke to FULL and turned the starter. An ominous, husky, grinding noise came from under the hood. Again. Again. Finally, the engine took hold, coughed, bucked, and settled down. Never in my life had I been so grateful to any mechanical device.

As soon as I could ease the gearshift into neutral, I got out and started running up and down the parking lot. My body was bitterly cold. After ten minutes, the cab was warm enough to thaw out in. It was so painful, though, that I had lost all taste for dinner. I had come within a hairbreadth of frostbite and perhaps severe freezing. I decided to go right back to the cabin. The thought of snowshoeing home at night in even colder temperatures was terrifying. One misstep—a twisted ankle, a fall through the ice, a bad leg cramp—could kill and kill quickly. Again I sensed that feeling of inexorable, pitiless, relentless winter. It gives no quarter at all.

That Christmas walk chastened my attitude about living at the cabin. Rather than continue in my self-imposed complete isolation, I now craved some form of communication, some line with the outside world. A telephone was out of the question since the nearest poles and lines were 5 miles away. But a citizen's band (CB) radio and tall antenna might serve as an emergency link with people in Hawk Hill or even as far away as Lake Serene where a volunteer ambulance and fire truck were on call.

I purchased a compact transistorized set and attached a 9-foot antenna to the roof ridge. A 12-volt truck battery provided power. The first night I switched on the set and turned to the one channel for which I had a crystal. This, I knew, was the Emergency React station for our section of the Adirondacks. It was monitored continually by the volunteer fire department and a few concerned citizens who kept CB sets in their homes and cars.

There was a crackling. I adjusted the squelch control and heard an acquaintance out at Hawk Hill calling for a wrecker to pull a car from a snowdrift. Suddenly my cabin did not seem so remote and winter not so bleak. A glow of comradeship warmed me. Voices and cracklings filled the air as instructions were given.

When silence fell again, I pressed in my microphone and said, "This is Anne at Black Bear Lake calling Hawk Hill; Black Bear Lake to Hawk Hill."

A faint hum, then a flurry of static. A deep voice replied, "KBX-5213 at Hawk Hill to Black Bear Lake. I read you. How you doing, Anne?"

"Fine. I'm testing out my new set. I hear you fine," I said proudly. "How are you?"

"10-4. This is KBX-5213. Over and out."

The set was silent again. I was perplexed by the quick conversation, code, and sign-off. Next day I found out about the rules and regulations of CB radio operation. One must apply for a federal communications license, receive a call number and letters, and pay a fee to be legal on the air. An emergency channel must not be used for chatting, but kept open at all times for trouble calls.

I applied for my license and bought more crystals. The set brought many fascinating hours of listening because of the "skip." The world came in staccato bursts to Black Bear Lake bouncing haphazardly off the ionized layers of the ionosphere. Mornings I might hear Texas shrimp boats arguing roughly off the coast of Yucatan. Around noon a garble of Spanish often came from Havana and San Juan. Toward evening, beaver trappers in Nova Scotia or fishermen off Georgia might radio ahead to their wives to have cod and boiled potatoes or catfish and hushpuppies ready for supper. Skip, however, was a nuisance, if not a hazard. It often interferred with the messages I wanted, or had to, transmit. Sometimes it was impossible to break through. Then a CB set was all but worthless. Nevertheless I kept my set on each evening for an hour. Each month or two I dragged the battery down by toboggan to my pickup truck and exchanged it with the fully charged one. In this way, I maintained a fresh power supply by simply driving and recharging it.

At the time I was improving my communication system, I was also experimenting with toilet and bathing facilities. First, I merely used a chamberpot by night and trudged out to the out-house by day. But as winter grew more severe, I was literally "freezing to the throne." I began carrying the toilet seat indoors to keep it warm and carrying it out as needed. Still it was a *big* inconvenience to put on winter clothing and snowshoes and walk 200 feet. Eventually, I installed a type of porto-potty in the kitchen with large plastic bags and a special deodorant-decomposer solution. Now my toilet facilities were in relative warmth and I only made one trip a day with the bag to my outhouse.

Never had I been more conscious of the functioning of the human body, especially the constant and predictable flow of wastes. These were not items to be flushed nonchalantly down a white bowl to pollute the nearest river. They were parts of me that had to be conscientiously disposed of in an ecologically sound manner. That incredibly balanced, magical, physiological act—whereby food, air, and water went in; glucose, pyruvate, lactic acid and oxygen chain reacted; energy and heat were re-leased; and feces, urine, carbon dioxide, and other wastes passed out—was running my body like a precision-built machine. Thus I was kept warm, moving, and breathing amid winter's deathlike immobility, lifeless snow drifts, ice sheets, frozen creeks, trans-fixed trees, immutable boulders, cementlike ground. I don't think that people can think of themselves as physiological masterpieces in the city where the environment is so transformed. But here in the woods in winter, one's life functions are strikingly self-evident.

As for bathing, I tried many techniques from sponge bath to Swedish sauna. The best method was to fill a round, metal horse drinking tub with three pails of hot water, scrunch myself in, and put a rubberized poncho over my head and tub rim. This held in the heat and steam. I usually took these "horse baths" on the back porch, often under falling flakes. But when the tempera-tures really dropped, I used two pails, a sauce pan, and a plastic dish tub filled with piping hot water. Carrying these right out-doors onto the snow, I stood in the tub which kept my feet warm

In winter, my drinking water has to be dipped up through a hole chopped in the lake ice. (PHOTO: DAVID ALLEN HARVEY: CHIMERA)

and poured the scalding water over my head and body. Steam rose from every inch of skin. I had approximately one minute to shampoo and soap down before the cold penetrated. Another hot sauce pan full and I'd be warm again. Pour. Rinse hair. Scrub hands and feet. Pour. Rinse. Two buckets exactly did the job. As long as there was *no wind blowing*, the heat of the water would sustain my naked skin at a reasonable temperature. Then for a tumble in the snow and/or a fast dash in to the fireplace. I've taken baths this way at minus 10 degrees and felt absolutely marvelous afterward.

Winter is a lonely time—even with occasional trips to town, birds at the feeder, a porcupine under the cabin, mice in my drawers, and a citizen's band radio on the desk. Loneliness is a pervasive quality in these mountains. It affects certain people more than others. It is worse for those who are ill, aged, divorced, widowed, or isolated. I've known intolerable hours at the cabin, waiting for a blizzard to blow itself out. Roads are blocked. The mail stops. Phone and electric lines are ripped down. Fierce winds endanger driving and prevent social visits.

I know one eighty-year-old friend who stares down the country road for hours, seeing nothing but snow devils kicked up by the winds. He says glumly, "Winter I don't love. I don't even *like* it! You just have to put up with it—or go to Florida."

Winters I try to keep busy writing, visiting good friends, consulting, traveling. It's a conscious battle against the loneliness. Many residents go to the local bars and taverns for companionship, entertainment, and human warmth. Here the local gossip is shared, current events are discussed, and bets are laid when a special barrel will fall through the ice on a certain lake come spring. Some natives drop into the bars for a cup of coffee; others come for an Adirondack haircut and stay a couple of days. We are all seeking solace from loneliness.

That first winter, one of my articles appeared in a regional magazine with a snapshot and mention that I lived in a log cabin.

I was away on a short trip and returned to find strange snowshoe tracks leading to my door. A letter was stuffed in the doorjam. I opened it and discovered a seven-page document with reference to my article and a love poem! The address was from a distant, tiny hamlet in the Adirondacks; the addressee was also a log-cabin dweller.

Amazed, I asked around Hawk Hill, Lake Serene, and other spots about my uninvited visitor. He had left a string of inquiries across the Adirondacks trying to find me. In those winters, before snowmobiles became popular, any strange face was a novelty. I was able to obtain a fairly detailed description of my visitor. A nice young man, decently dressed in old woods clothes, dark hair, blue eyes, medium build—that's how he was described.

I answered his letter with reservation. I said that I admired his persistence in reaching out, trying to find a possible soul mate who lived in a log cabin in the woods. Yet I told him that I was annoyed with his breach of my privacy. He answered with another poem. We corresponded for a while, but it seemed as if he were looking for a dream person, a recluse, a philosopher. Eventually our letters fizzled out. I never met this romantic snowshoer. Perhaps it's better, for I might have shattered his image. But I still feel a bond with him. He was lonely, too.

# 9

# Winter Today

Winter today is free and fun. It is ushered in by the first blanket of snow *and* the first whir of a snowmobile. Instead of burrowing into their homes like woodchucks to suffer from "cabin fever," natives are now able to get out and enjoy a social life. Many towns have experienced complete transformations. Snowmobiles bring fresh faces, conviviality, enthusiasm, and excitement to winter-weary hamlets. Devotees buy food, beverages, clothing, gas, and oil; they need lodging and repair service. Romance thrives on the heady sport. Within the space of a few years snowmobiles have made a direct impact on winter life in the Adirondacks, especially on my life.

On a good snowmobile weekend, every inn in the North Country is jammed with vacationers. They bring their machines, trailers, pickup trucks, sleds, colorful snowmobile suits, boots, helmets, mitts, goggles, and arm patches. Caravans roar down the roads and trails. People tromp in and out of local pubs and restaurants in heavy rubber and felt boots. Whole clubs like the Northwood Snowtravelers, Motor Mushers, The Polar Bears, Driftbusters, Boondock Boganeers, Winter Weasels, Paul Bunyan Riders, and Rump Bumpers race up and down the lakes.

Families plan Sunday snowmobile safaris. Groups travel from lake to lake over the smooth surface of the ice, stop for lunch, build a bonfire, cook hot dogs, tap a keg, sing songs.

A friend in Lake Serene, mother of five, confided to me, "I can remember six or eight years ago when I'd gaze out the kitchen window and see nothing but snowflakes go by. Dan had the car all day. I was stuck in the house. Temperatures might stay below zero for weeks. Now I use my snowmobile to have coffee with friends, take the laundry out, bring groceries in, play with the kids, and join my husband weekends riding, bar hopping, and visiting."

The first snowmobiles ever to come up Black Bear Lake and pass my cabin did so on a night about eight years ago. A pair, moving steadily and majestically, sped up the ice on a gloomy January evening. They made a wide circle at the head of the lake, and then as imperturbably raced back. Little did they know they had just made history. After centuries and aeons of creatures *walking* over the snow and ice, a mechanized vehicle had arrived that could reach maximum speeds of over 100 miles per hour on snow and ice. The red tail lights glowed like tiny UFOs. I felt exactly as if a pair of spaceships had just touched down on the lake.

Yet this visit, exotic as it seemed, started me thinking. I calculated the hours I spent snowshoeing up and down the lake for mail—at least one and a half or two per day. I thought of the heavy loads to be carried or towed on a toboggan—groceries, 50-pound sacks of dog food, kerosene, books. I considered the items which had to be brought up by boat before freeze-up or else they'd never get there at all—gasoline, cases of canned goods, propane tanks. I remembered that awful Christmas when my feet turned numb and one wrong move might have meant freezing to death. It seemed to me that a snowmobile would take much of the hardship out of winter and even more of the loneliness.

It did. My little Rupp Sprint (15-horse engine) has made life far less grueling in winter. I can come and go over the ice with almost the same ease and probably no more noise than in summer with my outboard boat in the water—except it's a hell of a lot colder! In my mind I link canoe and snowshoes, outboard boat and snowmobile, as two distinct modes of transportation, both necessary to my way of life. I'm tolerant toward snowmobiles in the Adirondacks because they seem to do less harm here than elsewhere.

One night I joined a group of acquaintances from Lake Serene and whisked miles up the lake to a lean-to nestled under ancient white cedars. Inside, a barbecue glowed beneath venison steaks and hash brown potatoes. A bonfire, whose flames leaped higher than our heads, roared out on the ice. A picnic table was loaded with bottles of liquor, cases of beer, plates, utensils, hot coffee, and cups. Snowmobiles surrounded the lean-to and campfire like patient horses hobbled around a covered wagon rendezvous. Beyond us, the lake stretched tautly away to coal-black hills as cold as chalcedony. A twilight glow hung above the hills—an apricot band transfusing into lettuce-green into lavender and finally into the royal purple which precedes black night. A few stars were already twinkling. By their very scintillation, I could tell we were in for a sub-zero evening. Everyone ate and drank heartily. We clustered around the bonfire for good conversation and warmth, turning back to side to front to side. Our shadows around the bonfire loomed grotesquely like spacemen—bulky bodies encased in full suits, huge helmeted heads, lumpish boots, and gloves. After dark, some of the men took their machines out to run circles, races, and cut capers. The throaty whine of engines echoed and reechoed across the lake. Twin headlights and single tail lights weaved and danced like a snowmobile ballet. It was a wonderful, companionable evening which did not break up until midnight. We left dirty dishes, empty bottles, blackened fire, pots, and pans for daylight. Nothing would disturb them and they would offend no one remaining on the ice for the rest of that arctic night. Streaking back across Lake Serene, I felt dwarfed by the great fingers and streamers of pale green and

rose which flickered on the northern horizon. The aurora bore-
alis was in fine evidence that night and made a beautiful finale to
our snowmobile picnic.

Snowmobiles, however, have many disgruntled opponents. A
Hawk Hill handyman exploded when he saw me ride up on my
new Rupp, "For Christ's sake, Anne, have you gone and gotten
one of those damn converted chain saws?"

Drawbacks and dilemmas crop up. Riders forget their manners
and wake up residents at 3 A.M. by revving their engines below
bedroom windows. One home owner became so incensed that he
beat up the leader of a snowmobile pack with the butt of his
rifle.

"You come back around this house at this hour again," he
thundered, "and I'll use the other end of this rifle!"

Snowmobile and dog stage an impromptu race on the solidly frozen
lake. (PHOTO: DAVID ALLEN HARVEY: CHIMERA)

Although New York State law insists that snowmobiles travel at a minimum speed and no closer than 100 feet of a dwelling between midnight and 6 A.M., it has not stopped this type of aggressive territorial encounter.

Thoughtless snowmobilers also litter and pollute. I've picked up empty beer cans right in the middle of Black Bear Lake. On windless days, one can often see a blue band of exhaust fumes stretching out behind a covey of machines. New synthetic oils are supposed to cut down somewhat on unburned hydrocarbon emissions, yet fumes still hang in our clear Adirondack air.

Noise is the chief complaint. Certainly it's mine, even owning a snowmobile. The engines are a definite hazard to healthy hearing. New models are supposed to be muffled down and produce a noise roughly equivalent to a vacuum cleaner. What a difference on recent weekend winter nights when I open the door of my cabin. That immensity of silence is gone. The hum, roar, whine, purr, and snarl of snowmobiles reverberate through the night, all night.

Perhaps the most telling, intangible disadvantage of snow-machines is the ease with which they can penetrate into once-pristine winter areas. A square-dancing buddy of mine, born in the remote hamlet of Beaver River which has no roads connecting it to anything, gave me this poignant epitaph.

"When I was a boy, I could step outside in winter and *hear* the silence. Nothing anywhere, just once in awhile a tree cracking or ice making up on the flow. It's not like that anymore. No, sir!" He contorted his lean, handsome face, thrust out both arms as if grabbing the steering handle of a machine, and bellowed, "Now it's 'Wruuuum, wruuuum, wruuuuuuuum.'"

Nevertheless, I believe that snowmobiles are here to stay. There are over 180,000 registered in New York State alone, and more than 1,600,000 in North America's snow belt. Combining Canada and the U.S., over 2 million machines exist.

The New York State Department of Environmental Conservation maintains approximately a thousand miles of official snowmobile trails in the Adirondacks. And the towns of Webb and Inlet alone, which call themselves "the Snowmobile Capital of the Northeast," cut, pack, and groom almost 500 miles of woodland trails.

One of the greatest benefits of the snowmobile is in emergencies, saving lives and helping injured people in remote and isolated areas. The second winter that I had my snowmobile, a frightening event occurred.

It was a sparkling, calm day in February, the first after about ten days of blowing snow, freezing rains, and keening winds. Coming back from the post office in early afternoon, I lingered outdoors near the cabin. The sun beat down on my back as I bent over the hood of my snowmobile, checking the spark plug and refilling the gas tank. At the moment when the tank gurgled

Venison steaks sizzle in the frying pan as snowmobilers gather around a roaring bonfire to enjoy a picnic in sub-zero temperatures.

full, I heard a distant shout, or was it a scream? I lowered the funnel and listened. Again. "Anne, Anne, come . . ." The rest faded out. The yelling was coming from over half a mile away on a point of land across the lake. It was carried on the crystal-clear, zero-degree air with amazing clarity.

"Anne, come quick! Bring your snowmobile!"

I scanned the lake. No one there, no dogs, no animals, nothing. Then I remembered that two hired men were walking in to various camps, cutting and laying up wood for summer folk. Could one of them have been hurt?

I reacted fast. Everything was ready, as if by a miracle. The snowmobile had just been run, was warm, and was full of gas. I cranked up the engine and raced toward the point. As I approached, a tall man came hopping wildly out of the woods. Every motion displayed panic and injury. His pants leg was ripped open to the knee and blood was pumping out over his white long johns.

"I've cut an artery in my leg with an axe!" he shrieked even before the machine came to a stop. "Losing lots of blood—may pass out. For God's sake, get me out of here!"

The man was 6 feet tall and close to 200 pounds. I thought fleetingly of my single-man machine, of trying to sustain or move him if he *did* pass out on the ice. Never having studied first aid, I had no idea what to do on the spot. The most reasonable course of action seemed to be to rush him to Lake Serene's health clinic as swiftly as possible.

"Get on," I shouted. "And grab my shoulders tight. Try to keep from fainting."

Never had the small Rupp taken so long to cross the lake, laboring under that extra weight. On the way, a sudden idea came to me. I swerved off to a camp nearby the landing which had electricity *and* a CB radio set. If worse came to worse, I was going to break in, throw on the power switch, and radio out for the ambulance. The woodcutter might need blood. I might need help transporting him. Again, as if by a miracle, the camp was occupied. It took only three minutes to give instructions, explain the situation, and enlist a helper. Together we got the man to the landing, still conscious, and into my truck.

The engine was also still warm from my trip to the post office and the snowy road was freshly ploughed. We whizzed over the mountain to Hawk Hill and turned onto the paved road for Lake Serene 20 miles away. Headlights blazing, horn blaring, I drove those snowy curved roads faster than I'd ever done before. Blood was covering the floor of my truck, our boots, the seat. My companion applied a tourniquet ripped from the torn trousers' leg. Five miles from Hawk Hill, the ambulance passed us traveling equally as fast. Both vehicles skidded to spectacular stops, then backed up. The woodcutter almost fainted from fright. But he was easily transferred to a stretcher and whisked off to the clinic. There a few stitches and pint of blood quickly restored him. Meanwhile, my helper and I went to devour steak sandwiches and cups of hot coffee to calm our nerves, and wait to help our patient home. It had been a close call, but the man recovered in time to finish his woodcutting chores before spring breakup.

A series of snowmobile accidents has marred every winter in the Adirondacks recently. It can be a dangerous sport with fractured knees, dislocated hips, slipped discs, and cut faces. Machines went through the ice on Black Bear Lake, Lake Serene, and others, into as much as 80 feet of water, although the riders miraculously jumped clear. Machines were hit trying to cross highways. Machines collided with each other due to running too close together on narrow trails. Worst of all, a young father of four was trick riding on a logging road, zooming around corners, leaning way out over the road for balance. On a sharp curve, he smashed chest-on into a loaded pickup. The machine was not even dented, but the man died of multiple fractures.

I had a near fatal accident myself on this same logging road. A girl friend flew up from Boston for a winter weekend. She had never been snowmobiling, so I decided to take her over the well-packed logging road. We bundled ourselves up heavily as it

was very cold. Beverly clasped me around my waist and I ran
the Rupp. As she became accustomed to the motion and road,
I started fooling around. We would swoop up on the right-hand
snowbank, coast down, cross the road, and curve up on the left
one, using centripetal force and downhill momentum to carry
us on. Suddenly, I saw a heavily laden log truck bearing down on
us around a corner. We were on the *left* side of the road. I
gunned the motor and jerked the handlebars toward the right
side. The driver, well to the left on *his* side, flailed his hands on
the wheel to bring his rig to the right and keep it from jack-
knifing. His astounded face passed scant inches above and to the
side of us, white, round-eyed, tense. We both made it, but barely.

The effect of our fright and of seeing the driver's face as he
was confronted by two pandalike females on a snowmobile set
Beverly and me into a fit of laughter. We fell off the machine
and into the middle of the road. I was doubled over from hilarity
when the local Environmental Conservation officer's car braked
to a stop a few feet from my head.

"Now, girls, for God's sake, what's going on?" exclaimed the
astonished officer.

Sobering quickly, I convinced the game warden that my
friend and I were not drunk, only relieved after our close brush
with a log truck. He shook his head gravely and suggested that
we do our riding in the woods where the only things that could
get hurt were the trees.

Game wardens spend a good deal of time in winter patroling
not only by car but by snowmobile as well. Unlike the situation
in other parts of the country, our wildlife and forest growth is
very seldom disturbed by snowmobiles. For one thing, the snows
are too deep and our woods too dense to permit much off-trail
travel. In most areas, it is just not possible to chase deer, coyotes,
bobcats, or foxes across open fields or brushland. And this type
of wildlife does not frequent the frozen lakes on which a large
percentage of the machines run. Since snowmobile trails are usually well-marked and groomed, they are preferred by outside

visitors and are heavily used. This means a minimum of back-woods snowmobiling. It is very rare to find anyone harassing or poaching deer in their "yards."

Yet this is not the complete picture. I've been back around deer yards in winter and was dismayed at the bitter existence of these animals. Most deer cluster in small groves and flats of balsams where they avoid chill winds and receive some protection from snow. But food here is almost nonexistent. After the adults have browsed the few existing twigs and branches of hardwoods and balsam tips, there is nothing left to eat. And as snows deepen, the deer refuse to venture out to browse. Snowmobile trails near such yards can, in fact, provide "trails" which may support the sharp hooves of these animals and enable them to reach new food sources. Such respites from continual fasting can help to cut down the high rate of winter starvation among Adirondack deer herds.

As for noise and its effect on wildlife, it seems to be a minor nuisance. If the deer which live within a few hundred yards of the New York State Thruway don't mind the traffic sounds, then it's doubtful that snowmobile noise will bother them up here.

The species which *are* affected by modern-day snowmobiles are the furbearers. In the old days, trappers had to lug their equipment by pack basket and limit their lines to distances they could cover on snowshoes. Nowadays, snowmobiles transport trappers three or four times the distance in the same amount of time. Therefore, a greater number of furbearers can be taken if a man or woman is willing to work hard. Coyotes, foxes, weasels, and bobcats are, at this time, completely unprotected. They may be trapped at any time and in any number in most Adirondack counties. Raccoons, mink, and muskrats may be trapped in any number during their open seasons. Fisher, otter, and beaver may be taken only during a certain short season in winter, but the numbers taken, unfortunately, are not controlled.

One winter day I joined a local beaver trapper on his line to learn something about this time-honored line of work which employs several hundred people in the Adirondacks. We met shortly after daybreak on a mild March morning, and took off with snowmobiles into wilderness country south of Tupper Lake.

"I like to trap where I don't see no other people," said Ernie after we had traveled about 20 miles through the woods.

Ernie is a hardy man. By law he must check his traps every forty-eight hours, tolerating whatever winter weather prevails and whatever problems arise.

"I've gone through a little of everything," he related. "Sub-zero days, cantankerous snowmobiles, bitches of snowstorms, falling through the ice, and even catching my hand in a trap."

I teased Ernie into letting me try to set a Conabear trap. With all the strength in my cold hands, I strained against the icy steel to force down the stiff springs. Certainly no beaver would ever know what hit him with this type of trap. With good reason, they are regarded as one of the most humane on the market. Finally I succeeded, winning Ernie's approval. Then at his next set, he casually pressed the jaws down and secured the trap as if he were going to catch a mouse instead of a 40-pound beaver. I watched him gaze into the ice hole with amber-tinted goggles—all the better to see into the water with—then plunge his rubber-gauntleted arm down to place the trap at the bottom of the lake. A stout wire secured the trap to a stake so it could not be dragged off. Still up to his armpit in the lake, Ernie delicately placed a sliver of poplar branch, partially peeled, on the trap lever as bait for the beavers. Then he withdrew his arm, pulled off the gauntlet, tugged off his goggles, and lit a cigarette.

Resting against his snowmobile, Ernie said genially, "I trap to help my income. Most of us don't have year-round jobs up here and trapping helps us survive. Besides beavers need some control or we'd be up to our asses in 'em."

"Didn't they used to be scarce?" I inquired.

"Very!" replied Ernie, dragging deeply on his cigarette. "In 1904 and 1905, the state had to import seven from Canada and fourteen from Wyoming to reestablish the Adirondack population. Fur-trappers had wiped them out in the 1800s when beaver hats and furs were all the rage. By 1890, the Adirondacks had no more than a dozen animals left. But after fashions changed, beavers had a chance. By 1940 they were so plentiful that trapping was allowed again. Now they're everywhere in the mountains. A real population problem in places."

I nodded my head in agreement, remembering the beaver swamp Betsy and I had found atop Jagged Mountain and the barrier it had imposed.

I was amazed to learn from Ernie that the Adirondack Trappers Association is 610 men, and 1 woman, strong; and that nearly 4,000 trapping licenses are sold in the Adirondacks each year. Between a half to one million dollars per year are sold in Adirondack furs, counting beaver, otter, fisher, weasels, raccoons, mink, muskrats, coyotes, and bobcats. This is one of the few areas in our populous East where a sustained harvest of these furbearers can still be taken. And where it's still a way of livelihood among mountain men.

Later that spring, Ernie gave me a couple of blanket hides, beautifully tanned, for my cabin. I accepted the sleek, glossy furs reluctantly. I still look at them with ambivalent feelings. That's because I know that only 51 feet from my window, a live relative of those skins may be swiming by at sunset, pushing his V-wake proudly and freely up Black Bear Lake. I'd *much* rather see my beavers alive than dead.

Having a snowmobile at the cabin made it possible to invite visitors of different ages and walks of life who otherwise would not have even considered making the trip. About the only people I knew who would attempt the snowshoe trek to my cabin in winter were a few hardy natives and one or two close city friends of my own age. I thought wryly what an unfortunate commentary this is on our urbanized way of life, as compared to pioneer days when folks would walk for miles any time of year just to see a different human face.

But now I could whisk guests up the ice in winter almost as

easily as by boat in summer. The weather, however, was not always to be trusted during these reunions. One New Year's, I had asked my dear friend, Frank, a city planner, and his new wife, Debby, up for the holiday. They were due back in New York City on January 2. Early on the morning of the 31, a strong wind began gusting from the south. Snow hissed across the ice. The hills around Black Bear Lake turned as grizzly-gray as the fur on a beaver's belly. Clouds lowered and the temperature rose. By noon, it was 50 degrees and pouring rain. By midafternoon, this unseasonable downpour had covered the ice with a shallow lake. An inch or two more and we might have paddled a canoe.

The lake would soon be impassable to snowmobiles if this continued, and the barometer gave every indication that it would. I decided I should start evacuating their gear. We piled suitcases, boxes, and briefcase on the toboggan and lashed it to the Rupp. Sprays of water shot out from the tracks and a great wave curled up from the lip of the toboggan. Everything was drenched by the time I reached the landing. On the trip back, the machine bogged down badly in several spots of rotten ice. We decided to walk out from the cabin rather than ride. I insisted everyone wear snowshoes because of the pocked ice and slush which now covered the lake. It felt like walking with webbed duck feet, but the support was safer. Debby almost didn't make it from exhaustion. It was dark when we reached my truck and their car. We were drenched to the skin. What should we do now, caught in a deluge on New Year's Eve without a home to go to in the Adirondacks?

Frank had a brainstorm. "You're not going back," he said determinedly. "Let's find the nearest hotel or roadhouse, get rooms, dry off, and celebrate."

The only accommodation we could find was at a small inn on Arrow Lake. It was bursting with frustrated but fun-loving snowmobilers. By great luck there was one room left with three beds—unmade. We took it.

By the time we made the beds, cleaned up, dried out, warmed

up, it was almost midnight. The crowd downstairs was exuberant and noisy. Yet we were too exhausted to join them around the huge stone fireplace to welcome in the New Year. Frank nipped down and brought back three double brandies. We drank our toast sitting on the edge of the beds while below us horns blew, balloons popped, people bellowed "Auld Lang Syne," an organ rollicked, feet pounded time on the floor, and the rain drummed on the roof.

It was one night I certainly didn't mind being away from the cabin. I still remember Frank's toast, "Here's to our friendship, but next New Year's, please, *you* come to the *City!*"

# 10

# The Breakup

The breakup is a prelude to spring. The breakup is a prelude to comfort. The breakup is a prelude to companionship. Through it, the lakes, ponds, and rivers are loosed from winter's rigid fetters —the ice.

I have never seen the breakup take place. Yet every year I watch for it, always expecting a great exodus of ice. Expecting a rumbling, crushing, tumbling, tilting, crashing, and scraping down the lake and its shoreline. But this rarely happens. Instead, it's a gentle, imperceptible dissolution with none of the stern precision of freeze-up.

Actually, the most exciting moment takes place a few days before breakup when a 55-gallon barrel placed on the lake ice melts through. Folks from all around Lake Serene have placed bets on this important event. Everyone compares the dates, hours, and minutes. My old guide pal, Rob, sage that he is, has guessed April 23 at 8:30 A.M. (a good solid average with the optimum time of day given). Jake, a pessimist, bets on May 1 at noon. Sally chooses April 30 at 6 P.M. I take an optimistic chance on April 15 at 10:15 A.M. The winner will receive twenty-five dollars from the local fish and game club.

Once the barrel has slipped through, the breakup is imminent. The eroded ice is rotten, spongy, and pocked with holes where melt water swirls through in miniature whirlpools to the great mass of dark lake below. My last few trips down Black Bear Lake are tentative and damp. Cracks are showing open water along the shoreline. The ice seems to warp and bend beneath my weight. The snowshoe webbing gets soggy, gelatinous, and heavy. I use an ice pole again, tapping carefully. Then, one day, intuition tells me to take to the woodland route until breakup is over. A few more days pass with treacherous "black ice" still spanning the lake. And then, miraculously, one morning there is blue water sparkling in the sun! It's April 25!

I shovel out my boat from under a foot of snow, haul up the outboard motor, screw in two new sparkplugs, and yank on the rope. Twenty-three pulls later, it coughs into life, disgruntled to be working again after a five-month vacation. The first trip down Black Bear Lake in April is like the last one up in November. The water is thick and turgid. The weather is raw and bleak. But now everything is reversed, especially my feelings. Instead of resignation to impending gloom, ice, isolation, snow, cold, short days, and hardship, there is anticipation of sunshine, green trees, visitors, movement, color, long days, and singing birds.

It must be the same for wild animals, I think. Beavers, otters, and muskrats are suddenly free to cruise on the lakes' surfaces rather than dive precariously from air hole to air hole under a heavy roof of ice. How *do* they find those lifesaving exits swimming through the murk of a cold Adirondack lake with 30 inches of ice and a foot of snow overhead? And what of the fish? Do they sense relief at the lightening, brightening, warming of water?

Loons, grebes, mergansers, geese, and ducks are migrating. Any day, familiar pairs will be dropping down to Black Bear Lake and Beaver Pond for the summer. I long for the shrill laugh of a loon at dawn. The Canada Geese have seen the open water and are heading northward, sure of a resting place come night.

Freak May snowstorm buffets Pitzi and me as we speed down the lake with the mailbag.

Their jubilant honking drifts down over the quickening streams, rivers, and marshlands.

All through the mountains, from steepest peak to lowest swamp, water is moving. Trillions of cubic feet of water have been freed. The immense watersheds of the Adirondacks are unfettered. The vast vegetative sponge is yielding up its moisture. Water is purging, flooding, surging toward the lowlands. Crystal drops are falling from ice-coated boulders way up on Algonquin and Marcy. Tiny trickles are gurgling out from under snow banks on south-facing slopes. From every height of land, water is pouring toward its appointed tributary or main river—be it the Independence, Grass, Cold, Opalescent, Cedar, Ausable, Oswegatchie, Boquet, Raquette, Moose, Beaver, Otter, Sacandaga, West Canada, St. Regis, Schroon, or Boreas—hence via the St. Lawrence or Hudson Rivers to the sea.

Our water is incredibly pure. I'll drink from practically any stream or lake in these mountains, unless they lie adjacent to human dwellings or below a town or busy lake. Such a condition is unique in our populated and polluted Northeast and Atlantic coastal plain. I often paint a mental picture of the East Coast as a relief map with a scum of bilious brown wherever polluted waters exist. By my reckoning, the whole map would be brown except for the Adirondack Mountains (largely above 1,500 feet), a few Catskill peaks, northern Maine, and the tips of the Green, White, and Appalachian Mountains. Elsewhere human beings live beside foul waters, never knowing the privilege of taking a drink as nature intended. Instead they often pay close to a dollar for a gallon of pure spring water!

It is the very bounty of Adirondack water that helped prompt and abet construction of the famous Erie Canal. The New York State canal system in the early 1800s was considered the foremost engineering feat of our country. Canals, the "thruways" of those times, opened up the wilderness areas of upstate New York and allowed easier access to the Ohio and Mississippi valleys, as well as the Great Lakes. Canals helped to develop wheat and dairy farming, mineral and lumber markets. The Erie, Black River, and Champlain Canals, especially, made it possible to harvest more timber and settle more land in the Adirondacks.

But water was vital. It was the lifeblood of the Erie. If water levels dropped, so did transportation and commerce. Since the Adirondacks were lavish with lakes, elaborate plans were made to tap this abundant supply. Between 1880 and 1888, a series of feeder canals, dams, and reservoirs were built, some at almost inaccessible points, strictly by hand labor and horse power.

A more grandiose scheme, involving the alteration of major drainage patterns, was proposed. The headwaters of the St. Lawrence were to be diverted into the headwaters of the Hudson, since the two watersheds were a mere 700 yards apart near Grassy Pond! Engineers reasoned that this plan would bring a bountiful water supply to the Champlain and Erie Canals. Although the proposal gained favor and formed the bulk of more than one New York State Surveyor's report, it fortunately never came to pass. Such flooding and diversions might have caused serious ecological damage.

Today, the old Erie Canal and Black River Canal are largely abandoned. Only a short stretch between Rome and Syracuse is navigable by canoe. Instead the New York Thruway carries our cars, trucks, and buses, flanked by railroad tracks and the modern Barge Canal. Passengers and produce travel at speeds undreamed of in the 1880s. From a wearisome six weeks by stage from New York City to Buffalo, to ten days by barge via the Hudson River and Erie Canal, to about eight hours by car—travel time has shortened. The watersheds of the Adirondacks have played their part in the transportation systems of this state. Yet, I cannot help but think, prowling along the banks of abandoned feeder canals, picking up a rusty spike, touching old stone bulwarks, that man's works—like summer days—have all too short a lease.

Before summer, even before spring, we must put up with a period which is bleaker, if possible, than November weather. Perhaps it seems so because of my impatience to see flowers, hear birds, feel sun. One of my colleagues has described the Adirondacks in early April as "the Siberia of North America." And as Robert Louis Stevenson wrote in April 1888, while a resident at Saranac Lake, "The grayness of the heavens is a circumstance eminently revolting to the soul."

Days go by without sun. Cold rains pelt on roofs. Snows are soggy and almost impossible for snowshoeing. Short, vicious snowstorms occur. Every morning I grit my teeth, fight off the frustration of being indoors so long, and try to endure another long day at my desk. Then, quixotically, one day of sun will transform Siberia into a Dr. Zhivago-land of glaring ice and flashing snow. I lie in my bikini atop a well-blanketed toboggan and get a prespring tan from the blaze of sun on white. Then, as suddenly, the weather turns bleak, raw, and rainy once again. My frustration level soars.

By early May, the rain has swollen rivers to flood stage. Taking advantage of this, a new adventure-sport begins. White-water canoers and kayakers throng to the Adirondacks, intent on running the most powerful and frenetic of our rivers—the Upper Hudson. Every May, the annual Hudson River White Water Derby takes place. In its seventeen years, this has become the largest and most popular such derby in the United States, attracting notables like the late Robert Kennedy and former Secretary of the Interior, Stewart Udall. The 1973 races drew over 700 entrants.

I don't feel qualified to enter the race, but I have a great hankering to run this mighty river. Calling a friend, I make arrangements to join a local canoe club on Sunday for an all-day white-water paddle. We plan the trip for the week before the races. The Upper Hudson is cresting at 4 feet, 9 inches. We'll put in 1 mile from the mouth of the Indian River and will pull out at North Creek, about 18 miles downstream. I am bundled in an orange life vest and snapped into a canvas cover which protects our canoe from taking on too much water. My friend, Edward, a powerful, 6-foot, experienced white-water canoeist, takes the stern. We have never paddled together, but it is apparent we'll do well. Ed shouts orders from time to time—"Pull left, *hard!*" or "Back-water, *fast!*"

It is a scary paddle. Maelstroms of waves, eddies, and whirl-pools surge and suck around huge boulders. The speed of the Hudson is terrific. We are thinking, working, panting, shouting, fighting the current every minute. Two canoes in our party of sixteen wrap around rocks and have to be abandoned, although we work for an hour with winches and cables to try to pull them free. In the space of a few seconds, the owners have each lost about $500 worth of boat, paddles, and gear. They were lucky not to be injured.

As we near Blue Ledges, a narrow gorge with steep cliffs, we ease up a bit. Ed points to a huge rock and yells, "We'll pull in behind 'er and rest."

Using the special technique of turning the canoe 180 degrees in midstream and then pointing the bow up behind a boulder where its back-eddy moves *up*stream, we can hold the craft in one spot with just the occasional dip of a paddle. My arms are aching and my legs soaked despite the canoe cover. Ed grins, de-lightedly. "Great river, eh? You're doing fine. The biggest rapids are still ahead."

I roll my eyes up despairingly and say, "I may beg off."

"Oh no, we'll make it. But first we'll stop and check out our best route."

A shiver runs down my spine. This river is more than I ever expected. I gaze up at Blue Ledges, towering 200 feet above us. This is one of the most dramatic gorges along the Upper Hud-son. Cliffs of blue-gray rock shut out the sun, and boulders dot the riverbed in a haphazard pattern. We push off again, letting the current wheel us around for our continued downriver dash. I fight hard as bowman to keep our canoe from becoming another wreck like the battered hulks we streak past on the slivers of beach.

True to his word, Ed stops above the most dangerous rapids

of all and strides along the bank, reconnoitering. I hop up and down, chilled to the bone, pigtails dripping, legs stiff from kneeling so long. Then he catches me under the elbow and says quietly, "I've got the route. Now you just do *everything* I tell you as *fast* as you can and as *hard* as you can. We'll make it."

I start to say no, to get someone else to run the rapids, but some wisp of pride prevents me. I crouch back in the bow, tighten my life vest buckles, shove the canvas more securely around me, and pick up the paddle.

"Eeeeeeeeeh-yeeeeeeeee," yips Ed jubilantly as we shove off into the raging river. He's as giddy as a teenager at a dance. Ahead of me, the riverbed is descending at an angle most unriverlike. I feel as though we are sliding down a hill, except that foam, spray, jets, waves, bubbles, and drops are exploding all around me. A paroxysm of fear goes through my body and then vanishes. I'm left with the exultant feeling of riding a wild horse,

A double kayak team practicing before the annual Hudson River White Water Derby.

landing a jet plane, skiing a high hill. Ed shouts directions. I obey. Our canoe handles beautifully. We are mastering the Upper Hudson with muscle, two stout paddles, and our brains. Two hundred yards downstream, the rapid tapers off and we are through it— and safe.

The trembling sets in a hundred yards below the big chute, but Edward reassures me that this is normal while running rivers. It takes me awhile to calm down, but from now on every other rapid seems tame. Ed scarcely has to call out instructions. We brazen our way through.

After running the Hudson, I come back to Black Bear Lake and step into a guideboat for contrast. Mine is red, pointed at both ends, and weighs 40 pounds. I have to admit I breathe a sigh of relief and contentment as I glide across the still lake. On calm water, one can travel faster in a guideboat with oars than in a canoe with one paddle. It is the only real native craft of our mountains. To the guide, "there was none other." Developed for the early guides and named for them, the boats were indispensable. No roads existed and all Adirondack travel went via water. The guideboat had to be light enough to portage, sturdy enough to cross stormy lakes, fast and silent enough to hunt, fish, and cover long miles.

Alfred Billings Street wrote in his *Woods and Waters* (1860), "These boats are 'dark-colored, slender as a pike, buoyant as a cork,' made gracefully of thin pine, with knees of fir, their weight from 90 to 120 pounds—though so small and lightly built, [that they] will live in the roughest swells." And Winslow Homer immortalized them in his Adirondack painting, "The Guideboat," and others.

The original makers of those dark-colored boats are gone now—the Chases of Newcomb, Rueben Cary and Henry Stanton of Long Lake, Dwight and Lewis Grant of Boonville, the Hanmers of Saranac Lake, and Riley and Ben Parsons of Old Forge. But a few, as yet almost anonymous, builders may keep the skill alive in their basements and garages where they fashion guideboats in off-hours. The Adirondack Museum at Blue Mountain Lake maintains a fabulous boathouse with unusual and vintage guideboats on display. A few fortunate private owners and estates own others. They seldom sell. Prices go to $2,000 for a 14-footer, and higher. Once, looking into the boathouse at the exclusive Ausable Club near St. Hubert's, I counted sixty guideboats on the racks! It was like seeing sixty Rembrandts hanging on a cabin wall.

To protect the precious rivers and streams on which our canoes and guideboats travel today, an inventory and study has been underway in the Adirondacks since 1972. Thanks to the passage of the New York State Wild, Scenic and Recreational Rivers System Act (1972), there exists a means to safeguard our remaining natural rivers. Once a river is recommended and incorporated into this system, it is afforded special protection by law against misuse and overdevelopment, especially impoundments. Without these safeguards, many waterways could soon lose their purity, beauty, wildness, and wildlife.

In our mountains, river studies have been carried out by the Adirondack Park Agency, with some help from qualified citizens and private groups. Almost 1,200 miles of Adirondack rivers have been included in this system, and 140 more miles are being studied. Probably no other area in the East offers so many miles of free-flowing rivers to nature lovers. If they were poured out end to end, one could canoe from here almost as far as Miami, Florida, on a wild waterway.

On a drizzly day in early May, I joined Clarence Petty, my favorite "old woodsman," with my canoe and dog for a survey of the west branch of the Oswegatchie River. Clarence, an expert biologist, has headed the Adirondack Park Agency's river field study since 1972. This particular piece of river, brown as bock beer, flows from Cranberry Lake through the forsaken, fir-forested flatlands of the northwestern Adirondacks. Clarence and other biologists in the team were busy making notes, taking photographs, toweling their clipboards dry, estimating depths, current flows, floodplain widths, pushing aside branches, listening for wildlife, looking for fish, and then stopping to drag their canoes through shallows. I marveled at Clarence's back. He has the shoulders and muscles of a thirty-year-old, although his face is seamed with over seventy years of outdoor work. Born at Upper Saranac Lake, Clarence lived in a tent camp and was raised by a guide-father. Clarence is more at home in the woods than any other man I've ever laid eyes on.

I was enjoying myself on this trip, actually helping to survey a "wild river," despite the cold, annoying branches, drizzle, and detours. And the Oswegatchie surely fits the definition of wild. It is free-flowing, has access only by water, foot, or horse trail, contains no structures other than footbridges, and is over 5 miles long. Other rivers in the Scenic and Recreational categories are usually more developed, yet are always free from impoundments.

At the end of our 22-mile, two-day canoe trip, I asked Clarence if he felt the west branch of the Oswegatchie deserved protection by law.

"It sure is wild and it *does* need safekeeping," answered the silvery-haired biologist slowly with a smile. "Not many places you can find a river this little used and this pure." As if for emphasis, he scooped up a palmful of tea-colored water and took a sip. The brown color came from the tannic acid of evergreens and was harmless. For this it was named—Oswegatchie—"black water." "We'll sure recommend this section of river to be included under the act," he said beaming.

When I returned to the cabin very late that second evening, towing my canoe behind the motorboat, the cold rain had stopped. A few tentative stars were winking above my big spruces. I tied up the boat and turned the canoe over on shore. Then I sat with Pitzi for a while on the dock, unwinding after the long drive and boat ride. Not a sound broke the early May night. There were no owls, frogs, or loons calling, no fish jumping, no beavers swimming. However, it was the silence that precedes a symphony. I knew it would start very soon. The stars, so long hidden by clouds, were brighter now.

And I noted with satisfaction that Orion, the mighty winter hunter, was sliding weakly off my roof into the west.

# II

# Spring

I wake at dawn to an absolute hush. It is 5 A.M. No rain drums on the roof. No frost flowers etch the windows of my sleeping loft. A pure, pale, yellow incandescence shines in the east, backlighting the bud-bursting trees. Something is different. I lie awhile in my soft, warm cocoon, drifting between sleep and puzzlement as to what has changed.

Rolling onto my belly, I squeeze open the locks on the window and raise it for a sniff of the air. That's it! Spring! Spring has come!

I throw back the blankets, scurry down my log wall, shock the dog into a flurry of barks (at seeing me up so early), brush my tousled hair, fling off my flannel nightgown, throw on jacket and jeans, and open the cabin door with a smile—to spring.

She won't stay long. Spring, on her fleeting journey north, shortens her visits the closer she comes to the Arctic Circle. Here at 42 degrees latitude, she graces us with perhaps two weeks of her vibrant, fickle, fertile presence. Her timing is unpredictable. She stalls, calculatingly, for at least ten days after breakup, letting us suffer the Siberia-like dreariness of late April and early May. She refuses to linger as she does in Virginia, for example, coaxing cardinals into cheerful concertos and wooing magnolias into creamy blossoms.

Instead, spring arrives unexpectedly as today, announcing her presence only by a softness and warmth in the air which have been absent for almost six months.

The glow is stronger now and a pearly pink light tinges the hills around Black Bear Lake. Three days of spring sun and the trees will leaf right out, practically bypassing that lovely, innocent period of frothy, pastel, baby-tender foliage. Instead they will turn quickly into a serious, deep green, adult covering. There is very little time for immaturity in the North Country. Life is hard, rough, and sober.

A flute pipes from the gloom under the balsams. Here is one touch of purity. A White-throated Sparrow is throwing his heart into a sunrise love song for an as yet unfound mate. His liquid whistle, translated by unromantics as "Sam Pea-bo-dy," is one of the most beautiful sounds in the Adirondacks. Clarence Petty says it *is* the sound of the Adirondacks.

The "flute of the woods" is followed by the effervescent trilling of a Winter Wren. Size for size, this miniature member of the bird world belts out a louder, longer song than any other species I know. He, too, is guarding his bit of balsam woods and advertising for a teeny female wren to join him.

One by one other species awake and give voice on this spring morning. The woods are alive with warblers, all in nuptial plumage, all flitting, feeding, preening in the still-naked trees. After breakfast I decide to spend this day bird-watching. I dust off my binoculars and pack a sandwich and dog biscuits, notebook and pen. Pitzi and I set off on a leisurely, circular walk which will cover only 3 or 4 miles but will sample several habitats. I may see close to fifty species.

Stepping east, we cut through the balsams behind the cabin to my little swamp. Rusty Blackbirds, Olive-sided Flycatchers, Red-winged Blackbirds, and Wood Pewees are sure to be there. Then we edge one of the shallow ponds which touch my property to

look for the usual pair of Hooded Mergansers, a Great Blue
Heron, Common Crows, and maybe a kingfisher. Next, the
stretch of hardwoods harbors dozens of warblers—Magnolias,
Myrtles, Blackburnians, Black-throated Greens and Blues. When
we come to the shoreline at Beaver Pond, I hush the dog and
creep out on the little point. A pair of Pied-billed Grebes is in
courtship display. They swim passionately toward each other,
then at the last possible second veer sideways and glide off side
by side, warbling cozily. A female Black Duck slips surrep-
titiously along the submerged stand of tamaracks. She is probably
guarding a clutch of eggs already. Other flycatchers call from
the dead limbs. "Quick, three beers. Quick, three beers," they
say, over and over.

The morning is uncommonly warm and I wish I had just *one*
cold beer. We walk on through a low notch and down a slope
toward another wilderness pond, Sunshine Lake. In the dry carpet of leaves, Pitzi hears a rustle. Despite being a huge German
shepherd, he "points." It might be a young hare or a baby squirrel. Ready to give chase, he suddenly drops his paw. An officious
Ovenbird hustles past, tossing leaves helter-skelter as it searches
for brunch. It makes more noise than an elephant.

At Sunshine Lake, we stretch out on a sliver of sand beach to
soak in the spring sun. How strong and hot it is. Bundled in winter clothes and long johns for the past five months, I'm as white
as a mushroom. I strip for the magnificent baptism of spring sun
on bare skin.

Suddenly a harsh screech sounds above me. I open my eyes a
slit, blinded by sun, and see a huge seagull hovering above me.
"Out! Out!" he's hollering. A glob of his excrement falls defi-
antly on the dog's side. I jump up stark naked. Why the fuss?
Scanning the lake with binoculars, I see his mate, a snowy-white,
ghostly-gray Herring Gull poised hesitantly on a rock jutting
from the water. Streaks of white pattern the stone. The gulls
have a roost there, or perhaps a nest. Clearly, Sunshine Lake is
*their* domain and the dog and I are not welcome. We'll have to

leave or put up with harassment for hours. But the birds will have to wait a moment.

I grab Pitzi's collar and we wade into the still icy water (which won't be fit for swimming until mid-June). Both of us cringe, but I splash his side clean and then dash water on my face and armpits to wash away the perspiration. Refreshed, I dress and we duck back into the woods again. The gull is not to be fooled. He soars above us, watching our progress. The gleaming white wings shear across blue sky and yellow sun. How fine to have a pair of seabirds in our landlocked mountains.

Near the lake's outlet, a "masked bandit" jumps out from an alder clump. This pert little Common Yellowthroat accosts us with a "witchity, witchity, witch." Possessive, he, too, is defending a nest and shy female.

Before continuing the circle which will bring us back to Black Bear Lake, Pitzi and I have our snack, sitting on a south-facing slope under a bare beech. I gaze around the sun-dappled forest floor. A clump of trilliums, or "wake-robins" as they're called locally, bob in the light breeze. This three-petaled flower grows in two colors—a pristine white with delicate red embroidery, and a passionate burgundy. Nearby, a single pink moccasin flower sways on its fragile stalk. I get up and scuff about, searching for its close cousin, the showy lady slipper. I can't help marveling at how these flowers have sprung so quickly from the drab, winter-flattened ground with just a kiss of sun. The ferns are also awakening on this warm hillside. I note the tender, green-curved "fiddleheads" poking up and make a mental note to pick some in just a few days when they are taller. I'll feast on "Adirondack asparagus" that night.

Pitzi and I walk on, pushing our way through thickets of hateful witch hobble. But at this time of year, anyway, I can forgive this plant for the hundreds of times its pliant, low-lying branches have tripped me up in the woods. Now, it's gracing the forest with wide, flat clusters of tiny white blossoms, as guiltless as any church flower.

By midafternoon, we break out on the shores of Black Bear Lake, not a mile from the cabin. The vigilant gull, still reconnoitering on high, wheels off to the west and leaves us in peace. To return, Pitzi and I walk past some of the summer camps, glancing at their roofs and foundation posts. It won't be long before the first of the "summer folk" will arrive around Memorial Day weekend to "open camp." It's always a time of surprises. Surprises left by the winter.

Did the winter wind drop any trees on the camp or in the woods? Did the roof leak? Have the posts shifted, the floor heaved? Did the heavy weight of snow buckle the rafters? Does the water system still work, or did it burst with frost? Was the dock swept away in the breakup? Is the chimney plugged? Was anything stolen?

Funny things happen. One family found a single electric light bulb burning, presumably left on since October when they "closed camp." Another cottage owner complained that his portable generator (nothing else) disappeared from his basement. Yet no windows were broken or doors forced. The strangest surprise that ever met any property owner was at a small private lake near Hawk Hill. The owner started a fire to warm the place up, but the fireplace kept smoking badly. The man peered up the chimney. It seemed to be blocked. Walking outside and looking up, he saw something like a big bag stuffed into the top. "Almost like Santa Claus coming down the chimney," he was to say later.

It wasn't *quite* Santa Claus. It was the body of an old lumberjack. He had apparently finished up a drunk in the city and come north looking for work again. Maybe he was trying to find just one more bottle before sobering up; maybe he was cold and thought he could squeeze down the chimney into the camp. No matter. His foot got caught in the heatalator, and he died half in, half out of the chimney. His body kept fairly well all winter. When the owners came in May, he still looked—almost—like Santa Claus climbing down the chimney.

On our walk back to the cabin I see and hear more birds—a Rose-breasted Grosbeak singing daintily atop a maple, Redstarts flitting through a spruce stand, Barn Swallows swooping over the lake, Yellow-bellied Sapsuckers drumming on sweet sap-laden birches. Back home, hot and sweaty, I go to the snow bank which still squats under the woodshed roof, 3 feet high and twice as wide. Digging in the granular, dingy snow, I retrieve an icy bottle of beer. I take this down to the dock to sit in the spring sun, rest, and write up my bird list. Forty-three species so far! And there'll be more as twilight approaches and birds renew their territorial singing.

Toward twilight, on that magical spring day, I finally hear them—the peepers. Water in the swamp has warmed to some catalytic temperature and their spring chorus has begun. I sit for a long time listening, watching the sun sink behind the budding hill, feeling conflicting emotions of sorrow and happiness. The peepers were trilling when I first stepped onto my land and sketched out the cabin plan. That was a time of great stress. Hearing the peepers I can't help but recall Morgan, my former husband, our divorce, my moving out of the hotel and into the cabin.

But then I think of the good developments. Those peepers have sung for five springs since that bleak period. I've come a ways—constructed my own home, learned many useful skills, found out how to balance a checkbook and work out income taxes, earned a degree, and built up a profession. I support myself entirely, maybe not in the manner to which I was accustomed, but in a style that's independent, healthy, interesting, sometimes even a little risky and risqué. I'm able to open my doors to people I like, and close them to those I don't. That means *a lot* after living in a hotel where my "home" consisted of one room (which got rented out on busy weekends), or at times a mattress on the attic floor, or a shivering waterskier in my shower, or a waitress impatiently thumbing through my record collection.

A warm trickle behind my ear interrupts my musing. Blood!

What can it be? Did I cut my head in the woods? Then I remember. Black flies! It seems too early, or is it? Any time after the witch hobble blooms, the tiny flies can appear. Yet this one seems an especially eager eater.

Black flies are a scourge in swampy areas and a nuisance everywhere in the Adirondacks in spring. They can effectively depress outdoor activities for a few weeks between late May and June. The black fly attacks like a miniature vampire. Its bite is almost painless due to a numbing agent in the saliva. Only the females need blood, and they may travel up to 10 miles searching for a meal. Most natives acquire a natural immunity and feel only mild irritation, but some people react violently to the bites with swelling and itching, even shortness of breath. I usually experience a day or two of sluggishness, swollen neck glands, and lack of appetite at the start of the season, but that soon goes. Like most locals, I have my own defensive techniques against the tenacious insects. Miniskirts, T-shirts, hot-pants, and bikinis only offer the flies human flesh on a platter; so I dress to minimize exposure. I apply repellents liberally every four hours, make smudges while working around the cabin, stay indoors on hot, cloudy days, or do things outside at night when black flies are inactive.

The state of New York has spent millions in research and control work. For years the chief combat trick was to tie blocks of DDT in fast-flowing streams where black fly larvae cling to rocks and submerged logs. My friend, Rob, used to have a standing contract for six weeks every spring to put out blocks in the swift waters around Hawk Hill. Then the dangers of DDT were uncovered, thanks to scientists like Rachael Carson, and blocks were abandoned. Next low-flying planes sprayed our lakes and valleys with newer insecticides, some more toxic than DDT, and others almost useless. In the towns and hamlets, fogging trucks liberally sprayed all the streets, gardens, lawns, and golf courses (even children) with insecticides of varying degrees of toxicity.

Now the pendulum is swinging the opposite way. At Black Bear Lake, several summer camp owners have written to the Town Board protesting the spraying of their property and the lake. "We'll use birds to kill bugs," says one intelligent neighbor. I couldn't agree more.

Having taken this stand, to save birds, fish, aquatic insects, amphibians, and other animals which can be harmed by chemical sprays in our mountains, I pick off the dried blood and scratch. Then I shrug my shoulders and say to myself, "So, let the little bastard bite."

The sun has set. A chill seeps out of the snow-damp ground and off the icy water. It pervades the evening with a gray mist. The peepers trill on louder and more incessantly. I stand up stiffly. After the day's euphoria, melancholia descends. From sun's warmth to mist's chill—all in one day—all in one lifetime. Spring will always be like this for me—fleeting—bittersweet.

# 12

# Summer

As spring merges rapidly into summer, I am reminded of a symphony shifting from *allegro* to *andante*. The high soprano peepers are replaced by baritone bullfrogs. The burbling Winter Wren's song is now overshadowed by the bell-like notes of blue jays. The pastels of debutante leaves turn to deeper tones of green. Charlie, an elderly friend and retired band leader from Chicago, visits me for the first time over a long June weekend. He complains, "It's so *green* up here. It's like hearing a tenor sax all the time."

His untrained eye, used to city cement, fails to notice the subtle shades of color. "Look," I say, pointing to my young white pines, planted close to the cabin where no deer or snowshoe hares dare to nibble. They are thrusting their frail new apple-green needles toward the sun, while last year's growth remains olive green. I take my friend into the little fir forest. "Look, Charlie." The fresh new tips are shiny chartreuse in contrast to the dull bottle green of the mature balsam branches.

Charlie nods politely. "Yes, but it's still all green, still unidimensional."

He brightens when we take a drive over the mountain to

Hawk Hill hamlet. The roadside is always a riot of color. White daisies, orange hawkweed, yellow butter-and-eggs, blue chickory, pink Joe Pye weed, ivory boneset, purple *Prunella*—all these wild flowers brighten the narrow grassy edges of our bumpy roads. But almost all are transplants, blown up or carried in from outside the Adirondacks. They've found a suitable niche along the mowed rights-of-way. In the untouched Adirondack woodlands and beaver meadows, however, few wild flowers occur naturally.

My visitor keeps harping about the vegetation around my cabin. "Why don't you plant some nice flowers?" Charlie suggests.

"Like what?" I ask.

"Oh, geraniums, hollyhocks, roses, begonias, or dahlias."

I groan inwardly. I do not *want* these domestic flowers intruding into my cabin life with all their attendant tools, fertilizers, insect sprays, trellises, boxes, mulches, limes, and so on. I do not even want to transplant native Adirondack flowers—wild azaleas, violets, sheep laurel, wild iris, adder's tongue—around my home. Then I'd have to watch where I walk, put fencing around for protection from deer, and keep Pitzi on a run. I really like my land just as it is, natural, original, untouched.

"One good reason," I challenge Charlie, "is that the climate is too severe for all those hothouse flowers. We only have two to three months of frost-free weather up here."

"My, my! I can hardly believe that, right here in the United States," says Charlie, shaking his head doubtfully. "Well, you could cut some of these tall trees down and get more sun around here. Start your seeds on the sun deck. In fact," he warms to his subject, "you could build a nice little greenhouse with heavy plastic and 2 by 2s right on your deck."

He prattles on. I shake my head despairingly, for how many cottages have I seen up here with the surrounding trees cut down, lawns put in, flower boxes nailed up, vegetable gardens planted. When the owners come up for a "vacation" weekend, they spend all their time mowing the lawn, fertilizing, weeding, and watering. They might as well have stayed in the suburbs.

As kindly as possible I explain to Charlie that if I'd wanted a flower garden I'd have stayed in New Jersey. He smiles, but is not to be put off.

"Let's try one, just a little one," he persists. "Let me put in a small garden for you while I'm here. Just to see what would grow and what wouldn't."

"Or what would eat it and what wouldn't," I finish. "Charlie, the only thing I'd ever agree to would be a lettuce patch."

"Fine, fine." He jumps at the chance. "I'll go buy the seeds. You'll see how nice it will be having your own homegrown salad."

I give in, partly because Charlie is too old and too good a friend not to humor him, and partly out of curiosity. Is the Adirondack climate truly so inhospitable to crops? The very name of our mountains suggests it—Hah-dah-ron-dac. "They Who Eat Trees" or "Bark Eaters." This name, apparently, was applied derisively by the Iroquois to the Algonquin Indians who were forced to eat tree bark and tips in order to survive the long, bitter winters here. And there are precious few farms today in the Adirondacks. Those that make it lie in the low valleys around Lake Placid, Saranac Lake, and Elizabethtown where pockets of good soil and a more favorable microclimate prevail.

We clear a patch of land 8 by 8 feet which lies in a sunny spot close to the lake. The water will help moderate the temperatures. Perhaps there'll be three entirely frost-free months. Charlie purchases a dozen packets of seeds, stakes, a hoe, and a bag of fertilizer. I buy lime for the superacid soil and stop on the way home to shovel some manure from a stable into a bushel basket. Maybe that will help, too.

After a pleasant Sunday afternoon planting five rows—*one* of lettuce and the rest all experiments of Charlie's—one of radishes, one of carrots, one of parsley, and one of corn—my old friend heads for home. He leaves strict instructions on the tender loving care of this garden. Even Pitzi is entrusted to guard against greedy hares, squirrels, or mice.

The June sun warms the garden. Nothing happens. The June rains pour on it. Nothing happens. Pitzi tires of waiting for hungry herbivores. The hoe begins to rust. There are no weeds to chop down. The lettuce patch appears sterile.

July arrives. True summer in the Adirondacks. Some say it arrives on July 4 and departs the day after. I forget about the garden and swing into a delightful summer routine. First thing in the morning, I go skinny-dipping, hurrying into the lake before any boats or canoes are about. As soon as the sun hits the sun deck I carry out my typewriter, paper, books, radio, and pot of camp coffee. About 11 A.M. the mail boat chugs past. Pitzi runs down to the dock to attend to that business. He prances back to the sun deck, carrying an almost empty bag. Good. No correspondence to answer. After three hours working and sunning, I'm ready for another swim, this time in a bikini. Pitzi leaps in behind and "rescues me" with his tail. A light lunch and then I take a short rest in my Brazilian hammock strung between two spruces. Winter was never like this!

Lazily, I remember that the cabin posts need creosoting, as do the porch steps and dock timbers. Hot dry days are the best time to apply the preservative so it soaks into the wood well. I climb out of the hammock, put on my oldest shirt and pants, pull on old leather gloves, and pry open the gallon can. The sharp odor jerks me wide awake. Taking care not to spatter the caustic liquid on my skin or in my eyes, I slosh the black preservative around post ends where soil and moisture can cause mold and decay. Some of the posts are hard to reach. I have to crawl halfway under the cabin, holding the dripping brush, sweating and cursing. This onerous task over, I peel down again for a swim, this time with soap and a scrub brush.

To dry off, I stroll down to the garden. What do I see? A tiny, fuzzy row of half-inch greens are pushing up through the dirt. It's lettuce! Charlie's neat, hand writing on the white stake identifies the row. Maybe I won't have to eat bark. I'll write to him this very evening. Three and a half weeks to sprout! When will I be able to *eat* it?

Before supper, I spend half an hour scouting around my woods for fallen branches, dead limbs, and old snags downed by winter. These I drag to the campfire circle and break up to make a pyramid of firewood. Lighting it, I go indoors to select my supper from the gas refrigerator. A small steak, two ears of corn, a salad, and whole wheat bread. I carry it outside and continue down to the dock for a glass of clear, cold lake water.

On these long summer nights, I can read a book outdoors until 9:30, perhaps 10 P.M. The afterglow lingers long after the sun sets in the far northwestern quadrant of the horizon. Whitethroats, Winter Wrens, Magnolia Warblers, and Purple Finches have all mated and are busy nesting; yet they continue sporadic evening concerts around the cabin. Bats, recently awakened, skitter over the water.

Fish are jumping in the gray and pink twilight. The lake lies fathomless, black as onyx. A lone fisherman's boat floats close to the spring hole across from my dock. I see the silhouette of a hunched human figure and a delicate sliver of rod. Suddenly there's a tightening from invisible line, a convulsive bucking, then the mercurial gleam of a trout breaks the black surface. The fisherman deftly scoops it into his boat with a net.

Although Black Bear Lake and hundreds of other lakes and ponds have been stocked by the Department of Environmental Conservation since the late 1800's there is still a population of good-sized wild trout here. The pride of pulling out a native "brookie"—full-bodied, pink-fleshed, bright-spotted—is tremendous. It makes the pale, flabby, liver-fed products of fish hatcheries a poor substitute. Yet without stocking, many of our Adirondack lakes would be virtually empty, and sportsmen would go fishless due to the public pressure on the resources. Moreover, a new menace is depauperizing Adirondack lakes. Acid rain from

Detroit, Chicago, and other industrial centers is apparently dropping chemicals as "fallout," changing the pH of our lakes (also in New Hampshire, Ontario, and other northeastern areas), and diminishing fish populations.

Nevertheless, seeing the fisherman's fortune puts me in mind of taking a jaunt with Rob to some clandestine place where really *big* brookies lie. Next morning I present myself at his brown house before 9 A.M. Rob never goes into the woods any earlier, preferring to wait for the dew to dry and the day's mail to arrive. He's glad to have company and suggests we go into Birch Creek, 7 miles by abandoned logging roads and faint trails. Trout fisherman extraordinaire, Rob's philosophy is, "the best trout streams are those which haven't been fished." To find those, he walks.

At Birch Creek I watch his gnarled hands attach a Grizzly King and gently guide the line out over the narrow stream. There's a lunge from under a shadowy bank of sphagnum moss. Rob hooks the fish easily, plays it, and soon lands a 12-inch native brookie at my feet. My technique is far less skilled; yet by noon we have our limit of trout. The scarlet-spotted fish glisten against fresh green ferns lining Rob's creel. From a worn pack basket, my fellow guide produces two flattened peanut butter sandwiches. We enjoy a fine lunch, washing them down with icy spring water. Supper will be even better—fried trout and Rob's special hash browns.

The only other type of fishing I like in these mountains is bullhead fishing. That's because it takes very little walking and very little work. All the rest—lake trout, small-mouth bass, walleyed and great northern pike, smelt—take time and effort. But bullheads literally catch themselves. Whenever I think of it, I scrounge up a few worms from under old boxes and cans at the garbage dump. I bait a couple of hooks and throw out the lines, making sure my casting rods are well fastened to the dock. Then I go back up to my desk or sun deck. Within the hour, there's bound to be a bullhead on the hook. Given half a dozen and a box of batter, I'll skin and fry the bullheads in butter, serving them with small pancakes and pure Adirondack maple syrup.

Summer is the season for fixing things, repairing winter damage, and carrying out new projects. Every year I relive the mistake of building a cabin from *un*peeled spruce logs. I have built-in carpenters which make themselves very evident munching and chewing their way between bark and wood. Spruce bark beetles inhabit my logs. Come breeding season, in June and early July, they suddenly bore out of the logs and wing wildly across the cabin. Shiny, blue-black, inch and a half long males, and smaller, duller females copulate on my typewriter, in the sink, beside the mirror, upon my pillow. On hot muggy nights when they seem most active, I patrol indoors with a killing jar, shoving pairs in, trying to clear the walls before going to bed. I have a horror of waking up at night with a beetle crawling on my face. I refuse to spray the cabin with commercial toxic insecticides, and there is no way to probe the bugs out from under the bark. The remedy remains for me some day to peel the bark off the logs, sweep away the sawdust, and varnish the wood.

But there are so many more important things to do in summer, like pleasuring visitors, going camping, sailing or scuba diving, and fighting water pollution. The outside world impinges in a dozen ways. The problem of water pollution leads to a constant battle, like the beetles. On Black Bear Lake, a few of us band together each summer to protect the purity of our water. We make polite calls on cottage owners, armed with packets of Pylam dye and lots of logic.

"Would you like to be able to keep drinking good clean unchlorinated lake water?" we ask. The answer is usually yes.

"Do you want your children and guests to be able to swim in an unpolluted lake?" we continue. The answer is always yes.

Having established that the camp owners desire clean water, we ask delicately where the sewage goes? where the septic tank is? how long since it's been checked? and, may we flush a packet of Pylam dye down their toilet?

Usually permission is granted and we all stand anxiously on the lakeshore, watching to see if the brilliant yellow-green dye will leach out from some unsuspected source along with sewage. If it doesn't show up in half an hour, chances are there's no serious leak in the septic tank and leach field. We express our thanks and move on to the next occupied cottage. Every year, to our surprise and dismay, we find a kitchen sink emptying right onto the ground behind someone's camp, or a sewer pipe which has heaved over the winter and come disconnected so raw sewage is seeping out, or a septic tank that's sixty years old and plugged shut.

If the owners become defensive or protest they cannot afford the repairs, we ask the Town Pollution officer to pay them a visit. Fortunately, the state of New York has strict public health and sanitation laws so this representative can issue a warning which has teeth in it. A number of camps at Black Bear Lake have conscientiously redone their sewage systems for the overall good of the lake and its inhabitants. With persistence, we may manage to keep our water pure, stave off that creeping bilious brown scum of the East, and continue to use our lake for drinking, boating, swimming, and other recreational pursuits.

One thing we cannot seem to control on Black Bear is the size of motorboats. Every year the engines get larger, the boats bigger, the noise louder, the wakes higher, the oil pollution factor greater. I speak hesitantly about this to a neighbor. He has a 100-horse Mercury with a fiberglass double-hull cruiser. It streaks up and down our little lake, pushing 2-foot waves against the shoreline.

"Look," he snaps, "I have eight children. Do you expect me to bring them up this lake after dark or during a thunderstorm in a *rowboat?*"

I shake my head, but can't help but ask, "What did the very first summer vacationers use on Black Bear Lake?"

"Guideboats and rowboats," Jim answers, "but they didn't water ski and aquaplane and go out nights like we do. Times have changed, Anne. Why don't you admit it? Not everyone wants to live in a log cabin without electricity like you do, with just a 10-horse motor. That's no fun!"

"All I'm suggesting, Jim, is that we *reduce* the size and power of motorboats on our lake, not *stop* them," I argue, now on the defensive. "Our shorelines are eroding. The loons don't nest on Black Bear Lake anymore because the boat wakes are washing over their eggs. There's an oil skim on the surface in the mornings. Sometimes I have to push it away with a paddle just to take my morning dip."

My neighbor looks at me oddly. "Well, I say tough luck for the loons. I'd rather go out and buy a drink at night."

We are not communicating on the same levels. I try one more argument. "Jim, I know of two exclusive clubs in the Adirondacks. You've heard of them, too. They don't even permit motorboats on their lakes. Yet they charge an outlandish fee to be a member. And the clubs are full! To visit there is a delight. People love it. No roar of motors intruding on the quiet, no crash of waves. It's really peaceful. So they must have the right idea."

He shrugs. I can tell by Jim's eyes that it's hopeless. We murmur a few noncommital remarks and part company. I've made a bad start on my campaign to limit power boats on Black Bear Lake. But someone has to try, else where will it stop? Our lakes are becoming like our skies. Faster and faster means of transportation are appearing. Soon we may have supersonic boats whizzing from camp to camp!

That evening is calm and warm. A heat haze hangs over the hills. Today at 3 P.M. the temperature reached 85 degrees—a high for our mountains. They must be sweltering in the cities. At suppertime, I skip a campfire and slide my canoe into the water. Placing Pitzi carefully in the bow, I put in a pot of spaghetti, a bowl of tiny lettuce leaves from my garden (no radishes or carrots have appeared), and an ice-cold beer. I prop two boat cushions in the center and tie my shortwave radio to a gunwale. As an afterthought, I slip a flashlight in my hip pocket.

We paddle quietly toward the center of the lake. Not a sound, not a soul, not a ripple anywhere. The haze has a touch of downstate smog in it, for the hills are a sultry gray-blue. A carmine-red ball sets behind a smoky curtain. The lake lies like a bowl of ebony oil. I tune in the radio to a Beethoven symphony being played in Berlin at that moment. The thunderous chords are amplified by the metal sides of the canoe. They emerge from their 4,000-mile trip, rise ponderously into the air, and move slowly off over the mountaintops. I wonder if the trout rising for flies and the bullheads resting on the bottom can hear this majestic music. A small puff of steam also rises slowly into the air as I take the cover off the spaghetti. Pitzi's nose twitches but he remains motionless. Good dog! I eat my supper drifting light as a leaf on the lake, stretching back on the cushions. The sunset has been snuffed out by the smog. Twilight is monochromatic—gray and black, pewter and onyx, silver and ebony. The entire world seems to be in a summery trance as the symphony throbs to its close.

Suddenly a motorboat starts up the lake. It swings out from the shore and roars down the lake, heading straight toward me. I grab my torch and blink nervously three times, three more times. It's Jim's boat. At last he sees me and veers slightly off-course. He and his wife grin and wave as they flash by at 30 miles per hour. Off to a bar for the evening. His massive wake rolls slowly toward the canoe. I rise into the seat, take a paddle, and position the craft to take the big waves bow-on. The bottle of beer tips over, Beethoven is drowned out, the dog lurches to his feet, almost tipping us over. Waves of fury, equal to Jim's wake, rise in my chest. This is *not* what I came to Black Bear Lake for, not by a long shot.

Maybe it's time to go camping. These busy July and August weekends see a large portion of the annual 9 million visitors coming to the Adirondacks. It's little wonder that our roads and waterways are choked with people and machines. After all, these mountains are within a day's drive of 50 million people or more. Who can begrudge them the rest, coolness, and solace they seek up here, with 78 percent living in cities and suburbs. Not I.

Next morning I close up the cabin. The packs are full of food and the canoe is loaded atop the truck. Pitzi is ecstatic. He knows we're off on a special trip. Usually in summer I go to a large lake which offers 50 miles of shoreline without a single dwelling, except at the state launching site, and large wilderness tracts around it. No matter how many campers or canoers are at the lake, there always seems to be an extra island, another point, or an unclaimed stretch of beach free for the using.

I put the canoe in at one of the big bays and paddle away from the state site. By going 8 or 10 miles up the lake, I'll leave half the people behind. At the northern end of the lake are a few fiordlike bays which look good for exploring. Usually by August, the lake level has dropped and strands of yellow sand are exposed. Pitzi and I find an ideal campsite. A sand spit stretches out from a pine-clad point. On the south side, the sand bank sheers off to depths well over my head. Fine for swimming. On the north side, a protected cove gives a shallow harbor to the canoe. I stake out the tent under a huge pine right beside the beach. The circle of stones from last year's campfire are still here, plus many big chunks of driftwood. These will make a fine blaze tonight. Then I remember. Full moon! With the weather hot and fair, it should be gorgeous.

I spend the afternoon setting up camp, swimming, and chatting with a flotilla of Boy Scouts who canoe by. Pitzi helps me carry in more firewood. But he loses interest when a mother grouse and her chicks amble across the forest floor. He stalks the mother, who performs her broken wing act to perfection. Pitzi is perplexed. Meanwhile, her dozen little puffballs have scurried to safety. By the time the dog figures out she's really not hurt, the whole family is out of his reach.

After supper, we stretch out on the sand, still warm from the sun, and wait for the moon. So peaceful. The lake is large enough that distant motorboats are muffled and dwarfed. The wakes which reach the sand spit are mere ripples on its placid surface. The closest campers are over 2 miles away. Their campfire flickers companionably with mine. The first stars peer

Pitzi and I start on our summer canoe camping trip at the same tim
the astronauts are speeding toward the moor

through the heat haze. The eastern horizon is awash with a soft silvery glow. And then an enormous summer moon starts edging over the spruce-fringed mountains. It moves very slowly, seemingly swollen three times its usual size.

On this particular date and on this particular full moon, two astronauts were walking over its surface. They were collecting rocks, taking pictures, setting up an American flag for posterity's sake. I had chosen my seat and row well. From the warm sand point I gazed across 2 miles of smooth water with nothing to obstruct the view. Millions of people on earth sat indoors before TV sets, but I preferred my vantage spot to watch this most incredible feat in man's history. The video tapes would be around for a long time and would be shown again and again. Even though I have no television set, there was never any doubt that I'd see them somewhere, sometime.

But *this* moon, *this* night, *this* view was only happening here and now. I could imagine the astronauts' every move, and it was all enhanced by the contrast of this wild setting. The immediate scene was as it had been fifty, five hundred, perhaps five thousand years ago. Everything was the same in this corner of the Adirondacks, but the moon would never be the same again after this laying on of men's feet upon its ancient dusty surface.

Finally my mind boggled at what was taking place. I looked up and pretended it was just another round, gold, empty summer moon. Then I stripped and took a luxurious midnight swim in the tepid water. I lay floating for a long time, looking up at the orb. Moonlight poured down on me. I felt very elemental. I thought of my body, so free compared to those men up there in complicated life-supporting space suits. I thought of the winter ice which had covered this lake just three and a half months earlier and was only three and a half months ahead.

Later, standing in front of the fire, I heaped on more driftwood until the flames were leaping 10 feet into the sky. I pivoted slowly in front of this beacon, drying myself, gazing upward, and praying that the astronauts would return safely back to earth. This was my tribute to the men on the moon that summer night.

# 13

# Human Visitors

As my new life developed at Black Bear Lake, my summers gradually filled with visitors. Between July 4 and Labor Day especially, friends were fleeing cities, driving through the Adirondacks on vacation, visiting the states from foreign countries. Many wanted to visit me and stay at a log cabin in the North Woods.

The company I enjoyed most came from abroad. Often they were familiar only with the megalopolises of our Northeast, Midwest, and Pacific Coast; hence their view of American life was distorted. I loved to invite foreign friends to Black Bear Lake and watch their astonishment on sensing the wilderness beyond my backdoor, seeing wild animals, drinking pure water, and meeting some down-to-earth Adirondack acquaintances.

One summer I received a series of airmail-o-grams from an Indian friend. He was a keen bird watcher, outdoorsman, and conservationist whom I had met at a conference in New Delhi. He was coming to the states and had asked me to help plan his itinerary. I was delighted to do so and included a stop at my cabin.

The gentleman was a top-ranking career officer in the Indian Army. He disembarked at the Albany airport as nattily dressed as a Fifth Avenue executive, bearing a diplomatic passport and dozens of gifts from his native country. To honor his visit I invited a few local couples to share steaks around my campfire. The handsome officer regaled the company with tales of Indian wildlife and shikaras in his clipped British accent. No one like him had ever come to Black Bear Lake before. The evening grew late, clearly a success. Midnight passed. Only the start of a light drizzle and dampening of the campfire drew our party to a close. Then my guest outdid himself by presenting colorful Indian silk scarves to each lady as she stepped into the boat to head for home.

The following summer another Indian friend toured the states and paid me a visit, no doubt intrigued by descriptions from the army officer, whom he knew also. This guest was a retired colonel and sportsman who lived half the year in the fabled land of Bhutan. My agreeable visitor captivated me with stories of the isolated, high Himalayan country. He spoke of fishing expeditions and tiger hunts.

"In the clear mountain streams of Bhutan, it is not uncommon to catch two or three 20-inch trout before breakfast!" said the silver-haired colonel modestly.

Realizing I had an ardent fisherman as a houseguest, I offered to take him around Black Bear Lake. We rigged up our gear and rowed across to the springhole. The springhole which never failed—the springhole which kept trout all summer—the springhole which was always cold—the springhole which was everyone's "ace in the hole." It failed. The colonel spent hours without so much as a nibble.

The colonel was the first and only guest who ever requested a hot bath every morning—and took it—despite the fact that the lake was a tepid 70 degrees and the weather balmy. Some intuition told me that perhaps the bath was an important ritual in this military man's daily routine. So, while we cooked and ate breakfast, the tub filled, a process which took half an hour due to the somewhat limited plumbing. I spread a small rug on the gravel floor, hung a huge bath towel on a nail, laid out soap, washcloth, scrub brush, bath oil, body powder, and mirror on the work table, pushing tools aside.

"Bath's ready, Colonel," I called, feeling like a valet.

Wearing an elegant satin robe he would walk around to the basement door, and squeeze into the narrow room, carrying a shaving mug, old-fashioned razor, leather strap, comb and brush, shoeshine kit, tweezers, scissors, a fresh change of clothes, and his boots. The colonel stayed there for an hour and a half, emerging as finely groomed as the King of England. I apologized for my primitive bathing facilities, but he assured me that they were luxurious compared to some of the field stations he had lived at during army maneuvers.

Occasionally, however, I had a guest who did not take kindly to the rusticity of my home. An aunt came from Germany. We had not seen each other for years, and I was greatly looking forward to the visit. My aunt loved sunning herself on the deck and swimming in the lake, but she balked at the presence of an outhouse, screamed at the sound of an owl, and fainted at the sight of a mouse. I could do nothing about any of this. After three tense days I rented her a motel room at Lake Serene and visited her every day on the manicured lawn under a giant aluminum umbrella.

Feeling somehow that I had disappointed her, I arranged an "open-cabin" champagne party so that the summer people could meet my guest. To my surprise, over thirty people arrived, some in coats and ties! The dock looked like a marina with so many boats tied up. The company went through a case of champagne and dozens of hors d'oeuvres. My aunt was completely captivated by the Adirondack cordiality. So much so that she forgot about the mice, owls, and outhouse, and told everyone that I had "a marvelously unique home" and that "the highlight of her American tour was coming to Black Bear Lake!"

Champagne appeared once again at the cabin when another foreign guest arrived from Central America. He was a wealthy businessman who dedicated much of his time to conservation matters. The purpose of his visit was to discuss national park development in his homeland. He graciously surprised me with two large bottles of Moët. We spent a good deal of time discussing conservation and a good deal of time sipping ice-cold champagne around the campfire.

Another native conservationist from Guatemala arrived in the fall and had the good fortune to see the first snowfall of his life. I felt as proud as if I had created the storm myself, listening to his exclamations of enchantment. He looked at a flake under a magnifying glass, stuck out his tongue to catch snow, and threw snowballs at me. He even wanted to build an igloo!

A wildlife colleague based in Nairobi also came to call during snow time. He reveled in the crisp, cold, sparkling world. As soon as the formalities were over, he retired to my front porch and drew a desk chair close to the huge picture window. He spent three days gazing into the snow-draped forest, writing up his notes, dictating letters into a portable tape recorder, catching up on journals, and relaxing. Later he told me, "This cabin, this peace, this snow—it's the first time in years that I've been able to get totally away from phones, people, city life, and the tropics. And I think it's been ten years since I saw snow!"

One of my most surprising visitors was a business friend of my former husband. He was a handsome, youngish executive in the export business who had rather suddenly retired. He hitched a ride with the mail boat and arrived at my cabin with a few hours to spare before leaving for Brazil! We spent a pleasant morning catching up on news. He now lived on an island and owned a banana plantation. He eagerly invited me to visit him over the Christmas holidays. He seemed very interested in the cabin and kept watching me intently. Back at the landing and his rental car, he once again asked me to be sure to come. He'd even pay half the fare! Then it dawned on me, he was "shopping." Shopping for a wife to share his island and new way of life.

On impulse I went to his island for Christmas. It was gorgeous. However, the group of holiday houseguests was a bit too sophisticated for my tastes, and at that time my host was displaying a rather pointed interest in a young mulatto girl. Since I didn't fit into either category, I flew back to Black Bear Lake two weeks later with a super sun tan and a lingering regret. How nice it would have been to share life with someone at an Adirondack cabin in summer and a Brazilian banana plantation in winter.

Visitors with different colored skins are rare in the Adirondacks. The local people's reaction to them spans the emotional spectrum. One summer day, shortly after I finished building the cabin, Ruthie, a roommate from college came for the weekend, bringing her pet raccoon, Freddy, and her best friend, Kathy. Kathy was a child psychologist, bright, beautiful, and black. She was the first black person ever to come to Black Bear Lake. The three of us and the raccoon motored up the lake, and I could imagine the various comments from wide-eyed cottage owners as the boat passed by. A Negro *and* a tame raccoon! What's that girl in the log cabin up to *now?*

We spent a fine weekend, swimming, sailing, taking the circular walk through the woods with a picnic at Sunshine Lake. Freddy thrived in the Adirondack atmosphere. He followed us everywhere on a leash, turned over stones in the lake, caught crayfish, and even slept outdoors in a tree stump. He'd never been out of a city before. Ruthie had bought him as a baby from a pet shop.

Shortly after my company left early Monday morning, I had a concerned visitor at the dock. He said in a terse voice, not getting out of his boat, "Anne, thought I'd better tell you, there's talk around town. They say you had a *Negro* girl up here. Listen, be careful. With some of the characters we have around here, someone's liable to burn your camp to the ground!" (This is the time-honored revenge in our mountains.)

I was stunned, then furious. Never before had I sensed any racism in the Adirondacks. Could it actually be true that certain people objected to having a black person here? Or was it only vicious gossip exaggerated by a neighbor's concern for me? My reaction was to raise the fire insurance and continue to keep my door open to any person of any color or creed whom I liked. Nothing happened that summer. In fact, five summers went by without incident.

Then a section of narrow, bumpy road near Lake Serene was resurfaced and widened. A large road crew from outside the Adirondacks moved up to do the job. With them was a young, lean, black flagwoman with an Afro hairdo, gamin face, and perfect teeth. I stopped a couple of times along the roadside to chat with Marcia. I liked her immediately. She was rebellious, tough, artful, liberated, idealistic, and funny. Watching her handle herself among fifty white workmen and listening to her talk, I knew she was a special human being.

I invited Marcia to the cabin, motivated as much by defiance as by hospitality. We spent a lazy afternoon lying on my dock and talking about women's liberation and black females. Marcia was twenty and determined to be a large tractor operator or a ballet dancer. Marcia's reception in the Adirondacks had been a "mixed bag," as she described it. Some people ignored her, others befriended her. One service station attendant refused her the key to the rest room. On the other hand, she was offered a free cottage, rides to work, dinners, and dates. No warnings, no alarm calls, no gossip followed this second black visitor. I decided that times and people must be changing.

The saddest visit that ever took place at my cabin happened when Ruthie, my former roommate, and her pet raccoon returned. She was convinced that the Adirondack outing was therapeutic for Freddy. This time she brought her boyfriend, Pete. It was hard to say which she cuddled more, the 'coon or the man. One was like her child; the other, her lover. Fortunately, Pete liked the little animal almost as much as Ruthie did, so there was no jealousy between them. We packed a picnic lunch and planned to follow the same trail through the forest. Freddy again walked on a leash.

I was captivated by this raccoon, with his lively brown eyes, mischievous paws, busy nose, and engaging black mask. Freddy loved to have his bushy tail stroked and would curl up in anyone's arms to receive this caress. I began to entertain ideas about having a pet raccoon at the cabin.

Arriving at Sunshine Pond, we changed into our suits and lay in the sun awhile before going swimming. We left Freddy tied to a tree trunk. Later, floating on my back, I spied him free on the beach, rummaging through my pack basket.

"Ruthie," I yelled. "Freddy's loose."

She stopped splashing Pete for a second and glanced toward the inquisitive animal.

"Oh, he'll be all right, especially with food in the basket. He won't run away." And she dove at Pete's legs underwater.

But Freddy did. Ten minutes later when we all emerged laughing, dripping, and hungry, two sandwiches and the 'coon were gone. Ruthie roamed around the beach, sure that Freddy would waddle up to her at any moment. Pete and I started eating. Two hours later Freddy hadn't appeared. Ruthie was in tears. Pete and I were dashing through the woods, stopping to call his name and hold out enticing bits of sandwich. We waited until almost dark. Pete and Ruthie had a long drive home.

I consoled my friend, "Freddy will probably turn up at the cabin tonight when he's hungry. He's probably taking a nap in the woods after eating those two sandwiches. He can track us back here with that sharp nose of his."

"But he's never been outdoors alone before," wailed Ruthie. "He won't know what to do, where to go. Something will eat him." With that, she broke into a fresh burst of tears.

"There's no animal big enough to eat him," I reassured her, not entirely convinced myself. Could a bear possibly relish young 'coon? Might a large owl attack him? "I promise to comb the woods tomorrow for Freddy if he doesn't turn up tonight. And I'll call you as soon as I have any news."

Ruthie, still crying, left in the boat with Pete's arm tight around her shoulder. Freddy never came back and never was found.

Over the years, a number of interesting professional people have come to the cabin. Each one has brought a mark of their professions, some special skill or idiosyncrasy which has been appreciated. An avian biochemist, working on the effects of pesticides upon birds, came up for a spring day with his binoculars and left me with a list of fifty-three species seen on my property.

A computer analyst spent ten days of vacation with me. Among her bags were two dozen detective stories. She read one a day and enlarged my library when she left.

A senior airline pilot whom I met on a trip showed up for the weekend with an enormous tool box. "I figured you might have some little jobs that needed doing," he explained. "That is if you don't mind." I didn't. Pleased to be able to putter, he performed several jobs that I'd been unable to handle or lacked the tools with which to do them.

A malacologist passed by on his way to a conference. He spent all afternoon wading in the lake with a net and bucket. He collected a few snails and mollusks, gave me a better understanding of the aquatic and shell life of Black Bear Lake, and left most of a bottle of Scotch.

Three different professional photographers worked in the area and stopped in for coffee or dinner. They talked shop avidly and showed me the latest equipment. From them I learned techniques ranging from how to photograph a Winter Wren on its nest to taking time exposures of the cabin in falling snow.

My most unusual professional guest was a marine biologist and deep-sea diver from the Virgin Islands where I had worked on a wildlife survey. Rugged as a marlin, he outdid himself by offering to climb a 90-foot dead spruce and top it with an axe and a chain saw because I had voiced my fear that the crown might snap off and fall upon the cabin. "You're a scuba diver, not a tree surgeon," I said, trying to talk him out of the hazardous operation. "Air tanks and regulators are one thing, climbing spurs and chain saws are another." But he insisted and performed the task with all the prowess of a French-Canadian lumberjack.

It was truly heart warming. Everyone who came to the cabin offered to help fix or improve things. It was as though they wished to repay me for the tranquility, beauty, and wildness of the place. They acted like pioneers, ready and willing to help.

Somehow my little home in the woods brought out the best instincts in visitors. Or the worst!

There are many old sayings about how to *really* know a person. I've heard, "Get him or her drunk." "Play eighteen holes of golf with your prospective employee, client or friend." "Take a person aboard a small boat for three days." "Watch how a man or woman treats a dog." And so on. . . . I'd like to add my own formula: invite a person to a log cabin in the woods for a weekend. The true personality emerges every time. Acquaintances I've worked with here and abroad, colleagues I've met at conferences, friends I've visited in cities—without exception their artificial outer shells begin to loosen at Black Bear Lake. Their characters change. They relax. Within twenty-four hours, I can usually see through to their essential traits and peg them as "good guys" or "bad guys."

All this means is: are they adaptable, helpful, fond of animals? Do they have a sense of humor, love of nature? Or, are they inflexible, selfish, uptight, scared of Pitzi, impervious to the surroundings? Even though "good guys" (in terms of log-cabin life) may be taken aback by the outhouse, feel uneasy without a phone ringing or a TV blaring, act disoriented in the woods, they *will* offer to carry water and wood, help tie up the boat or start the snowmobile, take time to look at wildflowers, and generally find serendipity in the setting.

Observances at my cabin are simple and logical. I don't permit smoking indoors or in bed. The threat of fire is too disastrous. Visitors must be careful not to hit their heads against the 5-foot, 4-inch door jamb (just my height). No one uses the chain saw except me and a few proven visitors. It's too far to take fractured skulls or lacerated hands to the health clinic. Houseguests had better like camp coffee, roast beaver, champagne, and venison steaks. And, at night, my friends should be prepared for a deer mouse darting through the guest room, an owl chuckling outside the window, and a slumber as deep as a woodchuck's in December.

# 14

## Animal Visitors

My first summers at Black Bear Lake, a number of wild animals visited me of their own free will. They soon found out that I provided no free handouts or shelters here, except for a bit of bird seed. Much as I love all wild creatures, I have no desire for any of them to become dependent upon me. This would destroy their survival skills and the ecological balances which have evolved over time in the natural world. So my policy has been to "live and let live." I have *my* work to do at my desk and on my little home in order to survive—and they have *theirs*.

Nevertheless, the local wildlife and I have maintained a close rapport around the cabin. Wild animals are just as cherished as my human friends. They seem to sense that they are safe on my property, that the human animal in residence will not molest them. In turn, I know that none of them will harm me. In ten years of living next to the wilderness, no wild animal has ever threatened me. Instead, I have found wildlife living comfortably on all sides of my cabin, and some *in*side it.

One evening, I carelessly left a hot apple pie to cool by the open window before going out. A mother raccoon and three young ones pushed in the screen and climbed onto my kitchen table. They had smelled the pie and also were curious. The 'coons had five hours to snoop and were still ransacking the cabin when I came home about midnight. They didn't hear a thing until I opened the door and shone the spotlight into four pairs of sparkling black eyes and masks. A second of absolute immobility passed, then panic set in. All four 'coons went in all four directions. Since I was blocking the doorway, they had to scramble to find the window through which they'd broken and entered. One baby scrabbled onto the stove; another fell in the sink. The mother leaped on top of the refrigerator, abandoning the littlest 'coon on the slippery kitchen table which was strewn with sugar. The fuzzy creature lost its footing and spread-eagled, crying to itself.

I gasped. The cabin was an incredible mess. First, the raccoons had scooped all the apples out of the pie crust and eaten them. Then they had knocked a cannister of flour onto the floor. When it burst open, they proceeded to parade back and forth through the powder, leaving little white paw prints upon the furniture. One youngster had discovered the honey jar. He obviously tried valiantly to unscrew the lid, scratched off half the label, then left it upside down by the fireplace. He had better luck with a jar of mango chutney from Trinidad. What wasn't devoured was tracked over the Navajo rugs along with floury footprints. Mango chutney on Navajo rugs! What a combination! The catsup bottle had met a similar fate except that its contents were streaked around the kitchen floor. My bright red, blue, and yellow enamel coffee cups swam in catsup, while the green, orange, and purple ones hung sedately on their hooks. One of the curtains swung askew, having evidently been used as a raccoon swing. The sugar bowl's contents were spewed all over the kitchen table. The sugar looked like hoarfrost on the red oilcloth.

Suddenly the situation seemed hilarious. I couldn't help but burst out laughing. Grabbing a broom, I began sweeping raccoons out the door. They hustled into the woods and noisily climbed the closest balsams. There, 15 feet above my head, they draped over limbs and peered down at me with luminous, remorseful eyes.

"You broke up a good party!" they seemed to be saying.

After this invasion, I made doubly sure not to leave any food out in my kitchen or discard any scrap of garbage on my land.

Nevertheless, my next encounter with 'coons occurred through my carelessness about five years later. By then my dog, Pitzi, was living at the cabin. After a strenuous day of woodcutting, I decided to take a hot bath before bedtime—always a treat to be savored in my rustic surroundings. It was well after dark when I lit the hot-water heater and began to draw a tub. Pitzi had followed me into the basement. He seemed inordinately intent on one corner where old boxes, empty cans, and a 50-pound sack of dog food were piled. Perhaps a mouse had crept in there for cover, I thought. Stepping out of my jeans I eased down into the steaming water, oblivious to everything except the delicious heat penetrating my sore muscles.

Suddenly Pitzi charged into the corner, tipping boxes and cans all over the floor and shouldering the sack aside. A cascade of dog ration flowed out of a large hole. Then he leapt backwards with a small grizzled animal in his mouth. A young raccoon! Drawing up my legs and grabbing the sides of the tub, I shouted to him. Pitzi flipped the 'coon into the air, paying no attention to me. Then I realized that the raccoon had been hiding in the corner, filching dog meal from the bag. Pitzi was doing no more than defend his home and his food. He gave another smart toss and the terrified youngster landed with a splash in the tub! Dumbfounded and stark naked, I jumped to my feet and scrambled out of the bath. The 'coon floundered unhappily in the hot soapy water while Pitzi and I stood excitedly at the rim, wondering what to do. Then my enterprising dog dove into the tub, grabbed the animal by the scruff of its neck, and tossed it back onto the basement floor. Afraid any further manipulations by my huge shepherd would kill the 'coon, I held Pitzi's collar, opened the door, and nudged the raccoon outdoors with my bare foot. Soaking wet, but apparently uninjured, it bolted into the woods.

Other interesting animals made themselves equally at home around the place. One night I was lying awake listening to the Barred Owls calling across the lake. Suddenly the deep "awwwh-awwwh-awh-awhhhhhhhh" chortled out right from my little balsam forest. I flopped onto my stomach in bed, pressed my nose to the screen, and answered with my best imitation. Almost immediately the owl responded. His hoot ended in a throaty chuckle. Grinning to myself, I caught saliva in my throat and hooted back complete with deep gurgle. The bird moved nearer to my sleeping loft and called again. Soon our dialogue was being conducted with only a sheet of screening, 20 feet of space, and one balsam tree between us. It was a beautiful night conversation. Part of my mind could imagine the look on a few of my friends' faces had they seen me sweating under the covers with the strain of producing owllike sounds.

Something in my voice must have told the owl that he or she was being deceived, for suddenly its responses ended. The balsam trembled slightly as if a large bird had launched itself from the branches. Not a sound in the air, yet the owl was gone. I *felt* it leave as surely as if I had seen it fly away. The night seemed empty after that and I was a long time falling to sleep.

Often in the mornings I wakened with a start. "Tap. Tap. Tap." Was someone at the door? Before Pitzi came to the cabin, I had no early warning system. The first time I heard this knocking, I scrambled out of the loft, down the ladder, and dashed to the backdoor in my nightgown. No one there.

"Tap. Tap. Tap."

On the porch post a strange-looking woodpecker about the size of a Hairy was jabbing for spruce bark beetles with his powerful beak. From its black back, black-and-white barring on its sides, and yellow crown patch, I recognized it as a rare male Arctic Three-toed Woodpecker. This species is seldom seen in our mountains except in winter; yet this diligent bird has returned every spring to my cabin posts, tapping and probing and otherwise acting as if it owned the place.

Another of the daytime sounds around the house is a high "kee, kee, kee." It is as familiar as the haunting whistle of the White-crowned Sparrow. Often I spend lazy summer afternoons in my Brazilian hammock, watching a Broad-winged Hawk cruise in circles above the cabin. Its plaintive "keeing" shivers down the spiraling thermals and heat waves to reach the ears of furtive mice, voles, and shrews.

I thought I knew all the Adirondack animal residents and visitors at Black Bear Lake. Yet I never realized that one of the smallest mammals in the world was my neighbor—the Pigmy Shrew. Then one day, Earl, a keen zoologist from a local university, stopped by and set a small mammal trapline through my woods. Checking it a few hours later, he ran back to the cabin triumphantly. He lay a miniscule soft gray shrew in my palm.

"These shrews are quite rare in collections and their life history is poorly known," he gloated. "I'll skin it and make a study specimen for the museum at school!"

I felt sad that the shrew's short, frenetic life had been snuffed out by scientific curiosity even if it *was* a "collector's item." I held it for a while. The tiny head was barely as big as my little fingernail. The creature weighed about ¼ of an ounce, little more than a dime. Yet, ounce for ounce, Earl assured me, this tiny insectivore could rival a Bengal tiger or Cape buffalo for fierceness. It attacks small beetles, earthworms, grubs, and grass hoppers and eats great quantities of food every day.

After Earl left I found myself listening at times for the softest rustle of a Pigmy Shrew in the night or sometimes searching for the miniature tunnels they make, which will barely admit a pencil.

Down by my dock, I found a different set of friends. From time to time, as I lay sunning in the late afternoon, a saucy, sleek mink leapt fluidly from rock to rock along the shoreline, looking for crayfish. I used to admire its sinuous body and, as I discovered, its overly bold manner. 'A few days later I had been bullhead fishing and had hung a string of eight fish in the water at the end of the dock. Then I walked up to the fireplace with the tasty thought of fresh bullheads fried in butter in mind. When the fire had settled down to coals, I hopped back down to the dock to skin and clean the fish. The line felt strangely light as I pulled it out of the lake. And with reason! Only the heads and backbones remained! I knew there were no piranhas in Black Bear Lake, so it could only be one animal—my much-admired mink.

Next day I saw it—her—and two babies, skulking along the rocks, eyeing the dock and my fish pole. This time I shooed her away with a clap of my hands.

After taking up scuba diving, I became as interested in the resident fish as in birds and mammals. Adirondack lakes are dark and cold, however, compared to the warmth of the aquamarine Caribbean waters where I had learned to skin-dive. Up here, the thermocline lies just a few feet below the surface even in summer. Once I penetrated this watery layer the temperature dropped dramatically. Little wonder bodies of drowned horses and people have been retrieved from the bottom of Adirondack lakes after several days or weeks with few signs of decomposition.

I did most of my fish watching in the upper, oxygen-rich, warm layer of the lakes, the epilimnion. Here I saw trout lurking below the quicksilver surface, their unblinking eyes turned relentlessly upward, scanning for insects. I saw bullheads nuzzling over the rocky bottom like little dark vacuum cleaners. I also saw crayfish scuttling across the sunny shallows and mussels gently siphoning water in calm coves.

One phenomenon I've noticed over the years of skin and scuba diving in the Adirondacks is that the fish populations seem to be declining. And Rob and other fishermen tell me their catches are smaller and fewer. The chief reason appears to be acid rain and snowfall. Rain is made acid by sulphur dioxide and nitrogen dioxide in the atmosphere. Some of these chemical compounds originate at the huge industrial complexes of Gary, Chicago, and Detroit. The rest come from fossil fuels burning in city power plants and from the exhausts of cars, all carried eastward on the prevailing winds.

Acid rain is particularly troublesome in the Adirondacks (as well as other northeastern ranges) because our high mountains create clouds, which results in higher than average precipitation. In addition, Adirondack lakes are lacking in acid-neutralizing qualities and may therefore be more seriously affected by acidic rains and snows.

Studies made at Cornell University have corroborated our local subjective observations. There *has* been a decline of fish in New York State, much of it in the Adirondacks. The loss was estimated at $1.54 million in overall revenue from fishing in 1973! And it will probably worsen unless air pollution in Canada and the U.S. is conquered.

Now I treasure every trout which Rob and I catch on our covert fishing jaunts. And I relish each bullhead that takes a worm off my line. And I worry. Who will feed the mink and otter, the seagulls and osprey, the raccoons and herons if man's acid rain wipes out all the fish? As humans alter the ecological balances of the world, will they assume greater and greater responsibility for its damaged, dependent denizens?

One afternoon I decided to walk up to Beaver Pond just to see what animals were around. Sometimes the best encounters occur by chance and when least expected. Choosing a slightly different route along the sunny slope of a low hill, I was surprised to see a mound of fresh dirt behind which a hole led into the hillside. The ground was strewn with grouse feathers. A faint pungent odor hung in the air. Instantly a nostalgic vision of Mapuche flashed across my mind. No doubt about it, I had discovered a red fox's den.

Not a sound. Yet judging from the feathers, it looked as if some fox parents were bringing food home to their kits. I hid behind a witch hopple bush downwind from the fox den and waited.

Before long, a pair of tiny alert ears appeared over the mound. Then two inquisitive shiny dots appeared, and finally a wet smudge of a nose edged with short whiskers. The fox pup peered this way and that, cautiously testing the air with its ridiculously small nostrils. Then it pranced into full view. At once three other kits frolicked out of the den and began tumbling around in the sun. Never had I witnessed wild young having such a good time at tugs-of-war, feather chasing, mock fights, and ear biting. It was almost with disappointment that I saw a gorgeous, stern, male fox stalk into sight, carrying a snowshoe hare. His "bush," or tail, looked as light and airy as an ostrich boa. His pelt shone chestnut-red in the sun. The dainty black paws and white-tail tip highlighted his look of fastidious grooming. The dog fox constantly moved his ears, nose, and eyes like radar scanners, and he greeted the kits with reserve.

Not so the youngsters. On seeing their father, the four imps romped to his side, colliding with his trim legs. The male stared for a moment, as if silently remonstrating with his flippant offspring. Then he skipped over to the mound and dropped the hare. Instantly the four babies surrounded the meat and began a tug-of-war. Their puppylike movements were still unsure; yet they knew how to use their tiny teeth effectively. The male moved off a few yards, satisfied that his youngsters were safe and well-fed. He lay down in the sun to groom his fur. I dared not make a motion for fear of disrupting this extraordinary scene.

While watching, I examined the ground around the den. In addition to grouse feathers and hare fur, I could make out the tiny white skulls of mice and voles glistening among the fox droppings. Small rodents usually compose the largest part of a fox's diet. In fact, fox populations often fluctuate in response to mouse cycles. In years when mice are superabundant, foxes thrive —be they Red, Grey, Kit, or Arctic. Their fertility is high and most of the kits survive. In years when mice are scarce, foxes (and other predators) must adapt to other food sources or go hungry and die.

As I pondered this cyclic phenomenon of nature, a slight rustle sounded behind me. Instinctively turning my head, I glimpsed another, smaller red fox. It was the mother. Our eyes met briefly. I saw the same amber wildness blazing up at me that had been Mapuche's. Again I felt a stab of loss. Then she wheeled and broke into a run.

Immediately, the idyllic family scene disintegrated. The male swiftly herded his kits into the mouth of the den. The pups squealed and fell over one another in their haste to reach safety. The dog lifted his lips in a single gleaming snarl before he, too, disappeared. A few puffs of fur wafted across the ground. That was the only movement anywhere. There was absolute silence.

I sighed and rose to my feet. The entertainment was over. It would be hours before the family was reunited and sure they were safe. But I'd come back to take pictures and watch the little ones grow. Backtracking quietly so as not to disturb the female, who was almost certainly hidden just a short distance from me, I bumped into a tree by mistake. At once, a hawk plummeted off a branch and swooped at my head. A blur of pearl-gray breast and slate-gray back rocketed past my ear. A female Goshawk. Unlike the female fox who defended her young with stealth and cunning, this feathered bombshell made direct attacks on intruders. Most certainly she had a nest and chicks in the tree I had hit.

Fortunately, I was protected by my red felt guide's hat; yet the persistent swoops of the hawk were unnerving. I took to my heels and jogged into a dense grove of balsams to lose my attacker. My escape path took me closer to Beaver Pond's western edge, so I decided to continue on around its shore and check for any new beavers. The old dam looked neglected and grass was growing out of the lodge; yet a few freshly peeled white sticks floated on the lake. This was a good sign. Then at the far end of the pond where a small stream rippled into the inlet, I found a short, narrow, new dam. Behind it a bit of forest had been flooded. This looked like the work of a two-year-old couple that had migrated over the hills from their native lodges. Finding Beaver Pond already dammed and most of the tasty timber chewed off of the shoreline, the young beavers had headed up the inlet until they found a suitable site. Impounding their own pond, they could now cruise the edges for untouched yellow birches, alders, and poplars. I knew the couple would quickly make use of these trees for instant breakfasts, lodge poles, dam timbers, and winter feed piles. Then they'd need more.

What looked now like a pitifully weak dam had all the potential of becoming a grandiose structure. As the beavers made it higher and longer to raise the water level, they would also dredge canals, make side dams, and increase the size of their lodge to accommodate their growing family. I had read that the longest beaver canal ever found was right here in the Adirondacks—654 feet. And the longest dam, 2000+ feet, somewhere out West. These youngsters had a long way to go. But who knows? I might return to Beaver Pond in fifteen or twenty years (still within their life span) and find the pair had built the Hoover Dam and Panama Canal of all beavers.

Struggling through the lush grass and ferns which already fringed the shoreline of the pond, I found the couple's lodge. Like most newly-marrieds, they had a modest home. It stood a mere 3 feet high and 10 feet around at the base. Give them a few years together and it might go 7 feet high and 25 feet around. I wondered if they had young inside; so I sat down, smeared on fresh insect repellent, and waited. Before long, I heard the faint squeaks and murmurs of baby beavers. In my mind, I could picture them lying on the sleeping-eating platform a few inches above the water, perhaps nursing their mother. Born in May or June, the babies should be bright-eyed, well-furred, and able to swim and dive by now. I tried to guess how many were inside. Two? Four? Six?

Just then the water at my feet seemed to rise imperceptibly. I held my breath. The male had probably slipped down the plunge hole from the lodge and was swimming underwater. So far from people, motorboats, and canoes, he had little fear about appearing in daylight. He swam right past me, not catching my scent, and headed for a narrow canal. Moments later, he headed home with a branch in his mouth. I could see his sharp orange incisors glistening in the sun. These teeth constantly grow and resharpen themselves as the beaver chews and gnaws on wood. If he or she stopped using them, the teeth would not get honed down and would gradually become a physical impediment to their owner! So it is in nature, I thought. Everything has its purpose. Whatever is not used often becomes a liability.

The male dove without a ripple and disappeared toward the lodge. Soon I heard the sound of munching, almost like several people chewing celery stalks together. No doubt, the family was having a snack. Now the male was out again, this time heading for the distant shore. I watched him waddle up the little slope, clasp a yellow birch trunk with his front paws, and start gnawing at its base. This was a rare treat. I glanced at my watch—4:15 P.M. The beaver's back was to me, but I could hear the sound of wood being cut. Five minutes passed. I wondered which way the tree would fall since beavers have no way of controlling this. I guessed there was a 75-percent chance the birch would topple toward the water. Most trees on a lakeshore or streambank lean out toward the sun. Sure enough. Seven and a half minutes from when he started, the branches quivered and the tree fell smoothly into the pond. The splash sent waves across the placid water. Perhaps they acted as a signal because minutes later, I saw the female and five tiny replicas making V-wakes toward the birch.

Fascinated, I watched them line up along the floating trunk, the father and one kit on one side, the mother and four on the other. They began chewing white furrows in the bark. They looked as contented as a farm family who had sat down to dine on a Sunday afternoon.

Not wishing to frighten them, I sneaked backward and away across their little dam. A trout rose to catch one of the myriads of insects buzzing over the new pond. Swallows swooped over the water; frogs chorused; a Great Blue Heron froze statuesquely at the inlet. Come dusk, a deer might appear to drink, and mink to hunt. All that was missing was a moose.

In addition to the rich new diversity of wildlife, I knew that beaver ponds made invaluable watering holes in times of drought, just as alligator holes provide refuge for other animals in southern swamps. They also serve as barriers to forest fires, maintain the water table, slow down flash floods, and catch rich silts which are eroded from higher lands. No doubt about it, I thought, beavers—even two—make an ecological impact on the environment! Just like humans.

On my way back to the cabin, I crossed an old, old beaver meadow. Years ago it had looked like the fresh pond I had just left. The usual Broad-winged Hawk was hunting above the thick grasses where small mammals lurked. Deer trails crisscrossed the flats. Bear droppings lay redolently next to some raspberry bushes. Flycatchers, phoebes, grackles, and swallows perched on the dead, still-standing timber. The area was rich with bird and mammal life even though the beavers had long since departed. Already I noted signs of the forest encroaching into the meadow. Decades from now, probably after my lifetime, the forest would reclaim the land and the circle would close.

I was almost home. I needed only to cross one little swamp and climb the knoll to my balsam forest. The ebony water lay like a mirror under yellow cow lilies. Their reflections were perfect. With a little imagination I saw a Japanese laquered tabletop adorned with lotus flowers. What tasty food these lilies would be for moose. Once again I yearned to see the awkward bulk of a bell-throated bull standing hock-deep in an Adirondack pond. I thought to myself how many magnificent animals have been extirpated from these mountains due to man's heavy hand. In addition to the moose, wolves, lynxes, mountain lions, wolverines, and Bald Eagles have disappeared. The osprey, raven, and loon are severely decimated. Many acts have contributed to the death toll of these wild creatures—overtrapping, "varmint" hunting, the bounty system, insecticides, poisoning, pollution, disturbance by hikers, boaters, and hunters. And the loss of each species has impoverished our woods and lakes.

I squatted on the bank to gaze at the lilies and tried to imagine how my life would be if loons nested on the low islets of Black Bear Lake and woke me with their crazy laughter at dawn, if a panther screamed at night behind the cabin, if a pair of Bald Eagles came stooping out of the sky above my boat for a fish, if the tracks of a wolf pack passed my water hole on the ice in winter. How much more exciting and varied my existence would be, and how much more balanced the ecosystem would be, with these true native animals in residence.

Then I turned discontentedly away from those perfect lilies and moved into the gloom of my balsams. I had a pretty strong and ugly hunch that most folks are still afraid of wolves, that 100-horse motorboats are more appreciated than laughing loons, that the screech of rock music is preferred to the caterwauling of wildcats at night.

About the only animal which is on the increase in the Adirondacks is the black bear. As more and more people flock into the mountains in summer and fall, the amount of free food for bears rises. Fishermen, hikers, and campers bring food into the woods. Garbage dumps are swollen with tasty scraps. I've even watched a crafty sow bear slip out of the forest, gobble up steaks sizzling on an outdoor grill, and pause for a taste of potato salad at a state campsite.

Bear watching is popular summer entertainment. Many people take their children and guests to nearby dumps in the evenings. There may be twenty or thirty cars parked on the landfill and crowds of people peering about with cameras. So intent are the bear watchers that they ignore the stench of rotting garbage and the buzz of a million flies. Suddenly a small child will shrill, "Look, Mommy, a big bear!"

Then people ease closer to their cars. Some climb inside and lock the doors. Others advance foolhardily on the bear. A flash gun blazes out in the Adirondack dusk. A big male, belly hanging almost to the ground, growls menacingly. Now even the teenage boys, intent on showing off to their girl friends, abandon bravado and retreat.

Although there is no record of a black bear killing or maiming a human in the Adirondacks, there have been incidents of biting, scratching, and threatening. Each summer I say to Rob, "This summer someone is going to get it at the dump." Bear watchers go so far as to feed bears marshmallows, drape their arms over a bear's back for pictures, or throw tin cans at them to elicit snarls. Given the unpredictable natures of both bears and humans, it's only a question of time before a serious accident does occur.

Meanwhile I hate to see wild bears frequenting garbage dumps, eating junk foods, getting fat and sloppy, being speckled with flies, and tolerating crowds of gawkers. To me the animals lose their dignity, their wildness, and their independence. Dump bears are on the way to becoming beggars and bums, in the same way that bar hoppers are heading for alcoholism.

As Adirondack towns and hamlets tighten control and management over the dumps, sanitary landfills, campsites, and other places where humans bring or dispose of food, bears may once again have to revert to their natural role. Then and only then will they regain their nobleness.

Meanwhile I'll keep looking for wild bears. I've seen them in the woods only three times. The most unforgettable encounter was on a cold winter morning when I had snowshoed back to my little swamp to take pictures of the freshly snow-covered balsams. As I webbed my way through the forest I noticed a thin column of steam rising from the top of a balsam mounded by snow. Curious, I clumped closer. Never had I seen anything like it. Suddenly the snow gave way beneath my left snowshoe, and a sort of hollow cave opened up below me. Balancing percariously at the edge of this igloo, I peered inside. It was very dark. As my eyes adjusted, however, I could make out a black bear curled fast asleep at the bottom. Its slow breathing was causing steam to form and rise up through the little hole. Carefully, I backed away lest the bear should awake and be in a bad mood. Then I turned and sped home to the cabin.

Watching wildlife, thinking about wildlife, loving wildlife, I often contemplate the probable future it faces. I don't think wild animals have much chance for survival as long as people keep gobbling up the natural resources for their super-comfort and super-enjoyment. As we keep doubling and tripling our demand for and consumption of energy and industrial goods, more and more dams, reservoirs, transmission lines, power plants, strip mines, super highways, supermarkets, shopping plazas, and housing developments will appear. And wild animals, forests, lakes, soil, and clean air will deteriorate and decrease.

It sounds pessimistic, yes. I don't think that people will voluntarily cut down on their use of material goods and energy. It's so easy and effortless to let machines do the work, to receive our entertainment secondhand. I only know a few people—naturalists, animal lovers, ecologists like myself—who have purposely and conscientiously made their lives more Spartan and cut down to the essentials. And so it seems inevitable that wildlife will survive only in places like the Adirondack State Park, national parks, national forests, refuges, sanctuaries, and reserves.

It would take a lot to make me leave my cabin on Black Bear Lake and force me out of the Adirondacks. But one thing that could do it would be the coming of a day when I can no longer call a Barred Owl to my sleeping loft, sweep 'coons out of my kitchen, or hear coyotes yapping along the ridges on a chill fall night when blue-black clouds chase across a full moon.

# 15

# A Man around the Cabin

It was autumn again. My seventh autumn since building the cabin. The woodpile was growing, the leaves had fallen, geese were winging south. Winter was in the wind. It did not seem quite the preordained ordeal my first winter had; yet a sense of aloneness never left me.

I drove out to town late one Friday afternoon. Pausing broadside a moment on the tracks of the New York Central's Adirondack Division, I gazed into the west. The sun was setting at exactly the point where both rails merged into infinity. The rusty rails were burnished gold, the yellow tamaracks in the swamp alongside were translucent, the sky above was saffron streaked with heavy purple clouds.

As I squinted into the sunset, a group of men came walking down the tracks, back-lit in its golden aura. One strode slightly to one side, taller, leaner, straighter than the others. He carried a rifle in one hand. They looked like hunters back from a day's drive along the railroad bed. Half-blinded by the sun, I fumbled for the key to start my truck. At that moment, the tall man raised his arm in salute and waved. All I could see was his lithe silhouette against the glow. I waited, wondering who he was. He broke into a jog and reached the truck well ahead of the group.

"Hello! Aren't you Anne? The girl who used to work at the lodge near Lake Serene?"

I nodded, squinting into the glare.

"I didn't know you were still up here. Haven't seen you for a long time."

Now he was peering into the cab. I shaded my eyes to look into a lean, weatherbeaten face with pronounced brown eyebrows, a ruler-straight nose, humorous wide mouth, and hazelgreen eyes. Yes, I remembered. This man had often gone horseback riding at the hotel stables and had always asked me to accompany him on the trails. We'd had some splendid gallops along the roadsides. I had been attracted then by his good seat and easy way with horses. He had carried a camera slung across his broad shoulders and occasionally stopped to take pictures of trees, flowers, or wildlife. The slides were useful, he said, for the biology classes he taught in a small college downstate.

"Well, hello. I'm so glad to see you again," I said, groping for a name.

"Nick," he offered, as if reading my mind. "Nick Robbins. We used to have some fine rides together. Remember?"

"Of course, Nick," I replied, smiling. "Gosh, it must be six or seven years since I've seen you. Are you still teaching down near Albany?"

"Yes," he answered. "Only I have a better schedule than before. That gives me long weekends free, not just summers. I come up all year now, hunt in the fall, snowmobile in winter, and canoe in spring. Say, what are *you* doing these days?"

I didn't know how much he'd heard, or whether he still rode at the lodge. But I decided to be candid.

"I no longer live at the hotel," I began. "Morgan and I were divorced a few years ago. I've finished working toward an advanced degree and I'm writing and consulting full-time."

"Well, I figured something like that had happened when I saw someone had taken your place there. I stopped riding the next summer. No one really seemed to care about the horses or trails, so I quit going. Where do you live now?"

"Near here," I answered, hesitating to tell him about the cabin. "I built a place on Black Bear Lake."

"Are you remarried?" asked Nick.

"No, afraid not. Once burned, twice cautious," I said lightly.

"I'm in the same boat," he confided, dropping his head slightly. A chill breeze ruffled his tousled dark hair. He shifted his rifle to the other hand uneasily and hunched his shoulders. I quelled a sudden impulse to reach out of the truck window and stroke his head comfortingly.

By now his friends had caught up and passed us. They reached their cars parked alongside the tracks. The last rays of sun glinted off the plastic-coated hunting tags which each man wore pinned to his jacket back. I didn't want Nick to go but could think of nothing to say. He was watching his companions unloading their rifles before laying them inside the trunks and starting the engines. Perhaps he wanted to leave and couldn't think of a polite way to end our conversation.

Then abruptly Nick said, "I wish there was more time to talk to you." He glanced at me quickly and shifted his rifle again.

Almost without thinking, I blurted out, "Would you like to come up to my place for coffee?" Then I explained. "We'd have to go there by boat and it would be dark when you left. Maybe you're tired from hunting." My voice trailed away.

"No, I'm not," he said, brightening. "And, I'd like to go, but I'm supposed to join those fellows for a poker game this evening."

He frowned a moment, then said, "Wait a minute." He leaned his rifle against the side of my truck and strode over to the nearest man. A curious sense of anticipation ran through me.

Returning, he said, "It's OK. They're not starting the game till eight o'clock. It's five now so I should be back in plenty of time. Shall I follow you?"

We drove our cars to the landing, parked, and got in my boat. It was twilight and turning colder. The purple clouds had obscured the entire southwestern horizon and looked ominous.

"We might have snow before morning," forecast Nick, point-ing at the sky. "That would be good for tracking." Then he was quiet, scanning the shoreline.

We arrived at the dock and I led the way up to the cabin. "It's kind of small," I began deprecatingly, "but I built most of it myself."

Nick stopped stock-still on the path and looked around. "You built this?" he queried. I nodded.

"Well, I'll be damned. A real log cabin. Great." And he began circling the building, noting its construction and location.

I went inside, put the coffee pot on the stove, and threw a fresh yellow birch log in the Franklin stove. Nick entered, glanced at the bright enamelware pots and pans decorating the kitchen, automatically ducked his 6-foot frame through my short doorway, and stood quietly in the center of the main room. The only sound was the crackling fire until he let out a sigh.

"This is what I call a home," he said simply. He moved about stroking Mapuche's pelt, picking a book from the shelf, hefting the handsome Collins axe on the wall. Then he sat down in the Boston rocker and looked straight at me.

"It's really great."

Self-consciously I poured coffee and offered Nick sugar and milk. The silence lengthened. The room was almost dark so I lit a gas lamp and opened the doors of the cast-iron fireplace. The flames drew highlights from the glossy black bear skin rug on the floor. We sipped coffee and began asking each other about our past lives. Gradually my self-consciousness faded and I be-came increasingly interested in this man. He spoke modestly about his job, his travels, his experience in the Armed Services, and finally, his divorce. It was a disturbing account, and I found my-self sympathizing deeply.

When Nick stopped talking there was a long pause during which the sounds of the cabin whispered companionably about us—the soft hiss of the gas lamp, snap of the fire, creak of the rocker as Nick moved, a low moan of wind outdoors.

"And you?" he asked softly.

A confidence had been given. A confidence would be returned. Acting with complete trust toward this newfound friend, I shared the sorrows of the past years with him. As I talked, I suddenly realized that a perspective had developed within me. There was very little bitterness left. Even more surprising, I found myself wondering what it would be like to be in love, deeply in love, with a man like Nick. Could it be my deepfreeze attitude had thawed?

I looked at my watch. It was 8:30 P.M. "Oh, Nick, your poker game. It's already started."

"Are you serious? Don't tell me it's eight o'clock already," he exclaimed.

"More than that. Shall I take you on down the lake?" I asked, hoping he'd say no.

"Well, I don't want to put you out. I've stayed way past your supper time, Anne. I'm sorry. But, believe me, it's really good to talk like this."

Still he made no move to get up.

"Why not let me fix some supper?" I suggested, speaking again from some deep-seated impulse. "It won't be much, but at least you won't play cards on an empty stomach."

"I'd love it," said Nick, and he got up to put another log on the fire.

I fixed a pot of hot soup, a platter of cold meats, cheese and pumpernickel bread, a salad, and tea. Somehow it seemed important to set a nice table, so I spread a gay red Guatemalan tablecloth on my desk and lit a slender red taper. Nicked watched appreciatively.

"Do you like music with your meal? There's a good FM station from Syracuse at night."

"Fine," he agreed, sitting down at the desk.

While serving the soup, a sudden quiver ran through me as I brushed against his arm. The candlelight touched his high cheek bones, straight nose, and strong chin. He looked very handsome. We ate in leisurely fashion, talking and listening to the music, darting quick looks at each other, being studiously polite. Before we knew it, the eleven o'clock news was being broadcast.

"Where is the time flying to?" I marveled out loud. "Some nights I sit here, reading or writing, and it seems as if news time will never come."

"That's what happens when two people hit it off," said Nick quietly. "I haven't enjoyed an evening this much for years. Usually I'm busy preparing classes, paying bills, or attending adult night courses."

Now a strange tension filled the air. Nervously, I cleared the table, piled dirty dishes in the sink, and put food away in the fridge. Smoothing my long hair self-consciously, I came back into the room and picked up the nearest conversation piece I could find.

"Have you ever seen a pair of horns like this?" I asked, my voice suddenly high-pitched. "They're from a chamois, taken in the Kamnic Alps of Yugoslavia." Moving across the room, I picked up a puffer fish from a shelf. "This puffer fish came from Jamaica. The meat can be poisonous if not prepared properly. In Japan," I went on, hating myself for prattling like a natural history textbook, "the fish is specially cooked and is considered a delicacy."

Why couldn't I be suave and confident like the *Cosmo* girls I was always reading about?

Nick gingerly took the spiny fish from my hand and placed it on the shelf. Then he gently took my arm.

"Come. Let's sit down on the bear rug in front of the fire. I want to enjoy this setting a few more minutes before I leave."

I allowed myself to be led like a little girl to the fireplace where I sat hugging my knees. My hands were cold now and my heart beating rapidly. My mind was reeling. I was afraid. We should start down the lake at once. I shouldn't have invited Nick to stay for supper. He must think me terribly forward. I longed to hold his hand. What should I do? I stared into the flames. Years of aloneness overwhelmed me. Suddenly I knew I was ready to take a chance and dive into love once more.

Nick was watching me with those greenish eyes when I turned my head toward him and unclasped my hands. He took them in his. "It's all right," he whispered. Then he pressed his lips to mine.

Two inches of snow carpeted the ground and plastered the trees when I took Nick to the landing next morning. Sullen pewter clouds promised more before nightfall. It would be a fine day for tracking deer. Nick's companions were probably wondering what happened to him after his mysterious departure yesterday afternoon.

I watched his car drive slowly away over the empty dirt road to Hawk Hill. I felt as every woman newly in love has felt since time immemorial watching her man—her predator, lover, roamer, provider, defender—leave. Would I ever see him again? Had I given too much of myself? Or not enough? What would he tell his friends? How sincere was he?

I climbed into the boat and headed morosely back up Black Bear Lake. The loneliness hit me like a heavy fist in the chest. Strangely it was just as severe as when I'd first come to the cabin alone. Now I had found somebody; yet I felt the same emotional despair.

Nick had said he would come back. I had only that to cling to, to wait for. No amount of writing, no repair work, no walks in the woods, no social visits could quell the awful exultation and anxiety in my heart, the fierce restlessness and passion in my body.

It was the beginning of a new emotional era. Nick did come back. We visited each other dozens of weekends and vacations. It was the beginning of a tumultuous, trying, romantic period at the cabin.

---

# 16

# The Adirondack Division

Nick was a railroad buff. Because of his interest, I became aware of the tremendous impact that railroads had on mountain development. He introduced me firsthand to the famed Adirondack Division. Although I had spent several years living a few miles from it and had occasionally taken the train to New York City, I had no idea of its colorful history. As Nick put it, "the Adirondack Division was a fairy tale of a railroad."

"Tell me everything you know about the line," asked Nick one morning at the cabin. "I have a reason for wanting to hear."

"It's not too much," I began, leaning back in my chair and sipping coffee. "It's the only transmountain railroad in the Adirondacks, coming out of Utica and ending up in Malone. Another track meets it there and goes on to Montreal. I'd say the line is roughly 200 miles long."

"One hundred ninety-one miles, to be exact," quoted Nick.

"How come you know so much?" I joked.

"I've been reading about railroads since I was twelve," he volunteered. "Anything else?"

"My first summer in the mountains, I rode the train from

Forestport to Lake Placid, just to see what it was like." I grinned at the memory. "The train came through very early in the morning. About 6 A.M. There was absolutely no one in the two passenger cars. I yelled up to the engineer and asked if I could ride in the diesel engine. He invited me to climb right in. I figured it was the best way to really see the countryside; and he figured it was the best way to relieve a boring trip. He didn't charge any fare and let me sit on his knee and drive the train."

Nick poured more coffee and murmured, "Hmmmmm."

"Well, it was a great ride, even though the rails clattered and the train never seemed to go over 30 miles per hour. The tracks ran through narrow cuts, wound around mountains, and climbed steep grades. The engineer called one "Purgatory Hill" where the train almost slowed to walking speed. We even went over a kind of gorge."

Nick's interest quickened and his green eyes narrowed. "Do you remember the name of that gorge?"

"No," I replied, "but it was about halfway to Lake Placid."

"That figures," said Nick cryptically. "What else did you see?"

"Oh, it was just like taking a wildlife tour by train. We surprised a mother bear and two cubs in a rock cut. The swamps and marshes along the right-of-way were full of ducks, herons, loons, and ospreys. I saw two deer and a mink along the sides of the tracks."

"What about the engineer?" said Nick mischievously. "Did he give you a kiss while you were on his lap?"

"For heaven's sake, Nick! He was over sixty years old, had a huge pot belly and a bristly walrus mustache. In fact, when we got to Lake Placid he told me to stand back so no one would see me in the engine. I guess it was against the rules to have passengers ride up front."

"Just a little," said Nick smiling.

"I remember we had a half-hour wait before turning around

and heading south, so I took a walk through town and then rode all the way back in the passenger car. I was at work again at the hotel by 2 P.M."

"Very interesting," said Nick. "How'd you like to cover those tracks again?"

"How can we?" I asked, sitting up straight now. I sensed an adventure. "There's no trains running anymore."

"I'd like to hike the Adirondack Division," he began, "not all 191 miles, but the central core. I really want to see the place where the two rights-of-way joined. It should be at that gorge you mentioned."

"Two rights-of-way? What do you mean, Nick?"

He pulled out a topographic map and laid it flat on the desk. "This railroad was built in record time—eighteen months—through some of the most rugged terrain in the Northeast and with only men and mules for labor. That's why it's a 'fairy-tale railroad.' When the line was about halfway done, two divisions began working, one from the south, one from the north. The southern team, made up largely of Negroes from Tennessee, laid track from Thendara; the northern group had several St. Regis Indian workmen and laid track from Childwold." He traced out the route for me on the map with his strong, blunt fingers. "The two sections met at the Twitchell Creek Bridge, which spans a small gorge. That's where the last spike was driven. I read about this feat of railroad history long ago and have always had a hankering to visit that spot, see the bridge, and find the spike. Now that the line is abandoned, the only way to get there is by foot. How about it? Would you like to take a camping trip along the famous Adirondack Division?"

"Sounds great," I exclaimed, eager to go. "How far is it? And where do we start from?"

"Your choice," said Nick. "One way it should be 35 to 40 miles. We can either walk up from Thendara or down from Sabattis."

"Let's walk south," I decided impulsively. "Our faces to the sun. We'll get good tans that way." (Nick and I were both sun worshippers.)

We drove to Sabattis in Nick's car after parking my truck in Thendara where we would come off the track. Each of us carried a pack, and Pitzi, his saddlebags. It was an ideal summer day— fluffy white clouds, faultless sky, temperature around 70 degrees, a northerly breeze. We welcomed this weather because walking the line would keep us exposed all day to sun and wind. After half an hour Nick had established a rhythm; his long legs hitting every other cross-tie. But after two hours I was still stumbling, two, then one, then two, then one, or relieving the awkward cadence by tightrope walking along a length of rail. In most places there was barely room for a footpath alongside the ties. The bed of crushed rock was very narrow and the sides steep. The forest pressed close to us. Except for the two ribbons of steel and the endless rows of wooden ties, we might have been walking a trail through one of the most remote sections of the Adirondacks.

As we came to our first cut, a narrow defile blasted right through solid granite, Nick sighed and said, "No wonder it's called the 'Tracks of Tears.' "

"How's that?" I called, stretching my legs to take the ties two at a time and catch up with him.

"There's a legend that says a dead man lies buried for every mile of track on this line," explained Nick somberly.

A chill ran over my back, despite the sweat under my pack. "Why?"

"Those Negroes I told you about, the ones working on the southern division; well, most of them came from down south. They were lured up by the promise of good pay and a steady job 'near New York City.' Imagine what they found here!"

"Black flies, sub-zero temps, blizzards, rain, granite outcroppings, dense forests, swamps," I enumerated in time to my pace.

"Right," said Nick. "Those poor guys had to blast out cuts, build bridges, fill in swamps, lay out tricky curves, carry ties and rails all by hand. I read they lived in little shacks or covered-type wagons. They must have been real homesick because a great many men deserted before the line was done. No grits and no banjos up here!"

"But why did so many get buried on the line?" I questioned.

"Rumor has it that some of the foremen were rough. They were rushing to finish the job in record time, even if it meant at pistol point. They didn't have time for funerals, so when a man died they just shoved his body into the roadbed and covered it up with steel and rock. No one knows if it's true or not."

We walked on in silence, the dog and I gradually slipping behind. We both had sore feet. In midafternoon we passed "Nehasane," the abandoned station stop for the famed Dr. William Seward Webb's estate and game preserve. He was the founder and builder of the line we were following. First he had called it the Adirondack and St. Lawrence Railroad, then the Mohawk and Malone Railway Company, and finally (after leasing it to the New York Central), the Adirondack Division.

Our tans deepened that afternoon as we headed into the sun. Nick was naked to his waist and I wore a brief halter top. By supper time we had arrived at "Brandreth," another station stop to a large private estate. Like Nehasane, the former owners had brought their families and belongings up from New York City, spending entire summers at their lavish camps. No roads existed into these areas at that time.

Again a shiver passed through me. "Let's not camp here," I begged Nick.

"Why?" he asked.

"I recall hearing about an awful thing that happened here shortly after I came to Lake Serene," I said, quickening my pace. "Part of the private land was being logged. One gloomy fall night the southbound train stopped because the engineer saw a body hanging from the station rafters. It was a lumberjack. I never heard who he was, or from where, or why he killed himself. But I'll bet he was far from home and that was his final remedy for the loneliness."

We managed another mile in the long July twilight before I gave out from exhaustion. We cut down to the Beaver River which ran near the track. Within half an hour Nick had the tent up in a little balsam grove on a bank above the river. A campfire was winking, our sleeping bags were rolled out, and the dog's food and freeze-dried rations were ready to fix. While waiting for the water to boil, I stripped and waded into the shallow, sandy-bottomed stream. The chill water felt better than a massage on aching muscles. Pitzi and Nick squatted by the fire, too hungry to swim.

After dark, the evening was completely silent. Only the distant hoot of a Barred Owl drifted over our campsite. The Adirondack Division was a lonesome line now, but it hadn't always been that way. In the early 1900s, more than a dozen trains a day ran between Lake Placid and Utica. The line had opened up new resort areas along the Fulton Chain, Big Moose, Little Moose, White, Otter, Okara, Limekiln, and many other lakes. Not until the first road went through, connecting the Fulton Chain with Raquette Lake and Blue Mountain Lake in 1929–1930, did railroad service decline. Even so, passenger service continued on the Adirondack Division until 1964, freight until 1973, making eighty-one years of service since its inauguration on October 12, 1892.

I relaxed in my sleeping bag, thinking back on how some of those trains looked. The wavering beam of the night engine's light slicing between black hills and probing through the narrow cuts. The whistle echoing like a desolate wail over still lakes and hushed hamlets. And then the tiny day train, "The Beeliner" (or "Toonerville Trolley" as locals called it), bustling by at noon. An electric engine pulled the single car whose back end was striped like a zebra. I laughed to myself, recalling a day Rob and I had taken a very rough, hot hike into a new area, bushwacking most of the way. Rather than walk 10 miles back to our car, we cut cross-country to the tracks and flagged down the Beeliner. Rob was carrying his perennial pack basket and wearing his ageless fedora cluttered with fishing flies. I was barefoot, in pigtails, and wearing a Daisy Mae-type blouse and patched jeans. A just-found Goshawk feather rose jauntily behind my ear. We climbed aboard, paid the conductor fifty cents each, received two clipped tickets, and walked down the aisle. I noted several ladies in hats, veils, and elegant suits. No doubt they were traveling from the Lake Placid Club to New York City and would be dining at the Waldorf Astoria that evening.

The Beeliner clackety-clacked its way through the woods. There was a buzz of conversation from the ladies. Ten miles later, Rob and I got off. As I passed the last row of seats, I heard one woman whisper to another, "Oh, look, Peggy, real hillbillies. And they *don't* wear shoes."

Next morning, after a dip, Nick, Pitzi, and I continued along the tracks. The day was as lovely as the last. Little Rapids slipped by and now we were on the open stretch of line above Beaver River. Water from the Stillwater Reservoir stretched away on either side of us. A late-morning mist still hung over this huge placid body of water, shrouding points and islands. Close to the right-of-way, two loons floated motionless. We stopped silently to watch. From where we stood, I could see a few hungry and determined black flies buzzing about the birds' heads. Their eyelids were the only places the insects could penetrate for blood. Then one loon broke the hush with a long, demented laugh and dove out of sight. The ripples spread in perfect circles over the satiny water. Its mate remained on the surface, carefully stropping its wing feathers and preening its snow-white belly plumage. The mist, loons, and stillness were enchanting. We hated to break it by once again scuffing over the rough crushed stone bed and pounding our boots on weathered ties. But Nick was impatient. He estimated that we were only 3 or 4 miles from the bridge.

Along this stretch we could walk side by side with the rails between us. Another mile of straight track beside water faced us. To make conversation I started telling Nick about Rob's early experience on this line.

"As a boy he used to come up to a family camp on Seventh Lake in the early 1900s. As he described it to me, that was quite a trip. He would leave Utica at 6 A.M. and take the train to Thendara, then change to another line for Old Forge."

"That would have been the Fulton Chain Railway," interrupted Nick. "It ran all of 2 miles to the boat landing on First Lake. Dr. Webb was president of that railroad, too, for some time. Go on."

"Well, after he got to Old Forge, he and his family boarded a *steamer*. Rob said it was a gala event. Crowds up to three hundred strong would pack aboard for the trip up the Fulton Chain. They'd sing and carry on. A stop was made at each hotel along First, Second, Third, and Fourth Lakes. Newly arriving guests were greeted by cheering sections at each one."

I chuckled, recalling the vision of Rob with his pack basket on, dancing along the trail and chanting something like:

> Hokey Pokey sis-boom-bah,
> Rickety Rackety rah-rah-rah,
> Razzle Dazzle kitty-kat-kin,
> What's the matter with this Fulton Chain Inn?

Nick laughed appreciatively. "Then what?"

"At the head of Fourth Lake everyone left and their baggage was unloaded and strapped onto *buckboards* to travel the mile between Fourth, Fifth, and Sixth Lakes. At Sixth, *another* smaller steamer ferried the remaining vacationers to their camps or resorts on Sixth and Seventh Lakes."

"That must have been an all-day trip," mused Nick.

"Eleven hours to be precise," I flipped at him, "compared to only one and a half hours by car today!"

We were at Beaver River hamlet now, the town without a road, accessible only by boat, canoe, snowmobile, snowshoes, or trail.

"Let's leave our packs here and let me show you something strange," I said. "This is the craziest place."

"How do you know?" he asked, eager to go on.

"Because I've come in here a few times for square dances."

"How'd you get here if it's so remote?" he asked, slipping one arm through his shoulder strap.

"Usually I took a boat in from Stillwater and then went out on the midnight train. It was quite an expedition."

We left our packs under a spruce tree and walked down one of the narrow sandy roads which crisscross the hamlet. Suddenly, we heard a noise that was neither car, truck, train, or plane, but something of all four. It grew so loud that I put my hands over my ears. After the serenity of Stillwater, this was blasphemy. Suddenly a caricature of a car chugged by, the driver waving with great gusto. The rear half had been chopped away and a crude flatbed built on. On it an empty 55-gallon gas drum bounced. The windshield of the cab was cracked and punctured by a bullet hole. The tires were of various sizes and all looked half-flat. A raccoon tail hung from a rusty radio antenna. Surprisingly, the blast of rock music came out of the windowless doors.

"Did you see that?" marveled Nick after the plume of exhaust fumes had cleared away. "Was that a car, truck, or wreck? No license plates, no stickers, only one light! Wow!"

"That's what I wanted to show you," I said excitedly. "Just around this bend you'll see several more 'cars.' Since Beaver River has no roads connecting it to anything and is probably the most isolated village in the Adirondacks, people bring in old clunkers and run them without plates, registration, or insurance. They need *some* way of getting their gas, kerosene, propane, and supplies to their camps. You can be sure that no troopers are going to come all the way up here just to write tickets on a bunch of derelict cars."

"Unbelievable!" exclaimed Nick. "And right in populous New York State. Sounds more like Alaska."

"What's more," I continued, "Beaver River has no electricity, only one telephone, but a post office."

"How many people live in this godforsaken place?" asked Nick, trying to get my goat.

"Around ten to twenty permanent population. Most of the children that grew up here have gone out to school, although one mother taught the first six grades for years. Summers, there must be a couple hundred people. At square dances and barbecues, there'll be five hundred!"

We were passing some of the old camps now, a motley assortment of log cabins, frame cottages, converted buses and trailers, and reconstructed railroad buildings. Homes at Beaver River looked a lot like the cars—sturdy, serviceable, and delightfully original.

We had reached our packs, so we put them on and started down the tracks again before I resumed my narrative.

"Beaver River square dances have been famous in the mountains for years. I think they got started when the lumberjacks were living here, cutting the timber down in order to create the Stillwater Reservoir. It's a big flow-ground, really, with over 70 miles of shoreline completely wild. Anyway, Beaver River has a tradition of at least two dances a year—one at Labor Day and the other at Election Day. A band comes in by boat and plays all evening. Most people who come up *know* how to dance, that's why it's so terrific. You don't get your feet stepped on by a 200-pound city slicker or have to show some drunk how to swing. And, despite being so far from 'law and order,' no one gets out of hand at Beaver River."

By now we had left the clearings of Beaver River and entered the forest again. Nick was back in his easy stride, while I hopped and strained to keep up with him. Pitzi was picking his way gingerly over the crushed rock and splintery ties. I hoped he wouldn't bruise his paws and be unable to walk.

"I'd drive to Stillwater, take a large boat-for-hire up the Flow, walk in from the marina, and dance. Mostly I danced with old-time Beaver Riverites. We had some wonderful sets and, wow, what great numbers the band played. My favorite number was 'Spanish Caballero,'" I continued. "Each lady got to swing with all four men, one right after the other. Of course, each man had his own way of doing it, ballroom style, cross-armed in front, crossed arms behind, or elbow swing, and some finished up a swing with an underhand twirl or a back-hand twist. You had to be very fast on your feet. Usually I'd get back to my partner so dizzy that he'd have to hold me up." I paused for breath. "During the intermissions, we'd take an ice-cold watermelon and go down to the lake to sit with our feet in the water, slurp melon, and cool off."

"Likely story," muttered Nick in jest.

"At midnight, the train from Lake Placid came through. Everyone would take an intermission and walk to the tracks to see off the unfortunates who couldn't stay overnight. Since I usually had to work the next day at the hotel, I had to leave. There were always a few guys who were feeling high and they'd shoot off their guns in the air as the train light came into sight. Then we'd get on, in our boots, jeans, lumberjack jackets, pack baskets, and rifles if it were deer season. The rest of the passengers were all dressed up to go to the city and they looked a bit startled."

"Sounds wild," commented Nick. Then he pointed ahead. "Look, Anne. I think that's our bridge."

The track made a wide curve here and a long steel span stretched airily over a deep ravine. As we approached, I saw that nothing but rails, ties, and steel beams crossed the chasm. There were no handrails or catwalks. There was nothing smooth to walk along. I could look right down over the edges and see Twitchell Creek boiling along a hundred feet below. At two places on both sides of the trestle, small square platforms with iron railings jutted out from the track. These seemed to be safety platforms where a person trapped on the trestle by an oncoming train could stand to escape being run over. Twitchell Creek Bridge made me nervous, to put it mildly. Then I remembered Pitzi. If it looked tricky for two feet, how about four? He would never make it across! I turned to discuss the problem with Nick, but he had already taken off his pack and was halfway across the trestle, peering down at the ties and spikes. In the middle, he knelt down, probably hoping to find a plaque or seal or engraved date to show where that last spike had been driven to join the lines and open up service to the public.

"Nick," I cried anxiously, but my voice was blown away in the strong breeze. I waited for him to come back.

"Couldn't find a thing," he said on return. "Guess no one thought it was important enough to mark. Oh, well, at least this is the place."

"Nick," I said worriedly, "Pitzi can't get across this. What will we do?"

He looked at me, then at the dog, then at the open work bridge. "Hmmmmm." He volunteered, "I'll carry him."

"A hundred pound shepherd scared out of his wits?"

"We'll *both* carry him. Or maybe he could make it by climbing down, crossing the river, and going up the far side."

We peered into the gorge and both reached the same conclusion. Pitzi could never negotiate the steep sides and rocky river.

"Look, I'll take the packs and his saddlebags across. You stay here or he might try to follow. Then we'll truss him up and carry him across."

"What if he gets his legs loose and starts thrashing? We might be pushed right off the trestle!" I warned, remembering his tremendous power when he was tied down and we tried to remove the porcupine quills.

"There's no other way," Nick stated flatly.

The plan worked fine until we were halfway across the bridge. Suddenly the dog started wiggling. One leg came free and Nick had to stoop down to get a better hold. Then I lost my grip. If we once let go of Pitzi there was no telling what he'd do. And in the process we might lose our balances and fall. We were in a precarious position.

Luckily, one of the little safety platforms was near. We made it there, half dragging the dog. Then we laid him flat, calmed him down, and retied the ropes. A few minutes later, we hefted Pitzi into our arms again and made it safely across. I was shaking from head to foot. We all lay down against the bank on the sunny side of the track. I stroked Pitzi. Gradually we composed ourselves and soon were ready to walk on.

As we trod toward Big Moose station, I thought of another incident that had happened along the Track of Tears.

"Nick," I said. "On one of my trips down from Beaver River, the train had to stop to pick up an injured hunter. It would have been somewhere around here. It was raining like mad, almost 1 A.M., cold and windy, a typical November night. The man had broken his leg while hunting. He was 5 or 6 miles from the nearest road and in too much pain for his buddy to carry him out. They got as far as the tracks and lay down to wait for the train. At that time there was only one up in the morning, one down at night."

"How long had he been lying there when you came along?" asked Nick sympathetically.

"About nine hours. All they had was a little two-celled flashlight that was half-shot, two sandwiches, and a pint of whiskey."

"So the guy must have been half-shot, as well," quipped Nick, adjusting his speed to my awkward gait.

"The engineer almost didn't see them," I continued. "If the train had passed them by, the man would have waited another six or seven hours and might have died from shock or exposure. We all got out and carried him into the freight car. We laid him out on some packing cloths and immobilized his legs with the mail sacks from Saranac and Tupper Lakes. Fortunately there was a bottle of aspirin in my pack so I played nurse. He had taken about eight by the time I got off the train."

"What stories you tell!" said Nick affectionately, throwing his arm across my pack. "Look ahead," he pointed, "the hamlet we're coming to, Big Moose, is the highest point of the Adirondack Division and on the entire New York Central line. It's also the station where supposedly Grace Brown and Chester Gillette came in Dreiser's book *An American Tragedy*, and where Chester did his dastardly deed."

"Good heavens!" I exclaimed. "This line really *is* steeped in history. I've read *An American Tragedy*, and saw *A Place in the Sun* with Elizabeth Taylor, but I had no idea Big Moose was the actual locale."

"Yes, ma'am, it is," said Nick.

Serious, I said, "Poor Grace. Do you suppose she had any inkling that she was going to be murdered in Big Moose Lake when she got off the train?"

"I doubt it," commiserated Nick, as we passed the well-built station house. "She was probably madly in love with the scoundrel, scared out of her mind at being pregnant and unwed, and tickled pink to be up here on a holiday with her lover. Let's face it, in 1906 girls didn't know much about the facts of life or have much savvy. Society was still *very* Victorian."

The Big Moose station still stands beside the abandoned tracks of the Adirondack Division of the old New York Central Railroad.

"I don't see how Chester could have done it," I said as I shuddered. "Take her rowing, hit her on the head, watch her drown, run off through the woods, and then go play tennis at a resort hotel." It reminded me of the narrow miss I'd had with another such psychotic murderer, Garrow, even more cold-blooded than Gillette, as I hiked the Northville–Lake Placid Trail.

"I'm glad he got his!" said Nick emphatically. "The electric chair in Auburn prison was too good for him. He should have been strung up from his heels by the local vigilantes."

We left Big Moose and its "Lake of Tears" behind, and started on the long, wide sweep of track which was to lead us toward Thendara.

"Do you think we'll make it out by night?" I asked.

"Doubt it. Besides we're in no hurry. I'd kind of like to camp at Carter. That used to be called Clearwater Junction and is the meeting point of another famous little railroad, the Raquette Lake line. If we stay there tonight, we can be out to Thendara in time for brunch tomorrow. I'll treat you to a pancake breakfast—all you can eat!"

Just then we saw what looked like the ski tips of a snowmobile. They were crunched up against the side of a rocky cut.

"Oh, Nick, you know what *that* is?" I cried.

"A spaceship rudder?"

"No! During the last few years that freights used the line, they only ran north on Saturdays and south on Sundays. Some of the trains were thirty or forty cars long. Weekends, they competed with snowmobiles which were running the tracks illegally. Every-one tried to figure out the schedule and be *off* the tracks when the freight went through; but because of the number of cars and changing snow conditions, the trains never ran exactly on time. Sometimes they were hours late."

"Oh, oh. Another horror story coming up," said Nick.

"Right. Local rumor has it that a pack of snowmobiles were heading *down* the track in a heavy snowstorm. The wind was coming from the southwest, right into their teeth. A freight was traveling *up*. They met in a cut. Of course the snowmobilers never heard or even saw the train above the noise of their machines and the snow in their faces until the last minute. All the riders dove off their machines and narrowly escaped being crushed by the huge snowcatcher on the engine. But the train totaled five snowmobiles. Flat as flapjacks. I'll bet that ski tip is from the accident."

Nick chuckled, tossed the metal scrap away, and shook his head. "For being in the middle of nowhere, the Adirondack Division sure had its share of adventures!"

Steady, slow hiking brought us to Carter by midafternoon. The sky was hazing over and a south wind was blowing up the tracks. It felt like rain coming on. My legs were aching and I was glad we were going to camp here. Nick left his pack by the old abandoned section house and went to reconnoiter the right-of-way for the old Raquette Lake Railway. I started poking around inside the building in hopes there might be a flat bit of floor where we could spread our sleeping bags. If it was going to rain, we might just as well stay under a roof and keep our gear dry. As I scrounged and scuffed around, I found bits of coffee mugs, links of chain from traps, curled pieces of ancient leather. These must be remnants from the one-armed hermit, Compo, who had lived around Carter for years. People say he managed everything alone, chopping wood, setting traps, trout fishing, and that he always had a pot of coffee and a good yarn for any stray passerby. Soon I had a little space cleared, the bags laid down, and a campfire blazing outdoors.

Nick came back, beaming. "Is supper ready?" he asked. "I'm ravenous."

While I cooked, he told me what he'd found. "The tracks are all gone; probably sold to the Japanese scrap iron market years ago. But the railroad bed is plain as can be. It runs due east right toward Raquette Lake 18 miles away. It looks to me like snowmobilers have been using it as a major trail."

"Tell me about the line," I asked, stirring hot water into

freeze-dried apple sauce. "We're not going to walk that, *too*, are we?"

"No, not this time, although it might be fun to do. For its size, the Raquette Lake Railway had the wealthiest board of directors in the United States. Dr. Webb was president for a while. Then there was Collis Huntington, president of the Southern Pacific; plus J. Pierpont Morgan; Vanderbilt; Whitney; Dix, the Governor of New York State in 1911 and 1912; and Sam Callaway, president of the New York Central. Most of these gentlemen and their families summered in the Adirondacks at their estates, so a railroad was to their advantage to get there. Many rode up from New York City in their private cars, as elegant as you can imagine. Some had marble table tops, gold water faucets, and even Japanese servants in the dining room."

"Well, here's *your* dinner on a wooden board and your water in a tin cup," I interrupted, handing Nick his "tray."

He grinned, patted me on the head, and began wolfing his food. Pitzi was also chomping busily at his bowl in the corner. The only other sounds were the restless rustle of the south wind in the poplar and wild cherry trees and the zing of sparks from the old wood scraps.

Nick finished his meal and reached out to kick the burning wood closer into the fire.

"Did anyone use the line besides its well-to-do directors?" I asked.

"I'll say," replied Nick. "There were a number of popular hotels at Raquette, Forked, and Long Lakes. Guests could leave New York City, arrive in Utica, switch to the Adirondack Division, arrive here at Clearwater, switch to this line, and go to Raquette. There, they could board steamers to go up to their inns or camps."

"Sounds just like what Rob went through as a boy," I murmured, stretching out alongside the fire.

"Oh, this got more complicated than that!" laughed Nick. "In 1900, the Marion River Carry Railroad began service as the world's shortest standard-gauge line. All fifteen hundred yards!"

"You must be kidding," I exclaimed.

"Nope," said Nick importantly. "Once people got to Raquette, they took the steamer up the Marion River as far as the rapids. Then they climbed aboard the train to cross the Carry. Then *another* steamer took them up Utowana, Eagle, and Blue Mountain Lakes, ending at Steamboat Landing."

"And how long did that whole expedition take?" I asked wearily.

"Anywhere from fourteen to twenty-four hours," replied Nick.

"Crazy. Absolutely crazy," I commented. "I'll bet not many people put up with that kind of travel."

"Ha! You'd be surprised. The two lines ran for about thirty years and during peak summers, the trains carried more than ten thousand people. And now today, thousands more go to the Adirondack Museum just to *see* those old engines and private cars. We'll have to go there someday."

"It's hard to believe," I said, shaking my head. "They sure couldn't have had much business in the wintertime though."

Nick sprawled out beside me and started untying his boot laces. "Where do you think places like New York City, Utica, Albany, and Syracuse got their ice in the old days, Anne? How do you think they kept the beer and lobsters and lettuce cold all summer? Not with G-E refrigerators in 1910."

"I don't know," I said naively.

"The New York Central contracted to cut anywhere from twenty thousand to one hundred thousand *tons* of ice each winter for the icehouses down in the cities. And most of it was harvested right at Raquette Lake and Old Forge Pond, and came over these two lines where we're sitting now. I've seen pictures in railroad books of freight trains sixty cars long loaded to the roofs with ice cakes. And that was a daily occurrence."

I was getting sleepy and a light drizzle was beginning to fall. "Let's go inside, Nick. That walk today really wore me out. I swear one leg is longer than the other from reaching for that second tie."

"OK, sweetheart." He stretched once more and kicked the fire together again. "I think I'll get some water and put this out. I'd hate to see a fire start with all this scrap lumber around here."

By the time he came in, Pitzi and I were snuggled together on the floor, half asleep. The soft patter of rain on the old roof of the section house was hypnotic. Yet, one question kept niggling at my mind.

"Nick," I murmured. "I can't quite picture it. How did they cut all those ice cakes out of a lake in one day? It's impossible."

"Simple," he answered, yawning. "The ice cutters used a horse-drawn plough or a gasoline rotary saw to cut the cakes." He unbuttoned his shirt. "Then they pushed the 'floats' down an open channel with pike poles and shoved them right up a conveyor into the freight cars. With sixty or seventy men working and several teams of horses, they could cut about fifteen thousand ice cakes a day."

"Mmmmmm," I mumbled, almost asleep now. "Nite, darling."

"Nite, yourself."

"Oh, Nick . . ."

"Ummmmm?"

"Isn't it amazing how times change? We've really had a walk through history. I mean not so long ago railroads were the big thing to save time and go places—now its planes and next those damn supersonic jets. I hope somebody cares enough about these old tracks to save them."

"They're trying. The Adirondack Park Agency, several government leaders, and a lot of railroad buffs like me are fighting to keep the lines alive. With the gas crisis, it's a necessity. Besides, there's so many things that could be done—history excursions, flat cars for hikers and snowmobilers to bring their packs, canoes, and snowmachines into the mountains, scenic fall foliage rides to Lake Placid. It would be a crime if they ever tore up these tracks."

The rain pounded harder now, drowning out our conversation. I rolled over drowsily in my bag. In my mind's eye I could see the rails glistening wet, the ties soaking up the moisture into their weathered old cracks, the stones of the bed turning darker gray, the rock cuts dripping and trickling rivulets of rain. Just one more rain in the long life of the Adirondack Division. How many more? I fell asleep.

# My Backyard

One spectacular September Saturday, Nick arrived at the cabin, grinning from ear to ear.

"I got something in the mail yesterday that you're going to enjoy," he announced, plopping down in one of the canvas butterfly chairs on the sun deck. "God! What a beautiful day! We've got to do something special, honey. I left Albany extra early this morning so that we could have a long weekend together."

As he spoke, he was sorting through papers in his briefcase. "Here it is," he said cheerily and held up a copy of *Adirondack Life* magazine. "There's a batch of quotes from elementary schoolchildren down in Missouri. They've been doing a study unit on the Adirondack Forest of New York State, but have never seen it. The kids wrote some pretty funny lines and I want to read them to you."

I poured us cups of steaming camp coffee and stretched spread-eagle in the other chair.

"Listen to these kids' quotes," said Nick, scanning the pages.

" 'The Adirondacks are mostly populated with mountains. People are only their second source of population.' Here's another. 'Mountains hump their way all up and down there.'"

I burst out laughing, spilling a few drops of hot coffee on Pitzi's tail. He looked up at me reproachfully.

Just then the low roar of a seaplane sounded above Black Bear Lake. I dashed to the dock to see if it was going to land. With a graceful swoop, the plane lit and taxied to a camp diagonally across from the cabin. Three people hurried down to the dock, got in, and slammed the door. Then the plane, visibly heavier now, roared down the center of the lake and slowly rose. Fifteen minutes later they were back.

"Those folks must have gone up to see the fall foliage," I commented to Nick. "What a day for sight-seeing by plane. Imagine how it must look on the High Peaks."

"I'll say. Do you know what it costs to take a short trip like that?" he asked. "I've never been up in a seaplane."

"Around $5 for fifteen minutes, I think. That's per person," I added.

"Hmmmmmm. So the pilot earns about $60 per hour with three people, $40 with two.

Nick sat tapping the magazine, now forgotten, against his palm. Then he nonchalantly asked, "Want to fly over the High Peaks?"

"Of *course*, darling. I'd *love* it," I exclaimed, "but it's much too expensive."

"Well, we'll make a deal with the pilot. You take your cameras and offer to shoot some pictures for him. Shots of the plane, shots of him, shots of the mountains. Whatever he wants. People in the tourist business up here must always be in need of good publicity pictures. I'll bet all he has are some instamatic snaps and he'd love a few good prints. I'll wager we get the trip for half-price. And I'll split that with you. What do you say?"

Impressed by his canniness, I nodded my head.

"Let's go see him this noon when he comes down for lunch. We'll ask him if we could go up very early tomorrow morning.

You might get some nice shadows and lighting that way. The weather is supposed to be beautiful again tomorrow. Does that sound OK?"

It certainly did. To my surprise the young bush pilot readily agreed. As Nick had predicted, he was lacking good photos for postcards or posters, having recently started service around Lake Serene.

Reminiscing back to my first fall flight in the Adirondacks years before with Morgan to Deep Lake, I was secretly relieved that we were to fly with a new plane and pilot. It would have been too poignant to fly with Mike again.

At 6:45 A.M. Sunday, with all the Adirondacks in a soundless sleep, the audacious rasp of a single-engine seaplane shattered the silence. Light skeins of mist hung over the lakes and ponds, but the upper end of Black Bear Lake was open enough for a landing. Nick and I stood on the dock, waiting expectantly. Not a word was spoken. The pilot shoved open the door, smiled hello, and beckoned us in. Nick pushed off the wing tip and leaped onto a pontoon. He squeezed into the back seat while I took the co-pilot's place in order to have an open window available for shooting. We fastened our seat belts and three minutes later winged back into the still morning sky.

The air was so clear that we could see practically all of the 100-mile-diameter Adirondack mass. The plane climbed to 3,000 feet and leveled off. Way ahead of us the High Peaks were "humping their way all up and down." Below, a rich palette of color—russet reds, golden browns, tawny yellows, flaming crimsons, dark greens, cobalt blues—undulated over the landscape. I felt that same curious sensation of elation over color when as a child, I found a basket full of bright jellybeans and colored Easter eggs and gaudy foil-wrapped chocolates.

"That's some backyard you have," yelled Nick playfully.

"Right!" I shouted back. "What we're seeing surpasses the combined acreage of Yellowstone, Grand Canyon, Yosemite, Olympic, Great Smoky Mountains, and Glacier National Parks!"

It took us less than half an hour to reach Lake Placid. Both it and Mirror Lake were still veiled by shadow and mist. Brilliant rays of sun were shooting up from behind Whiteface Mountain, dazzling our eyes and probing into dawn-dark valleys. Each of the High Peaks was thrusting boldly into the sky. As one Missouri child had put it, "Adirondack Mountains are made for pointing to heaven." And, today, of all days, they were really stretching.

"The main product of the Adirondacks is highness," another young student had written. This observation suddenly struck home as our pilot dove down behind Whiteface's summit. It seemed as if all 4,872 feet of that symmetrical mountain were towering over my head while three or four G's of force were shoving up my breakfast. I gasped, clasped my hands over my stomach, and closed my eyes.

Nick grabbed my shoulder. "Remember what we read yesterday? 'On top of Whiteface, the law of gravity is maintained *very enforcedly*,'" he said and laughed. "Hey, how are you going to take pictures that way?"

I swallowed hard, looked out the window again, and managed a shot of the mountain in full, early morning sunlight with the Atmospheric Science Center perched jauntily on top.

The pilot pointed up and yelled, "That's where they monitor our air pollution. The Adirondacks have some of the cleanest air in the country, especially on a day like today when we get a northwest wind right out of the Arctic Circle and across the wilds of Canada. Man, it's really *clear!* I've noticed, though, how the visibility up here has been getting poorer. A lot of the time the center picks up dirty particles on south and southwest winds which come from the smog-ridden cities—Chicago, New York, and Philadelphia."

There was no time to comment before the plane (and my stomach) had made an abrupt climb back up to mountaintop level. Mt. Marcy lay ahead. Its base was a blaze of color. Bright reds, oranges, and golds of maples and beeches cloaked the lower slopes, while higher up, patches of "black timber" (balsams) mingled with the clear yellows of birches. The summit itself reared to our right, bedrock-bare, blue-gray, and slightly menacing. I couldn't have agreed more with one schoolchild who wrote, "Marcy is the name of a monster in New York which has more than 5,000 feet." I was glad we had unlimited visibility and calm air. It would not do to bump into the monster.

Flying smoothly over the highest point in the state, I could really get a feel for the geology of these mountains such as I'd never appreciated when walking on the ground. They are not part of the Catskills or Appalachians, which include all our other major eastern ranges. Rather they are an extension of the Canadian Shield. The 9,000-square-mile mountain island pokes up into the state like an American afterthought.

"The Adirondacks have been there forever and maybe longer," Nick and I had read yesterday in the magazine. "It took millions of years to make them. I know it was crazy, but there was not much else to do in those days."

Certainly 1.1 billion years was plenty of time to "make the Adirondacks." They are considered one of the oldest ranges on earth, with ancient crystalized bedrock forming the mountain root zone. Surface features, however, are a lot younger. The last sheet of the Ice Age, which pulled back off the mountains about ten thousand years ago, was responsible for the landscape we were viewing from the seaplane. It had reamed out valley floors, chiseled grooves on mountaintops, dropped sand terraces and rocky dams, scooped out cirques, and formed over 2,000-odd lakes and ponds. Yet so stubbornly resistant is this mountain mound that it withstood this carving, plus several other sporadic ice sheets and great periods of erosion. Sweeping my eyes around the horizon, I decided it must be one of the most complicated and challenging geological works in the world.

The plane had been heading southeast. Now I began shooting pictures of the gold and purple hills around Lake George covered with oaks, hickories, and ashes. Dozens of pine-covered islets dotted the 32-mile lake. I longed to swoop down, land, taxi to

Climbing the rocks at Indian Head, which overlooks the Lower Ausable
Lake, made me appreciate the colossal geological forces that had
formed these mountains.

one, and set up a campsite. The roar of the engine and whoosh of
wind past the open window were nerve-racking.

A few minutes more and we were heading west over Ta-
hawus. An ugly black scar gaped through the colorful canopy of
leaves. "That's the National Lead Company's titanium mine—
probably the largest in the world," shouted the pilot. "That old
pit down there is 700 feet deep and 3,000 feet long. Don't know
*how* deep the new site is where they're working now."

Then he pointed vaguely over toward Gore Mountain, evident in the stark light because of its ski slopes. "The Benson
mines are over there," he added. "They produce most of the gar-
net used in this country."

Nick tapped me on the shoulder and looked meaningfully at
his watch. An hour and fifteen minutes had gone by since we
left Black Bear Lake, and the plane showed no signs of heading
back. My mind did a quick cash register act. I leaned toward the
pilot and yelled in his ear, "We better be heading home."

He yelled back, "Don't worry about the time. I'm enjoying
this trip. Don't often have a chance to fly the area on a day like
this. Usually I'm puddle jumping around Lake Serene with tourists. They're all still sleeping or at church, so I won't get any calls
till about ten o'clock. As long as I'm back by then, it's OK. Hey,
I'll show you something terrific. Get your cameras ready."

He swung north again, back toward the High Peaks, but kept
his elevation low. "We're going down over Avalanche Lake!"

I tensed, cameras ready. Avalanche is one of the highest, most
rugged, and isolated lakes. Its only access is through a narrow
ravine and along a boardwalk-catwalk-ladder-and-bridge trail
which clings to its westerly edge. The seaplane flew right between two mountains. I had a brief glimpse of an onyx-black lake
squeezed between two sheer rocky cliffs which looked more like
the Rockies than the Adirondacks. I felt a sharp pull upward as
the plane skimmed over tortuous, shadowy Avalanche Pass and
climbed high into the sky once more. I'd barely had time to snap
two frames.

"How are you doing, Anne?" shouted Nick, leaning forward.

"Want some coffee?" yelled the pilot.

"Where's the airsick bag?" I moaned.

"Hang on until Long Lake," answered the pilot. "We can land right by a coffee shop. You'll feel fine once you're standing on solid ground."

By the time we side-slipped down to a satin-smooth landing on Long Lake, my stomach was better, as predicted. It was nine o'clock. We tied the plane to a dock, walked up the beach, and crossed the road to a small restaurant. The first traffic was stirring in the village, and two sleepy-eyed customers were already seated at the counter. A pleasant, middle-aged lady was cutting up an apple pie.

"Three coffees?" she said brightly.

"*Two* coffees and an Alka Seltzer," I mumbled, trying not to look at or smell the pie.

In a short while, though, I had recovered and was ready to photograph the plane and pilot.

"This is a good spot," he motioned, hopping onto his plane. "Get the lake in the background, beach in front, and the pretty leaves. I'll just kneel down on the pontoon and you take the plane and surroundings. I want something representative for my advertising posters."

"Gotcha," I nodded.

After the pictures were taken, he dropped us back at Black Bear Lake. The little plane definitely had the feel of a waterborne taxi now, stopping here and there all over the mountains. Nick and I climbed out stiffly from the cockpit. He pulled out his wallet. All the bush pilot would take for our three-hour aerial extravaganza was $30. "Just send me those prints when they're ready," he grinned and pushed smartly off from my dock. Watching the plane dwindle away over the hills, I wished I knew how to fly and could keep my own float plane moored in the cove by the cabin. Maybe someday . . .

Dazzled and frazzled by the trip, Nick and I sat quietly in the sun deck chairs, letting the quiet and peace flow back into us again. We had seen the entire breadth and length, warp and woof of the mountains, encapsulated into one morning. A trip like ours *on foot* would have taken Verplanck Colvin, the first State Surveyor for the Adirondacks, *years.*

"Nick," I said solemnly. "I'm so glad we went. I learned a lot about my backyard. As one of those kids wrote, 'From now on I will put both gladness and wonder in my same thought about the Adirondacks.' They're really terrific! I hope to heaven I can always live here."

Nick gave me an odd look, then glanced away. "You never want to leave?" he asked casually.

"No, not as long as we can keep the mountains this way."

"That's why the legislature voted for the Adirondack Park Agency," he replied with a trace of irritation in his voice. "It's for the protection of all this parkland—public and private—to preserve the 'forever wild' character and to regulate growth. Basically you have to think of it," he went on, "as a master *zoning* plan for 2.3 million acres of State Forest Preserve and 3.7 million acres of private holdings." He shifted his chair restlessly into a sunny patch. "In my opinion, it's the most advanced land-use plan in the United States."

"As good as those of Vermont and Oregon and Hawaii?" I challenged.

"Even better!" he stated flatly. Obviously, he had made up his mind that the A.P.A. was a remarkable piece of legislation.

"But you should hear the terrible things local people say about it," I retorted, playing devil's advocate. "One man told 'me, 'I'd rather burn the woods to the ground than let the Adirondack Park Agency tell me what to do!' Another guy I know calls it 'the biggest land-grab since the Bolshevik Revolution.' "

"Sure," replied Nick, testily. "That's normal. All you goddamned rugged individualists living way up here. You'd be against *any* kind of control, *any* kind of zoning. You all want to live like mountain goats—free and wild. You're content just as long as no one tells you what to do."

I couldn't tell if he was kidding me or really serious.

"Well, one thing's for sure," I said, "in spite of the local dissension, the agency has brought the first sense of community *ever* to local people up here. Nothing held them together before—no historical traditions, no cultural traits, no . . ."

"Other than stubbornness and a glorified need for independence," interrupted Nick, cynically.

". . . no accent, no arts and crafts," I continued uneasily, hoping to placate him. "Up until now, geography was the only great unifying force in the Adirondacks."

Nick left later in the day. I sat for a long time, rocking, thinking, wondering about the bad mood which had developed between us. Somehow I sensed that Nick resented my deep attachment to the cabin, this piece of land, these mountains. I watched the late September sun gild the log walls, mellow the Mexican guitar, shimmer on the cedar-paneled ceiling, caress the coyote pelt on the wall. Save for the roar of our airplane, the entire day had been still, and now the evening's hush was more pronounced than inside any ancient European cathedral. Bathed in the holy incandescence of this sunset, it was as if the whole world was "pointing toward heaven."

I felt as though I was sitting at the very core of something. From this core, this hushed cabin room, my mind was raying out like shafts of golden sun all over the Adirondacks. I could plainly "feel" them, their "*Gestalt*," their ancientness, solidarity, reliability. They were very comfortable mountains, deep-rooted, well-preserved. They were not given to sudden outbursts of lava flows, landslides, earthquakes, hurricanes, floods, droughts, or erosion. It was like living with a grandparent who could always be counted on.

Here was no smell of clayey soils, no complacency of evenly rolling hills, no monotony of vineyards and dairy farms as I'd known around the Finger Lakes. Here was no scent of tropical lushness, no boredom of flat pinelands, none of the restlessness I had felt from rustling palm trees and surging Gulf Stream in Florida. Here was no pungency of Indian villages, no urgency of active volcanoes, no bewilderment at the bustle and vibrancy of life lived in Guatemala. Here was no tickle of desert dust, no tedium of sage-covered plains and bone-dry mountains, none of the estrangement I'd felt from spiny cacti and Gila monsters in Arizona. Of all the places where I'd lived and worked, none offered the same sense of total continuity as did the Adirondacks.

And it was continuity I craved. I wanted to know that when I was seventy, the Adirondacks would be the same, that Black Bear Lake would be the same. That I could go down to the dock on a September morning and still take a skinny-dip, still see otter eating bullheads on my rocks, still carry a bucket of pure water up to my cabin, still watch the rain dripping from my big old trees.

I didn't want to think that there might be a road around the lake, more cabins clustered along the shore, a chlorinator on my water supply, a monorail over the old Adirondack Division, a jetport at Lake Serene. I didn't want to think that the Adirondacks might not still be the wildest tract left east of the Mississippi; that it might be just a weekend suburb for Utica, Albany, Montreal, Watertown, and New York City.

The sun disappeared behind the hill across Black Bear Lake, but I kept rocking and thinking back to the crises in the life of these mountains. There had been the *first* crisis of lumbering and wildfires in the 1880s. *Then* the Adirondacks had been saved by creating the Forest Preserve out of state-owned lands, and by adding the "forever wild" amendment to the constitution to protect timber and watersheds. Then, as now, many people felt, "Those wealthy outsiders are trying to lock up the land and limit the lumbering."

The *second* crisis was the tourism and recreation industry. With over 9 million visitors a year, many with money, mobility, and leisure, the second-home craze had hit hard. Land prices had been rocketing. Developers had been buying huge chunks of land for speculation, commercial centers, or housing subdivisions. At this moment, five such major developers wanted to involve 72,000 acres of mountain land. One alone planned for a small, septic-tank city of 30,000 people!

It seemed to me that this was like the proverbial snake swallowing its own tail. Second-home owners demand more roads, better maintenance, increased police, fire, and medical services, even new municipal buildings. Yet, these same people are here only during the summer months and perhaps a weekend or two in winter. They leave lots and camps empty most of the year. The cost of local government goes up, and there's still a lot of unemployment in the winter.

The solution to this second crisis was the creation of the Adirondack Park Agency. Its action was to produce a master plan for the care and custody of *state* lands; then a land-use and development plan for *private* lands with strict density codes. Both were signed into law by then-Governor Nelson A. Rockefeller. The main purpose of these plans is to protect the parklike atmosphere of the Adirondacks and still consider the economic well-being of its residents.

The *third* crisis, as I saw it, was the public's reaction to this "second saving of the Adirondacks." For the most part natives fear the impact of the new controls, while outsiders welcome them. It truly is a "collision in the wilderness."

One morning as a waitress poured my coffee, she mourned, "A few retired, wealthy outsiders will get all the advantages from this agency. The park will end up as their natural history museum and playground." Her words (spoken seventy years after the first crisis) had a familiar ring.

Since the agency had been formed, I had talked to Henry L. Diamond, then-Commissioner of the Department of Environmental Conservation, who stated confidently, "We *have* to put some restraints on land use for the greater good of the people. There are already regulations on air and water. Why not on land?"

I had also discussed the future of the A.P.A. with Ogden Reid, the present commissioner. The courtly ex-paratrooper told me firmly, "I fully support the agency, and I want to see it upheld, kept independent, and strengthened. This entity is a principal safeguard, along with the Department of Environmental Conservation to protect the Adirondacks against the cumulative detrimental effects of our highly industrialized and complicated civilization. I also feel both APA and DEC have a responsibility to ensure open meetings and greater public input in relevant decisions. In the case of the Loon Lake housing development, for example, the DEC supported the APA decision. In addition, it insisted on a more stringent monitoring of the ground water. The decision was to allow 500 units instead of the 1,000 originally planned to be squeezed into the hamlet area; and to eliminate an airstrip due to noise pollution and its proximity to wetlands."

This was the collision. A lot of people were sitting back, watching and waiting to see what would happen. As I had read yesterday in the school child's composition quoted in *Adirondack Life* (was it only yesterday?), "How the Adirondacks can keep both their natural beauty and civilization should be part of everybody there's spare thinking."

My "spare thinking" had gone on long enough. The cabin was dark and chill. I rose wearily. A faint whine came from the back porch where Pitzi was sitting shivering, waiting patiently to come in for a warm meal and to curl up by the fire.

I stretched once and some words from William Chapman White's book, *Adirondack Country*, flowed through my mind.

> As a man tramps the woods to the lake he knows he will find pines and lilies, blue heron and golden shiners, shadows on the rocks and the glint of light on wavelets, just as they were in the summer of 1354, as they will be in 2054 and beyond. He can stand on a rock by the shore and be in a past he could not have known, in a future he will never see. He can be part of time that was and time yet to come.

This was one reason I'd chosen to build my home and live close to the wilderness where nature would provide a perpetuity to life. If the Adirondack Park Agency could provide the special security to ensure that, then God bless it.

"Come on in, Pitzi-burger," I called, opening the door. "Time for supper."

# 18

# **Survival**

Survival in a log cabin in the woods as a lone woman falls into three categories. They are simply the three rules for a full, good life that I learned as a Camp Fire Girl years ago. They are work, health, and love.

Survival in the sphere of work means maintaining and protecting my home, and providing an income through my profession. Accomplishing this as a single woman has taken a special mental attitude. The first thing was to convince myself that I could handle anything I had or wanted to. The time-old excuse of being a woman, hence frail, dumb, afraid, in need of protection and a man's assistance, has no place in an isolated and rustic life-style. I believe a woman can do whatever she sets her mind to, once she's learned how.

Some of the fictions I had to overcome had been planted in childhood and perpetuated in early adulthood. I learned that I would not damage my "delicate internal organs" by doing hard work. I discovered that callouses, firm muscles, or a smudge of grease on the nose would not make me unfeminine. I found it was possible to lift and carry heavy weights and large shapes through the simple use of leverage, traction, and balance. I saw that, given the proper instruction, I could do most any kind of work, whether it was changing a truck tire, making out income taxes, shooting firearms, scuba diving, or reupholstering. Slowly, the sexual dichotomy and double standard toward work which we still practice in the United States fell to pieces, leaving me freer and more competent.

From the beginning, I had made the cabin as simple as possible so that I could do most of the repairs and maintenance myself. This was partly because it is too difficult to get skilled electricians, plumbers, and carpenters to work way up at Black Bear Lake. And partly because I enjoy being self-sufficient.

People are always surprised and sometimes shocked when I tell them I have no electricity. I don't *want* electricity, even though it would now be possible to tap into a power line 500 feet back from the cabin. The reasons are that I don't want a right-of-way slashed through my woods for poles and wires; don't want dangerous hot lines lying on the ground after a storm; don't care to wait several hours or even days for the linemen to restore broken service; and can't think of anything to use electricity for anyway. All my comforts of living—light, heat, cooking facilities, and refrigeration—are provided by propane gas. Without electricity, I live more ecologically, less expensively.

Why do I need an electric hair dryer? I have the wind. Why should I use an electric carving knife? I have a sharp hunting blade. Why must I own an electric vacuum cleaner? I have a dust pan and broom. Why should I use an electric toothbrush? I have toothpicks and a strong arm and wrist. How could I bring myself to use an electric fingernail polisher or makeup mirror? For the cost of one of these silly appliances, an Indian family of four could live for a month in Guatemala. Besides, painted nails and powdered faces don't last very long in the North Woods.

My record player, radio, and citizen's band set all run off batteries. The big 12-volt ones I trade off in the truck, charging one up every month or two as needed. I wind an old clock each morning. I boil up camp coffee in a bright red pot. Bread browns nicely on a metal frame which sits over a gas stove burner. My three-burner range and little oven enable me to cook almost anything. Dirty dishes get washed in the sink in summer, or in a pail on the stove in winter. I'll never resort to paper cups, plates, and plastic utensils because they are not reusable nor ecologically thrifty. Dirty clothes I do in the sink or pails, or take out to the Lake Serene laundromat. It would be unrealistic to say that my life-style is independent of the modern technology of the outside world. I rely on it for dozens of things—bottled gas, tin cans, batteries, and dog food being the most essential. Without the technological world, I simply could not survive in the cabin or off the land in the Adirondacks. It is too cold, too severe, too impoverished in wild food and game. And after eating the meager harvest of Charlie's garden, I know that farming is impractical. Nevertheless, I try to be as resourceful and independent as possible.

As far as the maintenance of my cabin, I can handle most tasks myself: painting and repairing the roof, simple carpentry, cutting firewood, hooking up and draining down the water system in summer, creosoting posts, dock, and sun deck, simple repairs to the chain saw, axes, and tools, taking down any dead trees which threaten the camp, and digging new holes for the outhouse.

Two things, however, have me stymied—the propane gas system and the plumbing. Of the first, even the smallest gas leak can be potentially dangerous and crippling to the cabin. As a security, the system is divided into three sections and each can be turned off at the big tanks outdoors in case of a leak or fire. The kitchen lights and appliances and the basement hot-water heater and lights run off one line. The main log room, or studio, lights and floor furnace operate off another. The third line goes to the porch and guest room for their small heaters and lights. As backup, I have kerosene lamps, candles, the wood fireplace, and a campfire for cooking. Even so, if anything goes wrong, I have to rely on outside help to fix it. Someday I *must* learn how to flare tubing, add a T, connect a nipple, clean the carbon from burners, and run a new branch line to a gas fixture.

The plumbing also has me buffaloed, though it is very simple. There is a gas pump, yards of plastic line, a water-holding tank, a sink, and a bathtub. Yet I have managed to chop a line in two with the axe, shoot a hole in the tank, and strip the threads on a faucet. My backup, of course, is carrying buckets of water from the lake, using the outhouse, swimming in summer, and taking hot horse tub and pail baths in winter. But if the system fails, again someone has to come up to help me. I *must* someday learn to repair and reconnect plastic pipe after the bears have chewed holes in it, thread a metal pipe, change a washer, unplug the drain, and solder the tank if it leaks.

My survival as an independent ecological consultant and free-lance writer-photographer is quixotic—sometimes precarious, sometimes lucrative—but always fascinating. For this type of work, the cabin suits me to perfection. When writing articles or reports, I find the quiet and tranquility of my little studio a definite and necessary prerequisite to creative thinking and steady output. I couldn't function half as well if jarred by a city's noises or interruptions from office workers or neighbors. And when consulting, a house like mine simplifies packing and adds to flexibility. If called away on an assignment, I merely close the windows, lock the door, turn off the gas, drain the water, pour kerosene in the traps, and leave for any length of time without worry.

Despite its isolation in one of the wildest sections of the Adirondacks, leaving the cabin for distant places is sometimes surprisingly easy. On one job I left in my boat about 5 A.M. on a clear summer morning, drove to the nearest airport, boarded a plane at 8 A.M., landed in New York City by 9 A.M., and arrived in the Virgin Islands in plenty of time for supper.

Then again, it can be so complicated that I come close to considering an apartment in the city just for ease of having my equipment on hand. One February, an unexpected cable arrived, requesting my presence for an ecological survey in Panama within ten days. I had to order special equipment, prepare for a month in the field, pack and get everything down the lake through blizzards and drifts. It meant several snowmobile trips back and forth with suitcases, dufflebags, and cameras dragging behind on the toboggan; more frantic trips in and out to the post office. Then the drive to the airport took three times longer than usual. The plane was delayed. Connections were missed. I arrived in Panama a day late, completely exhausted, harried, and unacclimated.

The hardest part of leaving the cabin on professional trips is saying goodbye to Pitzi. Somehow he always senses that I'm going off, even though I hide my suitcases in the guest room and don't pack in front of him. Like a small child he sulks and follows me around nervously. I refuse to leave him in a kennel, and never have. He always stays with good friends who baby him until I return.

In terms of survival against the elements, I don't worry too much at Black Bear Lake. These mountains are not violent; however, they do go to extremes in temperature and weather. My main preoccupations are windstorms which topple tall trees, heavy snowstorms which can buckle roofs, and extreme cold which can freeze not only water lines, but people.

I worry much more about the machinery and tools which are an important link in my survival, yet are potential hazards. I don't want to be stuck in the middle of Black Bear Lake with a faulty outboard motor on a blustery November night, nor stopped dead on a lonely stretch of highway with a defective truck engine. Machinery must be kept running smoothly; so I spend generously on overhauls and repairs. And I always carry a bag of tools, extra shear pins, spark plugs, oil, spare tire, flashlight, and gas can. When using my machinery and tools, especially working alone, I try to protect myself. Running the chain saw, I wear ear protectors and heavy gloves; using the axe, steel-toed shoes and a hard hat.

I've been injured or ill a few times at Black Bear Lake. This happens to a lot of natives, and most survive. It usually means an exciting rescue and evacuation. Despite our remoteness, I feel we have better emergency medical help here in the mountains than in most major cities. As soon as someone *knows* you need help in the Adirondacks, your survival becomes of paramount importance to everyone.

One sultry summer Sunday about eleven o'clock in the morning, I began to feel queasy. Nick was up for the weekend and busy on the front porch, writing a paper. So I curled up in the loft, reading, strangely unwilling to lie out in the sun. At lunch, I barely nibbled on sandwiches. Nick prescribed some Pepto-Bismol. I dozed half the afternoon. By tea time, I was experiencing pains in my lower abdomen. They were worse by six. Nick suggested we visit a physician who happened to be vacationing down the lake. The thought of appendicitis never occurred to me until the doctor pressed tenderly on my right side (McBurney's point), and I let out a yelp.

"Better get out of here and down the lake to a hospital before dark," he advised.

"Why can't I wait until morning and go out when Nick goes?" I asked petulantly.

"Appendicitis is a 'twenty-four hours disease,'" he answered. "It might rupture by midnight or it might subside and be OK by morning. But you should go out in case it gets worse. It's your decision, but remember, if it goes, it'll go fast. You might be in trouble 75 miles from the nearest hospital with peritonitis."

Nick and I thanked him for taking his time to examine me and went back to the cabin. The lake was roughening. Black thunderheads were piling up in the south. There would be storms tonight.

Nick was nervous. "Let's leave right away," he cajoled. "You can come back tomorrow if you're better. But supposing I have to take you out at night in a thunderstorm? You know I don't run the boat or know the lake as well as you do. All we need is to be wrecked on a shoal when you should be on an operating table."

At the moment, my stomach felt better, so I pooh-poohed him. "Let me fix supper and see how I feel," I insisted stubbornly. "I have such a nice meal planned for tonight, and I want you to enjoy it."

Nick shook his head pessimistically, but gave in. So I took a thick steak out of the refrigerator and began to slice up mushrooms into the big iron skillet. The first light drops of rain were spattering outside, so I decided to cook on the gas stove rather than make a campfire and broil over the coals. As the smell of melted butter, frying mushrooms and steak filled the tiny warm kitchen, I suddenly passed out momentarily.

Nick heard the thump in the kitchen and rushed out. He helped me to my feet and sat me down in the rocking chair.

"Now, goddamn it, you'll listen to me," he scolded, more frightened than angry. "We're getting the hell out of here *before* dark, *before* the storm, and *before* dinner."

I nodded weakly. It was the first time in my life I'd ever fainted. Now I was scared, too. All my bravado had vanished.

"Darling, at least take the frying pan off the stove. The steak's burning up. Give me a couple of minutes to rest and then we'll go. You might as well eat *something*. You're going to have to do all the driving and work. We don't know what we're in for or when we'll find another meal."

My logic prevailed. Nick wolfed down some steak and then packed a small bag for me. He shut the door, turned off the gas, called the dog, and helped me down to the dock. A stormy twilight hung over Black Bear Lake. Lightning flashed and thunder muttered over the hills. Waves were almost 2 feet high from the gusty south wind. Only a few lights twinkled along the shoreline way down the lake. I realized the advisability of getting out to medical care. My stomach hurt so much that I could never have pulled the starting rope by myself.

After a few yanks and curses, Nick got the engine running. We started slamming over the high waves. Every jar seemed to concentrate the pain on my right side. When we got to the truck, I was doubled up. There was no way I could have driven alone. We made Lake Serene village a little after ten. I was half conscious. Nick was speeding through town when a police car appeared as if by magic. As soon as the officer heard of my plight, he escorted us directly to the Health Center and radioed the resident physician. Within fifteen minutes the earlier diagnosis had been confirmed. Appendicitis!

The doctor called long distance to the city hospital to alert the Emergency Ward and then suggested I get into a waiting ambulance. A volunteer crew had already assembled.

"Ambulance?" I protested. "What do I need *that* for? Nick can drive me down in the truck. I can lie down on the front seat of the truck. I don't want to feel really sick until I *have* to."

"All right. Do it your way," the physician smiled ruefully, "only get there as soon as you can—without a crash." He gave Nick a comradely slap on the shoulder and left.

Nick kept it between 50 and 70 miles per hour all the way to the hospital. It was 1:30 A.M. when we arrived. A doctor examined me at 3 A.M. The blood tests showed a white blood count of well over 13,000. I was operated on at 7 A.M.

While I was still recovering from my appendectomy that fall, another emergency took place at Black Bear Lake. The last day of October a deer hunter suffered a heart attack early in the morning. His companions radioed out on a citizen's band set for help. Within twenty minutes, a seaplane had landed by their camp with a resuscitator, nurse, and Emergency Medical Technician. They were all highly trained for dealing with heart patients in rural situations. Yet no amount of medical help could save the man. It was not his first attack, but it was his last. The plane flew back out an hour later with the body.

My next medical emergency happened a year later while I was busy preparing for winter. I had hired a young student, Alan, to help stack wood, chink cracks, put up storm windows, and clean the stovepipe during the week. He was up on the roof, putting the stovepipe back together again, and I was handing up freshly scoured sections to him. When I came to the short stovecap, he couldn't reach it, so I laid a short ladder against the edge of the roof and climbed a few rungs to hand it to Alan. Carelessly, I didn't bother to chock the legs of the ladder. They began to slide out from under me and the ladder dropped. Rather than swing in and crash against the porch railing, I grabbed for the edge of the metal roof with my left hand. This broke my fall. I dropped harmlessly to the ground, but my fingers were slashed to the bone and filled with paint and soot. Immediately a sense of panic at possibly having severed tendons swept over me.

Alan clambered off the roof and rushed inside where I was holding my hand under the cold water faucet. The sink was red with blood. Alan promptly became sick. The pain was acute, and I couldn't seem to unclench my fingers which scared me even more. Finally, Alan recovered enough to wrap my hand in a bath towel and get me down to the boat. He started the motor and drove me to Lake Serene. For never having run an outboard motor and not having a driver's license, he did magnificently.

Within ten minutes, a doctor was on hand at the Health Center and I was lying in the little emergency room. Again I was lucky. No tendons were cut and no bones broken. But I did end up with twenty stitches, a bad infection, a pinky with no feeling, and a perpetual mistrust of ladders.

My third and worst accident took place when I was alone. It was early fall and the foliage was stunning. I wanted to take a special picture to illustrate an article I was writing, a picture which would capture the essence of an Adirondack autumn. I needed rafts of Canada Geese floating on a misty lake at sunrise—tendrils of rosy mist rising against a backdrop of high mountains cloaked in colorful leaves—a balsam or two silhouetted in the foreground as a frame. I thought I knew of just the spot to take this picture. When a long spell of rainy weather finally cleared, I drove off with the dog to camp there. We slept in the back of the truck and woke to hear a faint musical babbling. This assured me that the geese were still on the lake. I drove along an old logging road and parked at the edge of the steep shoreline.

Crisscrossing two cameras with telephoto lens over my shoulders, I eased open the cab door and very slowly stood up in the doorway so as not to scare the birds. I hushed Pitzi, who was sitting on the seat, then reached up to the roof. The night had been cold. Frost whitened the grasses, bushes, *and* top of my truck. Not realizing this, I felt for a hand-hold, encountered a cold, slippery metal surface, lost my balance, slid backward, and spun out away from the cab, right down the embankment.

I must have fallen 12 or 15 feet, for the breath was knocked out of me, causing several awful groans. Next I realized that something was crushed inside between my hips. I managed to roll onto one side which felt better. After about fifteen minutes I was breathing more normally and thought perhaps I could crawl to the truck and get in. But the pain was too great. All I could do was pull myself a few feet to within sight of the road. Then I went into shock. Ironically Pitzi thought this was a game, and he barked and danced and jumped around me.

The seriousness of the situation was alarming. I was about 5 miles from the nearest building, on a seldom-traveled log road, lying helpless on the ground with the temperature at about 28 degrees. No one knew where I was. I had broken one of the chief commandments of the woods: always tell someone where you are going and when you expect to be back!

An hour passed. Then I heard the low hum of a motor. Miraculously a game warden cruised by on patrol. There was an early bear season underway and he was looking for hunters. He spotted the truck, then the dog, then me. When he saw me shuddering, his first impulse was to pick me up and carry me into his warm car. But some instinct warned me this was wrong. I begged him not to move me. Between shivers I blurted out, "Get my sleeping bag and pack in the back of the truck."

He covered me up and laid the pack down. I rummaged around in a pocket, hoping that the two small bottles of morphine and Demarol were still there, left over from my long hike on the Northville–Lake Placid Trail the summer before. They were.

"Please give me some water," I moaned.

"You're not going to take morphine," he warned "until I know what's wrong with you. It's the worst thing for back and head injuries."

He knelt down and gently unlaced my boots. Drawing them off carefully, he told me to wiggle my toes. I did.

"Well, that's a good sign," he said, leaving the boots on the ground. "I think your back is OK, but just to play safe you take the Demarol instead."

I took three and lay waiting for the pain to ease. The officer stood a moment, studying the situation.

"I'll have to leave you here a little while," were his next words, "and go find someone to help pick you up with some kind of a stretcher."

How I dreaded to be left alone again, but I nodded, knowing that this was the only way. After forty-five minutes, he returned with two men and a wooden door. They let me crawl slowly onto the hard surface, then picked it up and slid the door into the back of my pickup. One of the men drove while the officer knelt beside me to steady my body from the jolting and swaying. Those must have been the worst miles I ever rode. Fortunately he had radioed out to the nearest volunteer ambulance. We met them shortly. I was slid into the ambulance, still on the improvised stretcher, for I would allow no one to move me. Then we headed for the hospital, 80 miles away.

From the time I was found until arrival at the emergency ward, only three and a half hours had passed. It was an evacuation of great speed, efficiency, competence, and kindliness. At the hospital I was informed that my pelvis and ribs were fractured on the left side. It had been wise not to let anyone pick me up or jostle my body unnecessarily.

Because of the way in which I was whisked out of the woods, my truck, dog, $2,000 worth of camera equipment (none of it broken), sleeping bag, pack, and boots were left scattered behind. The men who rescued me went back to salvage things. One took the dog until arrangements could be made to have him stay with friends. Another took the truck and kept it until I could drive again. The game warden collected all my equipment and locked it up until I was safely home. Without the assistance of these wonderful people, I would have been completely lost.

A philosophy of survival has evolved out of these various misadventures. I still believe it is safer to live in the woods and take chances with accidents and sudden illness, than to live in a city and be subjected to muggings, robberies, rapes, harassment, and traffic jams. I figure the probability of slicing my foot open with an axe is probably statistically less than finding a knife in my back walking down a city street. Also I'm sure that we have better medical aid in the Adirondacks with our volunteer ambulances, seaplanes, snowmobile rescue sleds, search and rescue teams, citizen's band radios, concerned doctors, and Emergency Medical Technicians than in any big city. While talking to a lady friend in New York City sometime later, I learned that she had fallen on the third floor of her swank apartment and badly broken her arm. It took *her* three hours to locate an ambulance and be taken to a hospital in one of the largest cities of the world.

My personal reaction to these accidents has been to invest in a Merck medical manual, a *Physician's Desk Reference*, and a cupboard full of first aid supplies; and, most important, to take a course in emergency medical technician training, which requires eighty-one hours of classroom study and emergency ward work. In addition, I am *very, very* careful how and what I do at the cabin and back in the woods.

# 19

# Alaska versus the Adirondacks

It was a hot, sunny June day when Nick arrived at the landing. He was late, tired, and curiously quiet. The black flies were out in force, so we went right inside the cabin, despite the beautiful weather. Nick sat rocking in the studio while I prepared tea in the kitchen.

"School almost wrapped up?" I asked.

"Just about," he answered, as if from a great distance.

"How was the drive up? Lots of tourists?"

"Not too many."

"Can you stay a couple of extra days this time, love?" I asked hopefully.

"I don't think so. I have a lot of correspondence to catch up with."

"Couldn't you do it here, sweetheart?" I pleaded, carrying in a tray with cups and cookies, lemon and sugar. I set it down beside Nick, and saw an airmail envelope lying in his lap. I poured tea and handed him a cup, then sat down with my own in the desk chair.

"Sure you wouldn't rather have it iced?"

"No, thanks. Ummmmmmm. It's good. I'm a little uptight. This should relax me."

"What's the matter, Nick?"

"This letter," he paused. Never being one to hold things back, he handed me the envelope. It was postmarked Alaska. "I've been offered a teaching position in Anchorage."

I sat very still, a sudden turmoil of feelings in my heart and brain.

"I've always wanted to live in Alaska. All my life I wanted to be as close to the Arctic Circle as possible. And now, suddenly, this came through." There was a note of wonderment in his voice.

"When does it start?" I asked, softly.

"The job begins in September. They'd want me there by the end of August. Just time to wrap up my job downstate and drive out there."

"Have you told the school about this yet?"

"No, I wanted to talk it over with you first," he replied. "I haven't mentioned it to anyone." The strain was making Nick's lean, sinewy body move stiffly. His eyes had deepened almost to brown.

Pensive silence filled the cabin. From outside the kitchen window I could hear the chirps and trills of mating Magnolia Warblers, carefree and casual. They had no decisions to make. Only natural instincts and hormonal impulses to follow. My mind winged off to a branch in the balsam forest and sat beside the birds, as if escaping from the dilemma inside the cabin.

"I was wondering if you'd go with me?" said Nick harshly.

Here was the question. He had laid the future right square in my hands. Should I go with the man I loved, leave the cabin, the Adirondacks, and start a completely new life in a far northern country based on his professional career? Or should I stay here alone in the home I'd built, in the mountains I loved, with the profession I had created?

"Well?"

I couldn't answer. I stared at the log walls where the sun lay in warm shafts. I heard the faint munching of spruce bark beetles under the bark. I looked at the shelves of books, Mapuche's pelt, my Navajo rugs. Suddenly I had the overpowering urge to run outside and do something active.

Nick opened the envelope in a half-apologetic, half-defiant manner, reached over and laid the letter on my desk. "Here, read it, Anne. There'd be time for exploring the backcountry. Two months off in summer and a long Christmas vacation. Oh, man, how I've always wanted to get into that backcountry, take a dog team out in winter, climb in the Brooks Range, hunt moose in the Kenai, fly around with bush pilots. You know the Adirondacks are just a miniature Alaska. Everything up there is so much wilder, bigger, higher, and colder." He gestured impatiently toward the north with his hand.

Colder. Nick had said colder. At once my senses balked. More and more my research interests and consulting work were taking me south on short trips to Central America and the Caribbean. I loved what I saw and felt in the tropics. Palm trees, white and black sand beaches, lofty volcanoes, sunny mornings, the lush smell of fertility, charming people, coral reefs, the feel of hot sun on my skin. It was so different, so euphoric compared to the bleak Adirondack—or Alaska—winters.

I picked up the letter and read it. The salary was excellent; a house would be provided; the institution seemed quite reputable. "It sounds like a wonderful opportunity for you," I began.

"Yes," he said quickly, "it's really unbelievable. You *know* I don't want to spend the rest of my life teaching in Albany. There are no real ties left from my first marriage there. Only you up here. You *know* I really love winter sports and hunting. Alaska should offer all that right in *my* backyard."

"And for you, *too*," he continued. "It should be a great place for a wildlife ecologist. Think of all the game up there. Just take the Alaska pipeline problem for example. It must need a lot of conservation and management."

So does the wildlife in the tropics, I said to myself. Conservation barely exists in some developing Latin and Caribbean countries, and the natural resources are being destroyed at an alarming rate—even faster than along the pipeline.

"If it got too bad in the winter, we could always fly to Hawaii for some sun and sand," Nick added. He looked at me quizzically. I don't know what my face showed, but he abruptly stood up and said, "Let's go swimming. You think about it. We can talk some more this evening. I hope we can decide on something before I leave tomorrow afternoon."

We put on our suits and walked down to the dock. I dove in at once and swam as far as possible underwater toward the center of the lake. Here the world was jade green, shading down to soft amber depths. A lone trout finned its way nonchalantly behind a sheltering rock. There was nothing here except warm water, the fish, and the rock. I wished I could stay down for hours, avoiding the problem that waited up in the sun and air and trees, the bombshell which had been thrown into our relationship. My lungs were bursting as I lunged for the surface. And I knew in that shimmering second between gulping air or water that I would stay and Nick would go.

The need for a decision was drawing into focus much more than our professional differences and our climatic preferences. It was pinpointing certain psychological conflicts which had been building between Nick and me.

The process of learning how to cope as a woman alone had backfired to an extent. I had noticed that the more competent I became, the more insecure certain men acted, or the more aggressive others behaved toward me. It was as if their inferiority complexes were showing, as if they couldn't stand to have a female be better at anything than they. It had happened with Nick.

"You can do everything so well around here," he often complained when he broke an axe handle or spilled a can of paint. "It makes me feel like a dunce."

"But I had to learn, darling. It was a question of survival."

Yet this feeling of inferiority showed, in that Nick spent less and less time helping me around the cabin. He said it took too much time from his lesson plans, grading papers, reading about railroads, hunting, etc. So, generally, I did most of the maintenance and repair work while he sat indoors at the desk or ranged out in the woods. This made me feel like a drudge. I knew Nick thought of the cabin as a haven, more than he did his studio apartment in Albany. Yet, I carried all the responsibility of its upkeep, while he more or less took it for granted. Sometimes I even sensed he resented my preoccupation with home and land.

I was constantly faced with a choice. To go ahead and act competently and independently, as I had been doing, thereby alienated the man I cared for. Then I was forced to handle the situation in a most careful and diplomatic manner. Or, to act like a "dumb blonde" or "helpless female" to build up my man's ego. Then I compromised my integrity. This conflict, I often reasoned, must be a basic concern of women's liberation. It certainly was of mine.

The weekend dragged along. At various times we discussed the problems involved in a move to Alaska. How would I close down the cabin? How much packing would be involved? Should I ship my library by freight, or haul it by trailer? Would Pitzi fare well on a three-weeks' drive? Which of our vehicles should be driven to Alaska? What should be done with the other? Could I gracefully cancel the three Caribbean consulting jobs scheduled for fall? Would it be possible to stay in touch with editors and publishers in the East from way up in Alaska? Through it all, Nick never asked, "Will you marry me?"

When he left on Sunday afternoon, no definite decision had been voiced outloud. Yet, we both knew; but both were afraid to say. The mail bag on Thursday carried a note from him. It read:

Baby:
    I've got so much to do to get ready. Just a little over a month until it's time to start. We can both use this weekend to better advantage alone, I feel. I hope you are thinking about going. Take care. See you soon.

                                 Love,
                                   Nick

I saw him twice more before he left for Alaska. As much as we loved each other, he couldn't stay and I couldn't go.

Two years had passed between our meeting on the railroad tracks and our breakup. The loneliness which swept back into the cabin was different from what I'd felt when I first moved in. This time there was a tinge of relief, a feeling of having made the right decision; yet the heaviness was as bad as before. I was back fighting for my emotional survival. I have a great need for love—to get it and give it—but it's hard to find, living alone in the woods. I can pour out affection upon the cabin, land, dog, friends, colleagues, and two godchildren; yet a void still remains that can only be filled by a man's love.

Meeting Nick in the Adirondacks had been a quirk of fate. Locally, it is hard to find a man with the same interests, background, and education as mine. Most of the compatible and eligible men I know work and live in cities or at universities. I meet them only when traveling, attending conferences, or doing consulting jobs. Usually these types are fiercely dedicated to their own professional goals. Scarcely any could make a living at Black Bear Lake. In fact, some would consider the system of values which operate in the Adirondacks *detrimental* to their careers. No one needs to be a good woodsman in Washington, D.C. Knowing how to use a wedge and go-devil doesn't help one survive in Los Angeles. These men could hardly "get ahead" in certain circles living like the typical Adirondacker who can "wear what he likes, spit anywhere, and not go to work at 9 A.M."

The conundrum in my life is the cabin versus the city. I don't know what the ultimate answer is. I just keep working—and moving around the woods and the world—and hoping . . .

# 20

# Cabin versus City Life

My dream had come true. I had spent ten years in a log cabin in the woods, with time away only to do the necessary course work and research for a doctorate, and to carry out occasional short-term consulting and writing assignments for my livelihood. I had come to know the land, trees, water, and wildlife intimately. Here was my home.

Now I, too, had received a tempting offer. It offered me a highly paid position with a prestigious Washington conservation organization for the winter. Coming so soon after my breakup with Nick, I decided to accept. The change would help me get over my heartache; nevertheless, I faced the move from cabin to city with mixed emotions. This would be the first time since I was born in New York City that I would spend more than a week or two in a metropolis.

On a brisk November day, just before freeze-up, I carried several boxes of books, clothes, files, linens, and kitchen utensils out by boat, loaded them in the truck, and together with Pitzi, started on the 500-mile drive to our nation's capital. Little did I realize that this trip was to introduce the greatest contrast I'd ever known in my life, a culture shock more acute than any experienced in Central or South America, India, or the Caribbean.

My close friends, Sally and Loren, a young professional couple, had offered me a place to stay until I was settled at work. Since I'd never driven the route before, my time of arrival was uncertain. They were expecting me sometime over the weekend. With clear roads, I made the trip from Black Bear Lake to Georgetown in one day, arriving about 7 P.M. on Saturday. Loren and Sally were just leaving for a dinner party as I knocked at their door. We exchanged enthusiastic hugs and they showed me to my room.

"Make yourself at home," they chorused. "We'll be back about midnight."

"You'd better unpack your things from the truck before doing anything else," said Loren. "I wish I could help you, but we're late already."

"Why don't I do it tomorrow in the daylight?" I suggested. "I'm a little tired right now."

"Because your things won't be there then," he warned seriously.

"Are you kidding, Loren? Who'd break into an old pickup on this pretty street in the heart of Georgetown?"

"Sweetie, he's right," verified Sally. "Nothing is safe here in Washington, and we've been having a lot of robberies recently."

"Well, I have a dozen big boxes, three suitcases, a typewriter, camera case, a 50-pound bag of dog food, and a bicycle in that truck," I groaned. Does it *all* have to come out?"

"Everything," they said in unison. "Except the dog food," added Loren. Then they kissed me goodbye and urged me to bolt both safety locks on the front door.

I shook my head in wonderment and walked back out to my vehicle with Pitzi. The street was quiet, lined with charming old homes, each one no wider than my woodshed, and graced with tall trees. These homes looked more like they belonged in a country suburb than in a city of almost 3 million people.

Wearily, I opened up the camper door and eased out the bicycle. As I was setting it on the street, I saw a police car cruise up to the corner and park. Then another slid into view from the opposite direction. From still another street a motorcycle with helmeted cop appeared. Far down the sidewalk, two more were running with nightsticks and radios in their hands. Suddenly Pitzi growled and the hairs on his back rose up like a porcupine. Out of the second car an enormous police dog had leaped and stood looking obediently at its trainer. I grabbed my dog before a fight could get underway.

I was still hanging onto both bicycle and dog and peering around in amazement when a helicopter clacked overhead in the night sky and hovered directly above us. Its brilliant spotlight shone right in my face. Pitzi began barking furiously. From the corner of one eye, I thought I saw a shadowy figure dart over a rooftop and disappear into a tiny backyard. The raucous machine flapped like a malevolent prehistoric bird, ranging restlessly over the rooftops, its light probing in all directions. The policemen converged on a house only two doors from Sally and Loren's.

I quickly put Pitzi and the bike inside and hurried to finish unloading the truck. By the time I was done, the helicopter had made its arrogant way back toward the Potomac River, the police dog was back in the car, and the officers were leaving. The thief had gotten away. I locked up my empty truck, pushed shut both safety bolts on the front door, and collapsed into a chair. Aloud I said to Pitzi, "Welcome to Washington!"

The first intimation that I needed to learn a whole new set of survival techniques for this potentially threatening environment came to me. A sense of caution and fear such as I'd never known in the Adirondacks began and stayed with me until I left there.

The noises of the city were very much in evidence that first night. Sirens screamed as ambulances, fire engines, and squad cars zipped through the streets. A constant low roar of traffic vibrated like a backdrop with an occasional louder rumble of trucks three blocks away on M Street. I lay awake for hours, turning uneasily, longing for my wide, firm mattress in the fragrant sleeping loft of my cabin, with the wind in the balsams outside.

Next morning I told Sally and Loren of my adventure the night before. They didn't seem at all perturbed.

"It happens a lot," said Loren, filling the coffee pot from a plastic gallon jug of water.

"Just last week," added Sally soberly, "a dear friend of ours was raped and almost murdered in the basement laundry room of her apartment six blocks away."

I shuddered.

"You must promise us to be really careful while you're here," warned Loren, plugging in the coffee pot. "Don't go walking around late at night, even with that monster dog. Someone might shoot the dog, then attack you!"

I stiffened in my chair and began wondering if I'd made a big mistake to come to Washington, in spite of the benefits and contacts of the job. Musing, I watched Sally pour the coffee.

"This smells delicious. But how come you didn't use tap water to make the coffee, Loren?" I asked curiously.

"The water has so much chlorine in it that the coffee comes out tasting awful," he replied. "Here, try a glass."

"Chlorine cocktail," I spluttered, putting it down with a splash. "Oh, why didn't I think to bring a few bottles of Black Bear Lake water with me?"

"That's spring water in the jug," said Sally. "We buy it in the supermarket."

I reached for a jug and saw seventy-nine cents marked on top. "Seventy-nine cents?" I marveled. "Seventy-nine cents for a gallon of water!" I did some quick mathematics. "Holy crow! I could have filled up my truck with thirty bottles from Black Bear Lake and paid for the gas, oil, and tolls on the trip down."

"Well, next time you come, *do* that," laughed Loren. "And bring some firewood, too. We have to pay $95 a cord here."

"Ninety-five dollars!" I exclaimed, astonished again. "Up home it's free. You just have to put a little muscle and sweat into cutting it. The most I ever heard anyone charge for a face cord was $15 to $20."

"That's life in the city," sighed Sally. "Washington is one of the most expensive places in the United States."

"And one of the dirtiest," interspersed Loren, running his finger unceremoniously over the window sill. "Out of eighteen cities analysed in one study, D.C. had the highest air pollution counts."

Just how expensive it was I soon learned while shopping with Sally. Food in the supermarkets seemed exorbitant, even by Adirondack summer tourist prices. And usually the stores were jammed when Sally was able to shop after office hours or on Saturdays. I often watched her grab a stack of TV dinners, frozen pizzas, or a prepared barbecue chicken in exasperation, just to get out of the crowds. The food tasted terribly processed and artificial. I thought longingly of the fresh venison I always managed to obtain during hunting season or from road kills, and the tasty beaver meat I got for free from trappers who wanted only the pelts.

One Sunday I heard Sally and Loren arguing about taxes.

"How much do you pay on real estate taxes?" I asked.

To my amazement, their fee was twice as high as what I paid on 22 acres. And their "yard" was a postage-stamp-sized patio no bigger than the dimensions of my 12- by-12-foot log studio.

Another difference I noted those first few days in D.C. was the cars, especially those parked along the streets of Georgetown. My pickup looked positively dowdy next to the shiny Mercedes of my hosts, the Jaguars, Corvettes, Triumphs, neat little compacts, and officially plated Cadillacs and Lincolns.

One morning I discovered a ticket on my windshield. Storming into Sally's kitchen, I sputtered, "Why in the world did I get a ticket? Why? Why? I was close to the curb, far enough back from the corner, not near a hydrant, not blocking anyone's driveway, not in a yellow zone or a bus stop. My word, there are so many things to worry about here compared with parking at the boat landing at Black Bear Lake!"

Sally frowned and looked at the ticket. Something illegible had been scrawled across it. "I know the police chief in Georgetown," she volunteered. "Let me call and see what's going on."

After a lengthy conversation, it emerged that pickup trucks, being commercial vehicles, were not supposed to be parked on the streets of Georgetown except for short periods of time and for business purposes.

Sally's blue eyes blazed, but she grew deadly calm. "Chief," she said sweetly, "the truck under question belongs to my house-guest. It serves as her passenger car."

The Chief said something.

"She lives in the Adirondack Mountains and that's what people drive up there," Sally replied.

There was another volley from the Chief.

"The Adirondacks are in upstate New York, near the Canadian border," explained Sally succinctly.

There was a silence.

"My friend will be staying with us for several days," continued Sally courteously. "I trust we can tear up this ticket and that your men won't bother her again." And she hung up the phone. Shaking her blond head in perplexity, she told me, "He couldn't understand a girl driving a pickup truck around here."

"You should have told him that I camp and sleep in it, use it as a traveling dog house, carry my boat and motor inside, strap a canoe on top, use it as a photo blind, haul lumber, canned goods, cement blocks, gasoline, and 100-pound bags of ready-mix in it."

"No way," laughed Sally. "He'd never even heard of the Adirondacks; so how would he understand the value of a pickup?"

Anyway, no more tickets appeared.

As Sally had pointed out, cars in Washington were purchased by a whole different set of values. Prestige, glamour, compactness for parking, and comfort were the key. The tables were turned next summer when Loren and Sally came to Black Bear Lake on their vacation. They ran out of diesel fuel for their fancy little Mercedes twice and could find no local service stations which supplied it. I rescued them with my pickup truck and repaid a favor.

I'd been with Sally and Loren about a month when they decided to take a long winter vacation, combining the Christmas holidays with two weeks off from their respective jobs.

"Would you stay on and 'house sit' for us?" pleaded Sally. "We'd feel so much safer if someone were living in."

"Yes," chimed in Loren. "Otherwise I'd have to go around securing the whole place, get a couple of self-timers to switch the lights on and off so it looks like we're really here, and notify the police."

"Not to mention stopping the mail, milk, newspapers, drycleaning pickup man, and the cleaning lady."

"But I've overstayed my welcome as it is," I protested. "I haven't even got a lead on an apartment yet."

"Listen, we love having you," said Loren, ruffling up my hair. "We hardly see one another as it is with all of us working and you going into your office even on Saturdays and Sundays."

"Well, the deadline on our report will be here soon enough. Besides, if I finish my contract early, I can go back to the Adirondacks sooner," I said wistfully.

"We're just not going to make a city slicker out of you, are we?" said Sally with a smile.

"Afraid not," I replied. "Meanwhile, I'm happy to be here with you both, and I *will* 'house sit' for you."

After my friends left, I spent more time than ever at the office. Time dragged. I got into a steady routine which seemed the best way to survive. Everything operated on a schedule. Rush hours in Washington reminded me of so many rabbits hopping into their warrens, then out again. To beat the terrible traffic in mornings, I tried to catch an early bus. But since the doors of our building were not unlocked until 8 A.M., there was no way to avoid the first part of it. I'd sit on an overheated bus, gazing out at grimy concrete and macadam unblessed by the crystal whiteness and purity of winter snow and ice, watching the blank faces around me. They were all immersed in reading the morning paper or stock market reports, doing crossword puzzles, leafing through pocket murder mysteries, knitting, scanning reports. Some instinctual response, some internal self-timing device must have alerted the passengers when to get off, because I never saw anyone miss a stop.

No one smiled or chatted on those buses. No one showed any manners. One morning, a blind man tapped his way aboard. The bus was crowded full, yet no one moved to offer him a seat. After a moment, I leaped to my feet and helped him sit down. A few eyes rose to watch me. As I looked over the busload, I felt like screaming at the top of my lungs, "You goddamn selfish bastards! Whatever became of your brotherly love?"

Afternoons, our office building was locked at 6 P.M. to lessen the chance of robberies and rapes. I was forced to leave, no matter what train of thought or conversation was being pursued. I often wondered how the creative moods and impulses to which I molded much of my life at the cabin would fare under such a regime.

On Fridays, it was even worse. Then the bus was filled with people wearing their "Friday night faces," sucked dry by a week of office tensions and no exercise. I saw such depression, weariness, bewilderment, and loneliness there that I stopped taking the bus on Fridays and splurged on taxis. I learned from those faces and from being alone for a month in Sally and Loren's house in a strange city that a person can be just as lonely in a city as in the backwoods. Crowds of people are no more of a guarantee against loneliness than are forests of trees.

Riding the buses, nevertheless, gave me an opportunity to make "time and motion" studies, comparing the efficiency of living at Black Bear Lake versus Washington, D.C. Most mornings it took me exactly the same amount of time to walk from the house in Georgetown three blocks to the bus, ride into the District, walk another three blocks to my office building, go up an elevator three floors and step into my office, as it took to walk from the cabin to the dock, run down the lake in my boat or snowmobile, drive over the mountain to Hawk Hill and out to Lake Serene village over 25 miles away. The few mornings when it snowed or rained heavily, the local bus trip took as long as the ride from Black Bear Lake to the nearest city!

I also saw that city living was not conducive to general ecological economy. Many times I watched Sally jump into her car and run up to the corner grocery, pharmacy, or dime store for one item she had forgotten. At the cabin, every trip counted. Garbage, laundry, empty gas cans and tanks, mail and packages went out; groceries, drugs, sundries, dry cleaning, gas, and batteries came in. I remembered, or went without.

Nights after work, supper, and the news, my main diversion was taking Pitzi on long walks. In this I ignored my hosts' warning. But rather than sit watching their large color TV set and become "addicted," I preferred to gamble with Washington after dark. I didn't want to suffer a "TV withdrawal syndrome" when I returned to my nonelectric cabin. Also I craved the exercise. Pitzi and I never met a mugger, rapist, or murderer on our walks; however, I kept a perpetual eye peeled, wore running shoes, and carried my hunting knife. I was damned if I'd let anyone shoot my dog while he was trying to defend me, or take an assault without a struggle.

We discovered a nice wooded park not far away where we went most evenings. The park contained some of the largest oak trees I'd ever seen, evidently having been preserved by a large colonial estate. On homesick nights, I'd put my arms around one of those patient giants, think of my pines, and try to feel that same peace and life-force moving between us. A few times I came close, but there was always an Eastern, Allegheny, Delta, American, National, or United airplane a few hundred feet above my head, roaring disconcertedly down its flight path for National Airport.

One night, a Friday to be exact, I got into trouble. We were jogging through the crackly dead leaves in the woods when suddenly Pitzi stopped short. A large golden retriever was ahead of us, running, jumping, chasing its tail in circles. Its behavior seemed peculiar. No one accompanied the dog. I began to drag Pitzi away on his leash, but the retriever pursued us. In a matter of seconds, a vicious dog fight was underway. For the first time in his life, Pitzi was pinned to the ground with jaws around *his* neck. By the dim glow of city lights reflected off the clouds I could see the strange dog tugging and tearing at Pitzi's throat.

I leaped forward, straddled the attacking beast, and tried to pull him off Pitzi. In a frenzy he turned sideways and buried his teeth deep into my left calf muscle. Given that short respite, my dog rolled to his feet and began trouncing the retriever. Five minutes later the fight was finished. The golden-haired dog raced off down the nearby street with his ears torn and bleeding. Pitzi had fared no better. Both his ears were ragged and one paw was badly bitten. Together we limped out of the park.

Every minute, my leg was growing sorer and more swollen. By the time we had reached the house, I could barely walk. To my surprise, Sally's medicine chest only contained cold capsules, throat lozenges, decongestant sprays, and aspirins. Apparently people in the city were prepared for flu and colds, not for dog bites or sudden injuries.

Not knowing any doctors in town, I had no choice but to drive to the emergency ward of Georgetown University Hospital. After hours of waiting among appendicitis sufferers, knife-wound victims, sprained ankles, and upset stomachs, my leg was looked at by the emergency doctor. I told her what had happened. She grew concerned, then asked several leading questions about the stray dog.

"Given its unexplained behavior and aggression," she finally stated, "I'd recommend you start a course of rabies vaccine within forty-eight hours; unless, of course, you find the dog."

I cringed on the examining table.

"Washington has a strict leash law," she went on. "That dog should not have been running free. There's no way of telling whether it's healthy or sick; and rabies is 100 percent fatal in humans," she added, giving a final roll to my bandage.

I left the emergency ward on crutches, unable to use the leg because of the hematoma which had ballooned my calf out of all proportion. Now I knew how effective "hamstringing" could be as a predator's tactic while hunting. Incapacitated like this, there would be no way an injured animal could run away. Pitzi was looking woebegone when I got back to the truck. We drove home. He felt no better than I, yet seemed to have no injuries that would require a veterinary unless an infection set in.

Now the full impersonality of the city struck me. With the exception of Sally and Loren and my office staff and colleagues, I knew no one in Washington. There was no close friend I could quickly call on to help find a stray dog and save me from a painful set of shots. The police had been notified, but I had little hope that they would start searching a wooded park for a golden retriever when they had the usual weekend people problems of a large city on their hands.

If this had happened at Black Bear Lake, I could have called the local troopers, conservation officers, other emergency medical technicians, the volunteer fire department, my friends, and each would have made an effort to find the dog. I felt desolate.

Next morning, barely able to move, I crutched next door in desperation. I had to find *someone* to search, bring in groceries, walk my dog. I knocked. A lean, silvery-haired man came to answer. I introduced myself and asked for help. He invited me in and went to fetch his wife and two teenage sons who were relaxing in the den with the morning papers. Over cups of cocoa, they listened to my story. Then one son said, "I'll go out and begin looking in the park for the dog."

The other boy joined in with, "I'll try the houses along the street where you last saw it running."

The woman volunteered, "Why don't I call some of my friends around this neighborhood and see if they know of such a dog. He must be a sight today after that fight, and easy to spot. Now you go back to bed and let me bring over some hot soup later."

Her husband added, "I do the grocery shopping on Saturdays. What can I bring you?"

Suddenly my spirits soared. There *were* kind people in the city and they *were* willing to help. I hobbled back to Sally and Loren's house and stretched out on the couch. By afternoon, the dog had been found. Its owner, a respectable business man, rushed to my bedside. He assured me that his pet had had its rabies shots and was in perfect health. The dog had slipped out the night before when he wasn't watching and had merely been romping by itself in the park. The police came and gave him a $5 ticket for breaking the leash law. He readily agreed to confine the retriever for a ten-day rabies quarantine to be certain no disease broke out. He offered to pay my medical expenses, drive me to work while I was lame, and take Pitzi for walks. He couldn't have been more solicitous. By evening time, the world seemed a far brighter place. I was saved from taking those painful rabies shots and had found good people to help me through this unusual crisis in the big city.

After I could walk again, I began driving with Pitzi out to Maryland on weekends. Newly made acquaintances owned a farm where I could let the dog run free, take a long walk without fear, and enjoy a pleasant dinner with my friends. The farm was only 22 miles from downtown Washington; yet the drive usually took over an hour. There must have been forty red lights on the round trip. Whereas in the Adirondacks I could drive 75 miles without a stoplight, here it was stop-and-go, stop-and-go. I found my frustration level rising in the traffic. The exhaust fumes, the idiosyncrasies of city drivers, the dismal scenery on the outskirts of our capital all grated on my nerves. I noticed my driving habits becoming more aggressive. It was dog-eat-dog driving manners. At times I felt like screaming in exasperation. If I'd stayed permanently in Washington, I'm sure I would have had a serious accident, or given up driving altogether. As it was, it didn't surprise me at all to hear a story about the enraged driver caught in a huge traffic jam who jumped out of his car, walked up to the vehicle ahead of him, and shot the next driver in the head.

Fortunately, I didn't have to stay in Washington more than eight months. One happy day in June, I laid a completed report on my office director's desk, received a letter of commendation, said goodby to my colleagues, and packed up the truck. Then Pitzi and I headed north to where northern lights would be playing softly above the forests, replacing neon lights and their glow over the city. North to cloud-splitting peaks, streams brown as bock beer, sunny beaver meadows, somber spruce forests, trout-blessed rivers, and fragrant balsam flats.

The cabin never had seemed so beautiful. I found my energy returning, my responses to the environment quickening, my reflexes sharpening, my muscles hardening, and my body slimming again. Packing away my heels, I stretched my toes luxuriously again in mocassins and lumberjack boots. Corns which had appeared in Washington, gradually diminished. My streak of aggressive driving passed. I slept well. How contenting to spend summer mornings again at my desk or on the sun deck, writing, typing, answering correspondence, then dashing into the lake for a swim. How relaxing to rock by the crackling Franklin stove, reading or gazing out the picture windows at an autumn stained-glass sunset. How comforting to burrow into the soft blankets of my sleeping loft on those awesome, frigid winter nights. And how inspiring to wake at dawn to the smell of spring and the trill of peepers.

Yet to be completely honest, my sojourn in the city had been profitable. I came home flushed with success, having done a good job, earned a handsome salary, and made excellent contacts. Al-

Sunset on a wild Adirondack lake.

though I knew that I could never stand to live in a city again, I also realized that a small connection with it had become necessary to bring a balance into my life. The city (regardless which one it is) *does* provide a certain degree of sophistication and intellectualism. It offers the challenge of professional matters. It throws new and interesting people in one's path. There is a dynamic and an energy in cities which is diametric to the life-forces of the forest.

Still the cabin is the wellspring, the source, the hub of my existence. It gives me tranquility, a closeness to nature and wildlife, good health and fitness, a sense of security, the opportunity for resourcefulness, reflection, and creative thinking. Yet my existence here has not been, and never will be, idyllic. Nature is too demanding for that. It requires a constant response to the environment. I must adapt to its changes—the seasons, the vagaries of weather, wear and tear on house and land, the physical demands on my body, the sensuous pulls on my senses. Despite these demands, I share a feeling of continuity, contentment, and oneness with the natural world, with life itself, in my surroundings of tall pines, clear lakes, flying squirrels, trailless peaks, shy deer, clean air, bullfrogs, black flies, and trilliums.

Sometimes at night when a problem has me turning and twisting in the silent sleeping loft, I get up, wake the dog, and glide onto the lake in my guideboat. Slipping over the star-strewn surface of Black Bear Lake, I'm gradually imbued with the ordered goodness of our earth. Its gentle, implacable push toward balance, regularity, homeostasis. This seeps into my soul as surely as sphagnum moss absorbs water. Surely the entire universe must be operating in this way.

True, some trees get blown over by storms; some stars burn out; some people encounter crippling misfortunes of health or finances. But the forest remains; the skies keep twinkling; and human beings keep striving.

Drifting about under the night heavens, I think and hope that

I can weather the storms which will blow my way. And that these trials will give me depth and stature so that in old age I can be like my big white pines—dignified, lending beauty to the surroundings, and lifting their heads with strength and serenity to both sun and storms, snowflakes and swallows.

# Epilogue

Sometimes I sit in my log cabin as in a cocoon, sheltered by swaying spruces from the outside world. From traffic, and noise, and liquor, and triangles, and pollution. Life seems to have no beginning and no ending. Only the steady expansion of trunk and root, the slow pileup of duff and debris, the lap of water before it becomes ice, the patter of raindrops before they turn to snowflakes.

Then the chirp of a swallow winging over the lake reminds me that . . . there is always a new beginning.

**For the first time in paperback, the compelling story of how one woman single-handedly met the challenge of the wilderness.**

"*Woodswoman* is an exquisite example of what one person, Anne LaBastille, wanted to do, attempted, and did. Its 277 pages are the kind of stuff that is just likely to turn you green with envy, send you into uncontrollable fits of daydreaming, or cause you to consider kicking yourself for not having done what she has. Magnificent!"
— *Virginia Wildlife*

"Her poetic description of the seasonal changes and photographs of her environment and its wildlife make this one of the most interesting books of its genre."
— *The Explorers Club Journal*

"If you like strong and successful images of womanhood, and if you like the woods, you will enjoy going backpacking with Anne LaBastille." — *New Age Journal*

**And from letters to Anne LaBastille...**

"I greatly enjoyed your new book, *Woodswoman.* Changing life styles and learning to live a new way is never easy, yet you explain it beautifully."
— Hugh Carey, governor of New York

"I have just finished reading your splendid book and enjoyed it immensely. It is one of the best things I have ever read. I marvel at the intimate way you bring the reader into your own life."
— Roger Tory Peterson, author of the *Peterson Field Guides*

*Cover design by Mark Rubin*

ISBN: 0-525-48565-1